ORGANIC GARDENING

3 Manuscripts: Hydroponics for Beginners, Aquaponics for Beginners and Microgreenson for Your Health or Profit

Gordon L. Atwell

© Copyright 2020 - All rights reserved.

The content contained within this book may not be reproduced, duplicated or transmitted without direct written permission from the author or the publisher.

Under no circumstances will any blame or legal responsibility be held against the publisher, or author, for any damages, reparation, or monetary loss due to the information contained within this book, either directly or indirectly.

Legal Notice:

This book is copyright protected. It is only for personal use. You cannot amend, distribute, sell, use, quote or paraphrase any part, or the content within this book, without the consent of the author or publisher.

Disclaimer Notice:

Please note the information contained within this document is for educational and entertainment purposes only. All effort has been executed to present accurate, up to date, reliable, complete information. No warranties of any kind are declared or implied. Readers acknowledge that the author is not engaged in the rendering of legal, financial, medical or professional advice. The content within this book has been derived from various sources. Please consult a licensed professional before attempting any techniques outlined in this book.

By reading this document, the reader agrees that under no circumstances is the author responsible for any losses, direct or indirect, that are incurred as a result of the use of the information contained within this document, including, but not limited to, errors, omissions, or inaccuracies.

TABLE OF CONTENTS

Table of Contents
Introduction: What Is Hydroponics All About?...22
   Hydroponics Versus Traditional Gardening...24
   An Overview of the Latest Technologies Used in Hydroponic Agriculture...26
      Grobo...26
      Bright Agrotech...27
      Cloudponics...27
      SmartBee Controllers...27
      Earth Prime Inc...27
      Urban Cultivator...28
      Thrive Agritech...28
      VegBed...28
      Urban Farmers Pro...28
   Sustainable Farming for the Future...30
Chapter 1: The Benefits of Hydroponic Gardening...31
   So How Does the Hydroponic System Actually Work?....33
   Setting Up Your Hydroponics System...36
   A Suitable Space for Your Garden...37
   Suitable Plants...38
      Containers for Growing the Plants of Your Choice...38
      Room Conditions...39
      Water Quality...39

Nutrients...40
  Macronutrients...40
  Micronutrients...40
A Good Water Pump...40
Planting Medium...41
  Grains and Small Pebbles...41
  Foam Matrix...41
  Fibrous Organic Material...42
Lighting...42
Additional Equipment...43
  Water Thermometer...43
  pH Water Meter...43
  Humidity Meter...43
  Humidifier...43
  Fans...44
Labor...44

Chapter 2: Starting Out with Hydroponics...45
  The Best Basic Hydroponic Systems for the Beginner Gardener...46
  The Wick System...47
    The Wick System...48
    Requirements for the Wick System...48
      A Reservoir...48
      A Growing Tray...49
      Several Tet Pots...49
      Growing Medium...49
      pH Kit...49
      Nutrients...49
      Wicks...49
      An Air Pump...49

Silicone Sealer...49

An Air Stone...49

Lights...49

Getting Started...50

The Advantages of the Wick System...50

The Disadvantages of the Wick System...50

Deep Water Culture System...52

Water...53

Oxygen...53

How Will I Know How Much Oxygen Is in the Nutrient Solution?...54

Nutrients...54

When Should the Nutrient Be Changed?...54

Requirements for the Deep Water Culture system...55

Reservoir...55

Air Pump...55

Air Stone...55

Tubing...55

Net Pots....55

Growing Medium...55

Hydroponic Nutrients...55

pH Control Kit...55

Getting Started...56

The Advantages of the Deep Water Culture System..56

The Disadvantages of the Deep Water Culture System...57

The Ebb and Flow System...61

Requirements for the Ebb and Flow System...62

A Submersible Pump...62

A Timer...62

A Reservoir...63

- Airline Tubing...63
- A Grow Tray...63
- Net Pots...63
- Growing Medium...63
- Nutrients...63
- pH Kit...63
- Overflow Pipe...63
- Good Quality Silicone Sealer...63
- Getting Started...64
- The Advantages of the Ebb and Flow System...64
- The Disadvantages of the Ebb and Flow System...65
- The Best Plants to Grow in the Ebb and Flow System...65

Chapter 3: Hydroponics Versus Traditional Gardening...66
- The Advantages of the Hydroponic System...68
  - Minimal Water Usage...68
  - Increased Oxygen...68
  - Better Temperature Regulation...69
  - Less Land Required...69
  - Improved Yield of Food Per Square Foot...69
  - Reduced Fossil Fuel Use Due to Flexible Locations...70
  - Reduced Soil Erosion...70
  - Preservation of Precious Forests...
  - More Versatile Options for Farming the Hydroponic Way...70
  - A Reduction in the Use of Toxic Chemicals...71
  - Control Over the Environment...71
- Disadvantages to the Hydroponic System...72
  - Time Constraints...72
  - The Initial Financial Outlay and the High Cost of Infrastructure...72

Unexpected Delays and Setbacks...73

High Humidity...73

Lack of Sufficient Knowledge of the Physiology of Plants...73

  Roots...74

  Stems...74

  Leaves...74

Inadequate Knowledge of the Requirements for Plants...75

  Oxygen...75

  Nitrogen...75

  Hydrogen...75

  Carbon...75

Chapter 4: Successful Plant Choices for Your Hydroponic Garden...77

  Plant Options for Your Garden...78

    Vegetables...78

    Herbs...78

    Fruits...79

    Cannabis...79

  Some of the Healthiest Fruits, Vegetables, and Herbs to Grow in a Hydroponic System...81

    Tomatoes...81

    Lettuce...82

    Cucumbers...82

    Spring Onions...83

    Peppers...83

    Spinach...83

    Strawberries...84

    Blueberries...84

    Basil...84

Coriander...85
Swiss Chard...85
Bok Choy...85
Chives...86
Oregano...86
Parsley...86
A Final Word of Caution...87

Chapter 5: The Variety and Flexibility Offered by Hydroponic Gardening...88

  The Choice of More Advanced Hydroponic Systems...89

  Bubbleponics...90

    Requirements for the Bubbleponic System...91

      Reservoir...91

      Submersible Pump...91

      An Air Pump...91

      An Air Stone...91

      Rubber Tubing...91

      Net Pots...92

      Growing Media...92

      pH Kit...92

      Polystyrene Sheet...92

      Irrigation Tube...92

    Getting Started...92

    The Advantages of the Bubbleponic System...93

    The Disadvantages of the Bubbleponic System...93

    Questions About the Bubbleponic System...93

  Drip System...95

    How the Drip System works...96

    Variations to the Drip System...97

      Recirculating/Recovery System...97

The Non-Recovery/Non-Circulating System...97
The Advantages of the Drip System...97
The Disadvantages of the Drip System...98
Getting Started...98
   Drip Emitters...99
   Thin Rubber Tubing...99
   Thicker PVC Tubing...99
   Water Pump...99
   A Draining Tray/Grow Tray...99
   Nutrient Pump...100
   Drip Manifold...100
   Reservoir...100
   Net Pots...100
   A Garden Timer...100
   Aquarium Grade Silicone Sealer...100
   Hydroponic Growing Medium...100
   A Power Drill, Hacksaw, and Clamps...100
Plants Best Suited for the Drip System...100

Kratky Method...102
Requirements for Building the Kratky Hydroponic Method...103
   Reservoir...103
   Grow Tray/Lid...103
   Net Pots...103
   Suitable Area...103
   Light...104
   Seeds or Seedlings...104
   Nutrients...104
Setting up the Kratky Method of Gardening...104
Plants Best Suited for the Kratky Method...105

The Advantages of the Kratky Method...105

  The Disadvantages of the Kratky Method...105

 Dutch Bucket...107

  How the Dutch Bucket System Works...108

  The Advantages of the Dutch Bucket System...109

  The Disadvantages of the Dutch Bucket System...109

  Which Growing Medium Is Best for This System?..110

  Plants That Are Best Suited to the Dutch Bucket System...110

    Climbers...110

    Root Vegetables...111

    Capsicum and Chilies...111

    Leafy Vegetables...111

Chapter 6: Advanced Techniques for Enthusiastic Hydroponic Gardeners...112

  The Nutrient Film Technique...113

    The benefits of the Nutrient Film Technique...114

    The disadvantages of the Nutrient Film System...115

    What You Need to Build a Nutrient Film System...115

      Reservoir...115

      Air Pump...115

      Air Stone...115

      Airline Tubing...116

      Water Pump...116

      Nutrient Film Tubing/PVC Pipes...116

      Net Pots...116

      Growing Medium...116

      Hydroponic Nutrients...116

    Getting Started...116

    The Advantages of the Nutrient Film Technique...117

The Disadvantages of the Nutrient Film Technique...118
The Vertical Garden...119
   Vertical Hydroponic Cultivation...120
   The Vertical Garden...121
   Requirements for a Vertical Garden...122
      Support Structure...122
      Weightless Growing Medium...122
      Effective Watering System...122
      pH Kit...122
      Timer...123
      Irrigation Line...123
      An Air Pump...123
      Drainage...123
      Recycling Tank or Water Source/Reservoir...123
      Vertical Grow-Box...123
      Lights...123
      Plants/Crops...124
   The Advantages of the Vertical System...125
   The Disadvantages of the Vertical System...125
   Types of Vertical Gardens...126
      Hanging Pots...126
      Tiered Gutters...126
      Trellis...126
      Tower Pots...126
      Vertical Trays...127
      Bottles...127
      Free-Standing Tiered Type...127
      Beam Garden...128
      Stair Garden...129
The Aeroponics System...130

The Process of Aeroponics...130
　　　The Advantages of Aeroponics...131
　　　The Disadvantages of the Aeroponic System...131
　　　Setting Up an Aeroponic System...132
　　　What Can Grow in the Aeroponic System?...132
　　Fogponics...134
　　　Let's Take a Closer Look at the Process of Fogponics...135
　　　The Advantages of Fogponics Versus Aeroponics..135
　　　The Disadvantages of Fogponics Versus Aeroponics...136
　　　New Designs in Grow-Boxes...138

Chapter 7: Challenges Hydroponic Gardeners May Face from Time to Time...139
　　Common Pests and How to Eradicate Them...140
　　　Spider Mites...140
　　　Thrips...141
　　　Aphids...141
　　　Fungus Gnats (Fruit Flies)...142
　　　Whiteflies...142
　　Suitable Ways to Rid Your Garden of These Pests...144
　　　Spider Mite Control...144
　　　Thrips...145
　　　Aphids...145
　　　Fungus Gnats...146
　　　Whiteflies...146
　　　　Biological Control...146
　　　　Cultural Control...146
　　　　Phytosanitary Treatment...146
　　Plant Diseases Common to Hydroponic Gardens...148
　　　Powdery Mildew...148
　　　Downy Mildew...148

Gray Mold...149
  Protecting Your Plants Against Gray Mold:...149
Root Rot...150
Iron Deficiency...150
Solutions to Steer Your Garden Back to Vibrant Health...152
  Cleanliness Is the New Buzzword...152
The Value of Using Good Quality Products...153
  Nutrients...153
  pH Solution...154
  Growing Media...154
  Temperature...155
  Tools and Equipment...155
    Scissors and Shears...155
    Spray Bottles...155
    Measuring Cups...155
    Buckets...156
    Brushes...156
Support for Getting Your System Back on Track...157
  Rhino Skin...157
  The Importance of Calcium and Magnesium...157
  Plants Come Alive with "Revive"...157
Other Potential Challenges to Hydroponic Gardening....158
  The Growth of Algae...158
    Suggestions to Resolve the Problem of Algae...159
  Leaks in the Hydroponic System...159
    Suggestions to Resolve the Problem of Leakages..159
  Clogs...160
    Suggestions to Resolve the Problem of Leakages..160
  Easy Cleaning Solutions...160
  Unpredictable Issues...160

The Dangers of Recycling Materials...161

Stay Alert!...162

Chapter 8: Starting Your Own Hydroponic Garden...163

What Qualifications Do I Need to Start?...164

So How Do I Get Started?...165

Which Hydroponic System Can I Use?...166

Kit Systems...166

Building Your Own System...166

Build a Basic, Easy-to-Operate Hydroponic System..168

The Kratky Bucket Method...168

Requirements...168

Assembling the Kratky Bucket System...169

The Simple Bucket System...170

Requirements...170

Assembling the Simple Bucket System...171

The NFT System...172

Requirements...172

Assembling the NFT System...173

Conclusion...175

The Need for Progressive and Inventive Agriculture...177

From Basics to Successful Gardening and Good Food...179

Amazing Veggie Tortillas...180

Ingredients...180

Method...181

References...182

Aquaponics for Beginners...187

Introduction...189

Chapter 1: Understanding Aquaponics in the 21st Century...191

Deciding What You Want...193

Systems Currently Being Used...195

What Can Be Grown Using your Aquaponics System...198

    Arugula:...198

    Basil:...199

    Chives:...199

    Kale:...199

    Leafy Lettuce:...199

    Mint:...203

    Most house plants:...203

    Watercress:...204

    Cucumbers:...205

    Broccoli:...206

    Peas and Beans:...207

    Peppers:...208

    Swiss Chard:...210

    Tomatoes:...211

Benefits of Growing Your Own Fruit, Vegetables, Herbs and Fish Using Aquaponics...213

Chapter 2: Different Aquaponic Systems...217

    Deep Water Culture (DWC):...221

        Building Your DWC System...223

        Important Tips for DWC Aquaponics...226

    Flood and Drain or Ebb and Flow System...228

    Nutrient Film Technique (NFT):...230

Chapter 3: Understanding the Nutrient Cycle...232

    Understanding the Importance of the Nutrient Cycle:...234

    Understanding the Role that Nitrogen Plays in Aquaponics...234

    Cycling Your System in Three Easy Steps:...236

    Monitoring Your Cycling Process...238

Temperature:...238
pH:...239
Nitrification:...239
Chloramines and Chlorines:...239
Light Sensitivity:...240
Dissolved Oxygen (DO) Levels:...240
Salinity:....240
Micronutrients:...240
Absorption:....241
Ammonia:....241
Denitrification:....241
Avoid the following:....241
Important Points to Remember...243

Chapter 4: Identifying the Best Fish for Aquaponics...244
Angelfish...246
Bluegill or Sea Bream....247
Crappies....250
Black Crappie...252
Goldfish...254
Guppies...257
Koi...259
Mollies...261
Tilapia...262
Channel Catfish...264
Largemouth Bass...266
Rainbow Trout...268
Jade Perch...271
Carp...272

Chapter 5: Common Mistakes in Aquaponics and How to Avoid Them...274

Ensure that your Water Quality is Correct...275

Ensure that your Fish to Water Ratio is Correct...277

How to Lower the Nitrite Levels in Fresh Water...280

Choosing the Right Growing Media...283

Using Harmful Additives to Lower the pH...287

Growing the Wrong Plants...288

Temperature Changes in Growth Cycles...290

Incorporate a Pest Control Strategy...293

Organic Water...294

Feeding Your Fish...295

Not Waiting For Your System to Cycle Completely...296

Lack of Oxygen Circulation...297

Choosing Your Fish...298

Keeping Ratios Right:...300

Overfeeding...302

Chapter 6: Advanced Techniques – How to Level Up Your System...303

Thinking of Going Commercial?...304

Interesting Facts About Aquaponics:...307

Understanding Fish Diseases:...309

Chapter 7: Maximizing Your System...312

Ebb and Flow:...314

DWC or Raft System:...315

Conclusion...317

References...321

MICROGREENS...325

Introduction...327

Chapter 1: What are Microgreens, and Why Grow Them?...332

What Are Microgreens?...334

History of Cultivation...337

Why Microgreens Became Popular...339

Chapter 2: Nutritional and Health Benefits of Microgreens...342

  Why Are Microgreens So Healthy?...345

    Vitamin K...345

    Vitamin C...346

    Carotenoids...346

    Potent Micronutrients...347

    Tocopherol...349

  Nutritional Benefits of Microgreens...351

    Nutritional Value of Individual Microgreens...353

  Health Effects...356

    Improved Digestion...356

    Cellular Regeneration...356

    Kidney Disease...358

    Cardiovascular Health...358

Chapter 3: How to Choose the Best Seeds...363

  Decide on Desired Crops...365

  Purchase the Best Seeds...370

    Organic...370

    Find a Trusted Supplier...371

    Go for a Limited Variety...371

    Purchase From Bulk Sellers...71

    Take Good Care of the Seeds...372

Chapter 4: How to Grow Microgreens...374

  Tools and Supplies...376

    Containers...376

    Water...377

    Growth Media...378

    Illumination...379

The Process of Growing Microgreens...380
  How to Plant Microgreens...380
  How to Harvest Microgreens...382
Important Considerations (Safety, Hygiene, Fertilizing, etc.)...385
  Quality of Lighting...385
  Harvest and Postharvest Factors...385
  Nutrition/Supplementation...388
Chapter 5: How to Prepare and Consume Microgreens...390
  How to Incorporate Microgreens Into Your Daily Diet...394
    Salads...395
    Wraps and Sandwiches...395
    Cooked Meals...395
    Juices and Smoothies...396
  Cooking Guide for Best Nutrient Preservation...397
  Tips and Ideas for Delicious Meals...399
Chapter 6: Marketing Microgreens...404
  Can Microgreens Be Profitable?...407
    The Production Economics...407
    How Much Can You Profit?...408
    Start-Up Costs and Supplies...408
  How to Sell Microgreens...412
    Evaluate Competition...413
    Reach Out to Potential Clients...413
    Advertise Your Business...414
    Be Flexible...414
    Get to Know Your Customers...415
  Legal and Other Considerations...416
Conclusion...420
References...425

INTRODUCTION: WHAT IS HYDROPONICS ALL ABOUT?

If you are already an avid gardener, you may have heard the term "hydroponics," although you may not know what it means.

Hydroponics is essentially a way of growing plants without soil. For those of us uninitiated in this growing system, we may find the concept difficult to grasp. Gardening, after all, means digging in the dirt. Right? So, let us examine this new idea of gardening without dirt.

The word hydroponics has its roots in a combination of Greek words "hydro" and "ponos," referring to water and work (Thu, M., n.d.). It is interesting to note the theory of growing plants in water instead of soil has been around for a very long time. This type of gardening was developed way back in the days of the Old Testament when the Hanging Gardens of Babylon were a good example. The Floating Gardens of China are another good example of hydroponic agriculture (Espiritu, & Teodoro, 2019).

Modern hydroponics, however, has become a very successful, speedy, and lucrative way to grow stronger, more robust plants in a fairly small area within a shorter space of time, compared to traditional agricultural methods.

Almost 80 years ago, William Frederick Gericke, known as the pioneer of hydroponics, experimented with growing tomatoes in water and soluble nutrients. Imagine the excitement of growing tomato plants to a height of 25 feet without soil! His work was so successful that other scientists and botanists were encouraged to follow in his footsteps.

You may think this sounds like a tall tale, if you will pardon the pun, but in reality, it is a wonderful example for anyone interested in diversifying their gardening talents to emulate. If you're interested, join me now to discover more about this interesting and rewarding, soilless gardening technique!

HYDROPONICS VERSUS TRADITIONAL GARDENING

There are many positive aspects of hydroponic gardening when compared with those of the traditional soil-based method. Essentially, hydroponic gardening uses significantly less water. This is mainly due to the water being recycled. We will discuss this in more detail in Chapter 1.

Hydroponic farming techniques produce an increased amount of produce for the same area under cultivation in traditional farming. Few, if any, pesticides and herbicides are required in hydroponic farming as there is little exposure to external parasites.

Hydroponic gardening methods produce an increased number of crops in half the amount of time it takes in a traditional soil garden. Hydroponically grown crops also reach their harvesting point sooner than those grown by the traditional method. Additionally, temperature and climate are easier to control in the hydroponic agricultural system because the hydroponic techniques are mainly used in an enclosed area, such as a hothouse.

The table below gives a quick and easy guide to the positive aspects of hydroponic gardening.

ORGANIC GARDENING

The Benefits of Hydroponic Gardening Over Traditional Methods

💧	↑	A dramatic increase of around 90% in the amount of water saved in hydroponic farming.
🌱	↑	Increased production of up to 50% of crops for the same area under cultivation in a traditional farm.
TOXIC	⊘	Pesticides and herbicides are not normally required due to the limited exposure plants have to the outside world.
🍅	↑	Up to 50% more crops are produced in half the time in the hydroponic system than with traditional methods.
🥗	↑	A decrease in up to 50% of harvesting time is a huge benefit to the hydroponic farmer.
🌡	↑	The temperature controlled environment encourages plants to grow better, quicker, healthier and more robust.

(Benefits of Hydroponics, n.d.)

AN OVERVIEW OF THE LATEST TECHNOLOGIES USED IN HYDROPONIC AGRICULTURE

With the emphasis on preserving what remains of our already highly stressed and compromised environment, many interesting technologies for sustainable, eco-friendly farming are making their debut. It is believed these methods will improve the opportunities for hydroponic farmers and gardeners to not only grow a wide variety of healthy, toxin-free fruits, vegetables, and herbs but flowers too.

Among the latest technologies on offer are the following:

Grobo

Grobo is a sophisticated, Canadian product. This is an "app-controlled" growing box, elegantly designed for home use. Users type the specific information about the plants they wish to grow into the app and the Grobo Technology adjusts water, nutrients, and temperature to suit the plants. The

Grobo system is button-operated and extremely user-friendly (Shiffler, 2018).

Bright Agrotech

Bright Agrotech, a hydroponic product from Wyoming, offers a wide variety of innovative growing structures that promote vertical farming for use in smaller spaces. This technology has a very positive impact on the challenge of optimizing space for maximum food production.

Cloudponics

Cloudponics offers a fully automated, compact "GrowBox" for home use. The "GrowBox" adjusts the amount of water and nutrients as well as the pH level in the growing system. This technology, which is operated via an app, is, although highly technical in nature, simple enough to operate, even for someone with no experience growing their own food (Shiffler, 2018).

SmartBee Controllers

This modular, versatile, app-operated, indoor hydroponic system is suitable for anyone interested in growing vegetables and fruits from the comfort of their home. Growers can add to the modular system as they become more proficient and require increased space for plants.

Earth Prime Inc.

Earth Prime Inc. has developed an innovative, compact, and

very attractive hydroponic system for both internal and external use. Combined with other features such as a pergola, or a platform or some other structure, Earth Prime Inc. units become an aesthetic eye-piece as well as a functional unit for growing vegetables, herbs, and fruit.

Urban Cultivator

This innovative hydroponic mini-farming system can be used commercially or as a do-it-yourself farming project in your home. It is a wonderful, easily accessible device that can fit into the average-sized kitchen. It is used for growing top-quality microgreens, herbs, vegetables, and fruit. Here's an opportunity to serve your family with fresh foods daily.

Thrive Agritech

Thrive Agritech produces high-tech, easy-to-use LED lights for hydroponic farming. The company is now busy working on the production of photosynthetic lighting to encourage optimum plant growth and early harvesting of produce.

VegBed

VegBed produces cost-effective synthetic foam for easy, hygienic germination of seedlings. These sheets are easy to clean and more resistant to mold, bacteria, and fungus. The VegBed is a great way for the beginner hydroponic gardener to start out growing seedlings on the floating garden tray.

Urban Farmers Pro

Using hydroponic technology in their upright growing frame, Urban Farmers Pro "Vios" growing system encourages up to 90% water conservation while crops can be produced at 10 times the rate of normal farming. The Urban Farmers Pro growing system offers grow lights, a special growing medium, a perpetual watering system, a unique growth formula, and functional hydroponics. This versatile mini-farming system is also app-operated (Shiffler, 2018).

SUSTAINABLE FARMING FOR THE FUTURE

Hydroponics farming methods appear to be considerably more successful than those of traditional gardening when the crop size yield is compared to the labor input. With the advances in technology, it is little wonder that great strides have been made in the development of sustainable farming methods that aim to produce increased quantities of nutritious food for the ever-increasing populations of the world.

So without further ado, let us get into gardening the hydroponic way.

CHAPTER 1: THE BENEFITS OF HYDROPONIC GARDENING

As we have seen from the examples already mentioned, there are many options available for the home gardener to use for the production of hydro-eco-friendly fresh produce.

Hydroponic gardening is soilless and involves a diversity of methods where the plant's roots come into direct contact with nutrient-rich water filled with life-giving oxygen. Nutrients and oxygen are dissolved in the constantly recycled water thus ensuring the plants have the best opportunity to grow to their fullest.

This may sound really simple. We have all put cut flowers into a vase filled with water, only to discover their life span is pretty short. So how can the hydroponic gardening system keep plants alive long enough for them to bloom and bear fruit?

The hydroponic garden, being a water-based system for growing a variety of different plants that may be specifically cultivated for flower production or farmed as a food source, operates best when it is undercover as in a hothouse or a tunnel. Some hydroponic gardens are worked from indoors from a special room set aside for this function. Others operate out of specially designed portable units, some of which were mentioned in the introduction.

Essentially, the plants are either suspended in suitable containers or they are grown on raft-like structures that "float" on the surface of the water. Other hydroponic gardeners may make use of different sized pipes or tubes, with holes cut into these at regular intervals for the plants.

There are other gardeners who prefer the simple bucket system and others whose hydroponic gardens are more complex.

SO HOW DOES THE HYDROPONIC SYSTEM ACTUALLY WORK?

A Simple Hydroponic Garden Plan

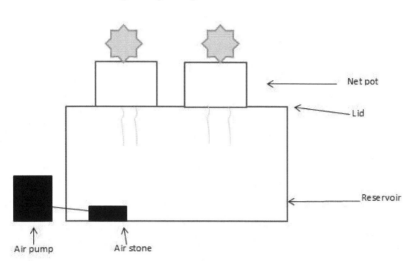

As can be seen in the example above, individual plants are placed in a horizontal pattern on top of the trough on a solid surface such as a lid. The plants' roots protrude through the ready-made holes in a net pot and then pass through the corresponding holes in the lid. Now their roots hang into the nutrient-rich oxygenated water.

The leaves of the plants are above the water-line. Water is continuously circulated through the system by the air pump, situated on the left of the diagram. The water in the reservoir is constantly oxygenated by the air stone, which has been placed at the bottom of the reservoir.

In order for this basic hydroponic system to operate successfully, lights need to be suspended above the plants. If, however, the plants are placed in a well-lit area of the hydroponic garden, there may be sufficient natural light for their growth to continue.

Consistent monitoring of the water level, the position of the plants, and the amount of light they receive are crucial for the success of any hydroponic garden.

Because the basic system above is a closed system, with the lid keeping the water in the reservoir from evaporating, there is less likelihood of the loss of water. The plants' roots, however, will continue to draw water from the reservoir as they grow.

There are a number of important elements that are vital to the success of every hydroponic gardening system. Let us take a look at some of these.

SETTING UP YOUR HYDROPONICS SYSTEM

Planning and setting up a viable hydroponics gardening system takes a great deal of time and careful planning.

The system can be intricate or simple, depending on the space available, the number of laborers working the area, the type of plants that are intended to be cultivated, and obviously, the financial considerations.

The aspects you will need to consider before embarking on this new and exciting gardening venture should include:

A SUITABLE SPACE FOR YOUR GARDEN

Although any type of gardening requires adequate growth space for the plants, a hydroponic system can be extremely successful in far smaller areas than those required for traditional gardening.

Decide on where best to establish your hydroponic garden. Bear in mind that it will need to be an enclosed area close to a water supply, as well as an electrical outlet. The area should be sufficiently spacious for you to move around in order to complete maintenance, replanting, and harvesting activities.

SUITABLE PLANTS

As an enthusiastic beginner, you may want to start off with the biggest and best plants. However, it is advisable to first start small and familiarize yourself with the hydroponic method of gardening.

Your best choice will be herbs and plants that are low maintenance with a quick turnaround from planting to harvesting. In other words, those plants that grow quickly and can be harvested without too much fuss. This will give you ample time to learn what works best in your hydroponic system and how to better manage your system for optimum production.

The more confident you become and the better your system operates, the more variety of crops you can grow. Eventually, you may reach a stage where you are able to supply a local market with fresh produce from your garden. That will be a success story in its own right!

Containers for Growing the Plants of Your Choice

A wide variety of containers can be utilized for hydroponic gardening. The important thing to remember is that these should be well cleaned and disinfected before they are used. It is also vital that you use containers that are non-toxic and will have no negative reaction to the nutrients or the acidic nature of the water mixture. The containers should also be suitable for ease of handling, especially where they may need to be lifted onto a shelf or growth tray.

Containers should be best suited for the size, height, and weight of the plants you intend to grow. Research the potential size of the plants when they reach maturity. As a guideline, the container should comfortably hold at least ⅓ of the plant (mainly the root system), while the remaining ⅔ rests above the container.

Room Conditions

For optimum success with hydroponic gardening, the room temperature, carbon dioxide levels, air circulation, and humidity levels are crucial factors for consideration. Maintaining the fine balance between the best relative humidity level of around 50° F with an ideal temperature of about 68° F (20° C) can be quite challenging.

When the humidity level is too high, powdery mildew and a variety of fungal infestations can result. On the other hand, when the temperature is too high, plants can develop root rot and their growth may be stunted (D'Anna, 2020).

Good circulation of air and CO2 is important for adequate plant growth. Maintenance of the correct temperature and humidity levels is essential for the successful operation of most hydroponic systems.

Water Quality

The quality of the water used in your hydroponic system affects the success of plant growth. Essential nutrients for the plants cannot dissolve in "hard water" because of its high mineral content. Hard water will first need to be filtered well before it can be used in your hydroponic system.

The ideal pH of water is between 5.8 and 6.2, which is slightly acidic. Your water may require added chemicals to adjust the pH accordingly.

Nutrients

Nutrients are an essential component of your hydroponic system. These fertilizers may be organic or synthetic and may be in a liquid or solid form. Nutrients are available from many gardening stores or outlets. Remember to ensure you read the instructions and check for the specific nutrients required for hydroponic gardening. Irrespective of the manufacturer, the best nutrients should include the following:

Macronutrients
Macronutrients refer to the chemical elements that are required by the plant in large amounts and that are essential for optimum growth. These include calcium, nitrogen, magnesium, phosphorus, as well as potassium (D'Anna, 2020).

Micronutrients
Essential micronutrients, which include trace amounts of boron, copper, zinc, molybdenum, chlorine, and magnesium, are all important for sustaining plant growth and development (D'Anna, 2020).

Make sure the nutrients you choose are specific for your hydroponic gardening project. There are those nutrients better suited to flower growing than vegetable farming. Fertilizers used in traditional soil gardening are not suitable for the hydroponic system.

A Good Water Pump

A high-quality water pump is an essential requirement for all successful hydroponic gardening systems. The pump, which is like the heart of the entire system, needs to work 24/7 keeping the nutrient-rich water constantly flowing through the entire system. Buying a cheaper pump may cost you dearly in the long run, so make this a priority choice from the start.

As the lack of access to a reliable electrical source may be a challenge, solar power is a very good and cost-effective option for consideration. The only negative in this regard will be on cloudy, overcast days when the pump's operation may be negatively affected.

Planting Medium

Because no soil is used in hydroponic gardening, a good planting medium—or substrate, as it is also called—is required. The first important aspect of the substrate is to be able to hold and support the plant securely in its container for the duration of its life. The second aspect is for the planting medium to be porous enough to retain sufficient quantities of valuable nutrients essential for plant growth. There is quite a wide variety of choices for planting media. Some of the more well-known types include Rockwool, coconut fiber, perlite, or vermiculite.

The best planting medium to use will be dependent on what type of plants you intend to grow and which hydroponic system you prefer to use. The more robust the plant, the more support it will require. Below are some common options.

Grains and Small Pebbles
Grains and pebbles are usually used to support heavier plants, although light-weight clay aggregate, perlite, and vermiculite for smaller varieties of plants are included here.

Foam Matrix
A planting medium is considered to have a foam basis when it is relatively soft and porous, allowing for good absorption of water. This type of growing medium is more suited to Rock-

wool, and cubes of florists' foam are the best examples of this type of growing medium (Pulsipher, 2019).

Fibrous Organic Material
As the name implies, this type of growing medium is lighter and easier to pack into the plant containers. It is suitable for lighter plants with a sturdy stem. Fibrous organic material is an excellent growing medium as it traps air between its fibers. Examples include coconut fiber, pine bark, and vegetable husks, such as those from rice or maize.

Lighting

As most successful hydroponic gardens operate within an enclosed space, there is an absence of natural sunlight. Between 6 to 12 hours of good light is one of the essential elements for successful plant growth. High-intensity discharge lights with orange-red lighting are best for promoting optimum growth in plants.

Other types of light that offer low heat and low energy consumption while giving high output are the T5 variety, which is suitable for plants with a short life span. They are also useful for cloning and germinating plants (D'Anna, 2020).

Consider investing in a good quality timer switch. This is a great investment that will ensure lighting is turned on and off as required. This device can substantially cut electricity costs, power usage, as well as time.

It is a good idea to invest in a reliable backup system for the eventuality of an unforeseen power outage. A fuel-driven generator is a great option. A solar-powered backup system may also prove a useful addition to your hydroponic gardening essentials. The only draw-back to this will be those cloudy or rainy, sunless days!

Additional Equipment

To ensure the ultimate success of your exciting new venture into hydroponic gardening, you will need to invest in some extra, high-quality equipment. The bigger your enterprise, the more expensive the outlay for this equipment will be. However, the returns on your investment are sure to outweigh the initial costs.

Water Thermometer
A water thermometer for maintaining the correct temperature is a vital component for successful hydroponic gardening. By maintaining the correct temperature, your plants are less likely to suffer from root rot.

pH Water Meter
A pH meter is essential for keeping a close watch on the acidity level in the water. The ideal pH for most plants to survive and thrive is between 6.5 and 8.5. Plants are unable to grow successfully if the pH is too low or too high. Think of the times when you may have swum in a freshly chlorinated pool and your eyes became instantly red from the excess acidity. Your plants suffer in a similar way.

Humidity Meter
Maintaining the correct humidity level in your hydroponic system is crucial for optimum plant growth and ensuring the good health of your crops. If you work in an enclosed hothouse or tunnel, the humidity meter will allow you to ventilate the area with greater ease and control.

Humidifier
It is important to keep the humidity levels constant. Where the climate is too dry, a humidifier can be the one device that keeps your plants alive because it helps to restore the correct humidity level.

Fans

Fans are important to keep the air in your hydroponic system circulating. A build-up of stale air will do nothing to improve your crop production. CO_2, which is absorbed by the leaves and which is vital to the process of photosynthesis, should be made readily available to the plants. One of the by-products of photosynthesis is the release of oxygen. Well-circulated air will ensure crops have sufficient opportunity to absorb and utilize CO_2 and then release O_2. You may have experienced the exhaustion of working in a poorly ventilated environment which left you tired and listless. Your plants experience a similar reaction by not thriving if there is inadequate airflow.

Labor

Hydroponic gardening and farming can be quite labor-intensive, depending on the system you have chosen to use. There are essential tasks that should be done daily so that the system operates to its fullest potential. The more complex your hydroponic system, the more effort it will require. However, the yields you will eventually enjoy are likely to outweigh your hard work.

CHAPTER 2: STARTING OUT WITH HYDROPONICS

If you are an avid traditional gardener who is looking for an exciting and very rewarding new gardening challenge, hydroponics may well be the best option for you.

Although this method of gardening may initially appear a little overwhelming, the principles are based on good old common sense. That is, plants need water with nutrients and a balanced pH, a suitable and protected growing area, oxygen, light, and a well-controlled temperature in order to grow well and produce fruits and flowers.

Let us take a more in-depth look at the options most likely to suit the beginner hydroponic gardener's needs.

THE BEST BASIC HYDROPONIC SYSTEMS FOR THE BEGINNER GARDENER

The hydroponic gardening system may initially appear to be quite complicated to the uninitiated gardener. As a start-up gardening project, there are three basic systems to choose from, all of which are composed of easily accessible materials and which can be constructed in your own yard. There is, of course, the option to purchase hydroponic kits that come with instructions for assembly. Depending on how handy you are with a set of tools, the second option may work better.

The three best systems to consider include:

- the Wick System, in which water is drawn up from the reservoir to the plants via a "wick,"
- the Deep Water Culture System, in which plants effectively float on the surface of the water, and
- the Ebb and Flow System, where the roots are periodically flooded with water that then drains away before the process is repeated (D'Anna, 2020).

THE WICK SYSTEM

The Wick System is the simplest way to start your hydroponic garden. A suitable container filled with a growing medium is suspended over a tank or reservoir filled with water and nutrients. The two containers are connected by a "wick," which draws water from the reservoir into the growing medium. The growing medium becomes saturated with water that the plants will begin to absorb.

This system of water transportation from the reservoir to the growth medium can be slow and may create a challenge for larger, thirstier plants like lettuce. It is likely, however, to be the perfect starting device for growing microgreens, peppers, and a wide variety of herbs (D'Anna, 2020).

The Wick System

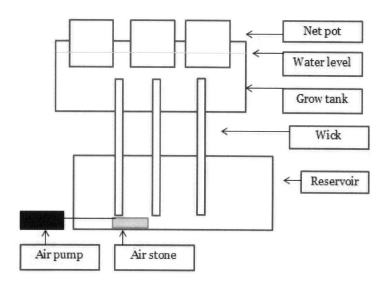

The Wick System uses an air pump and an air stone to oxygenate the water which is then "sucked up" to the plant via the wick. The wick will only pull up sufficient water for the plant's needs, and so the chance of the plant drowning is highly unlikely.

Requirements for the Wick System

The following items are required if you plan on setting up the Wick Hydroponic Gardening System:

A Reservoir

ORGANIC GARDENING

To hold nutrient-enriched water.

A Growing Tray
To support the net pots.

Several Tet Pots
These will be used for plants.

Growing Medium
A suitable growing medium for the plants you wish to cultivate.

pH Kit
This is an essential piece of equipment to help keep the acidity level in the system at about 6.5.

Nutrients
This is the plant food required for optimum growth and production.

Wicks
You will require 2-3 lengths, depending on the number of pots used.

An Air Pump
This is important for keeping the water circulating.

Silicone Sealer
A good-quality water-resistant sealer is essential to guard against leaks.

An Air Stone
To produce oxygen in the system.

Lights
As all plants require light to stimulate the development of chlorophyll, lights play an important role in successful plant growth.

Getting Started

- Fill the reservoir with water and add sufficient nutrients and acid, as per instructions on the containers.
- Attach the air pump to the air stone via a suitable length of rubber tubing.
- Secure the "wicks" into pre-drilled holes in the base of the growing tray.
- Place net pots filled with growing medium and seedlings into prepared holes in the growing tray so that the base of the pots are in the water.
- Place the air stone in the reservoir.
- Turn on the pump.
- Position a suitable light above the growing tray, unless, of course, you are fortunate enough to have sufficient natural light.

The Advantages of the Wick System

- The Wick System is one of the simplest and most reliable hydroponic methods.
- The system takes up relatively little space.
- The wicks keep the plants watered for quite a while, so the system does not require daily monitoring.
- There is no wasting of water.
- The Wick System requires little maintenance.
- Plants grown in the Wick System produce fruit and are ready for harvest in approximately half the amount of time it would take them under traditional gardening conditions (D'Anna, 2020).

The Disadvantages of the Wick System

- Pump failure is perhaps the biggest challenge to this system. However, the system can continue for a day or two without circulating water.
- Maintenance of water temperature is important.
- The water level can drop in the reservoir within a few days, so it should be checked at least twice a week.
- The system is limited to fast-growing, smaller plants like lettuce, some herbs, and a variety of microgreens.

DEEP WATER CULTURE SYSTEM

The second hydroponic system under consideration is the Deep Water Culture System (DWC), which is one of the simplest and easiest to operate. It is one of the most chosen types of hydroponic gardening techniques and results in very successful plant cultivation.

The basic requirement for the Deep Water Culture is to start with a suitable trough, sufficiently deep to hold a substantial volume of water. The more water the trough can hold, the less monitoring is required. A 5-gallon bucket is perfect for starting the system.

The plants are placed into the net pots, which are then inserted into holes in a polystyrene sheet that floats on the surface of the reservoir with the plant roots dangling in the nutrient-rich water. An air pump, connected to an air stone, circulates oxygen through the water.

In essence, the Deep Water Culture System requires the roots of the plants to be suspended in nutrient-rich, well-oxygenated water. The roots should be totally submerged in the water all the time. Take care to ensure that none of the foliage is in the water (D'Anna, C. 2020).

ORGANIC GARDENING

The Deep Water Culture System

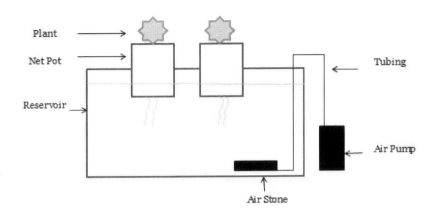

The water solution is vitally important to the survival and success of plant growth in all hydroponic systems. It behooves the gardener to consider and monitor the following aspects:

Water

Water forms the basis for the Deep Water Culture System, hence its name. The trough of water you use will keep your plants hydrated throughout their lifetime without you having to physically "water" them as you would do in traditional gardening.

Oxygen

Oxygen needs to be continuously pumped through the water so that it surrounds the roots. Some of the oxygen becomes trapped in the roots as small pockets of air. This is what keeps the roots from drowning and ensures the continued life of the plant. A good submersible pump is required for the successful execution of this process.

How Will I Know How Much Oxygen Is in the Nutrient Solution?

A number of different dissolved oxygen meters are available to monitor the nutrient solution in your hydroponic system. Unfortunately, some of these do not always deliver accurate readings. If you ensure the solution is at the correct temperature and the air pump is operating properly, you should not need to check oxygen levels.

Nutrients

Because of the absence of nutrient-rich soil in the hydroponic gardening system, added nutrients are essential for plant growth and sustainability. Consequently, micro and macronutrients are added to the water in specific, well-measured proportions to ensure optimum plant growth (D'Anna, 2020).

When Should the Nutrient Be Changed?

This is largely dependent on the size of the reservoir and the stage of growth your plants are at. However, a good rule of thumb is to change the nutrient every three weeks.

If you notice any change in the development or health of your crop, you should check, among other things, the nutrient levels in your reservoir.

It is, however, important to note that the under-nourishment of your plants is as dangerous as over-feeding them. A good balance in nutrient levels is what you should be aiming for.

Requirements for the Deep Water Culture system

The Deep Water Culture System is slightly more complex to operate but yields improved crops over a shorter period of time when compared to traditional growing methods.

Reservoir
A suitable container in the form of a 5-gallon bucket should be perfect.

Air Pump
A simple air pump is required to circulate oxygen-rich water through the system.

Air Stone
This vital piece of equipment connected to the air pump, which generates the oxygen.

Tubing
Suitable airline tubing for connecting the air stone to the pump.

Net Pots
The number and size of the pots required depends on the type of crop and how many seedlings there are.

Growing Medium
The choice of growing medium depends on the type of crops you will be growing. For soft-stemmed plants, vermiculite should suffice, while you may use Rockwool for plants with more robust stems.

Hydroponic Nutrients
These are essential for feeding the plants.

pH Control Kit

This kit is obtainable from a swimming pool outlet.

Most of these items are available from an online store such as Amazon, or from a gardening outlet (Espiritu, 2019).

Getting Started

- Fill the reservoir of your choice with water.
- Add the correct amount of nutrients and acid to the water. The pH should be between 6.5 and 8.5.
- Connect the pump to the air stone using a suitable length of tubing.
- Place the air stone into the reservoir.
- Start your seedlings in the net pots. Depending on the surface area of the reservoir, decide on the number of net pots that will fit comfortably into this space.
- Cut a piece of polystyrene to fit the surface of the reservoir.
- On the polystyrene, mark out sufficient spaces for the number of net pots you will be using.
- Carefully cut out holes that each net pot will snugly fit into.
- Place the polystyrene "lid" onto the surface of the water so that the base of each net pot is well into the water.
- Turn on the pump.

As soon as the plants begin to germinate and their roots reach the water, you will notice a sudden abundance of growth. This happens in half the amount of time as it would take for the same process in soil.

Ensure the water level is constant and regularly check the pH and nutrient levels while keeping the water well-aerated.

The Advantages of the Deep Water Culture System

- The Deep Water Culture System is one of the simplest and easiest systems to install
- It is fairly inexpensive to set up and run.
- There are fewer moving parts and complications than in other systems.
- The Deep Water Culture System is a low maintenance one.
- Plants grow at twice the speed in the Deep Water Culture System as they do in a traditional garden (D'Anna, 2020).

The Disadvantages of the Deep Water Culture System

As with any system you choose, there will be certain negative aspects to be considered.

- If the Deep Water Culture System is too small, there are likely to be constant changes in the water level and, therefore, in the pH and nutrient concentrations, which can play havoc with crop production.
- It is sometimes challenging to measure the correct amount of nutrients and acid required in a smaller system. Overdosing the water with either nutrients or acid will spell disaster for your crop.
- Electric outages or pump failures can cause roots to drown, which ultimately leads to the death of the plant.
- Maintaining the correct water temperature is more difficult in a smaller volume of water.

What is the best pH and PPM/EC level to have?

The best range for most plants is between pH 5.5 and 6.5 when they are still young. As soon as they start growing leaves, adjust the rage t0 about 6.5. When they begin to flower, lower the pH accordingly to around 5.5 (Espiritu, 2019).

With regard to the PPM/EC level, try adjusting it to half the recommended dose on the package and then monitor your plants going forward. Overdosing your plants with nutrients will do more harm than good. Instead, begin with a small amount and gradually increase this if necessary.

What is the optimum temperature for the reservoir?

Temperature control of the water in the reservoir is a challenge to maintain at around 60 - 68° F (16 - 20° C). Hotter temperatures will damage the plants, and lower temperatures will encourage the plants to start flowering or stop producing altogether.

How much of the roots should be submerged in the reservoir?

To be safe, approximately all the roots should be submerged except for the top area closest to the leaves, which should measure between 1 and 1 ½ inches. Do not submerge any of the leaves.

What is the best way to propagate plants using the Deep Water Culture System?

For the best success in propagating plants, use an aeroponic cloner. This useful gadget assists with propagating your favorite plants in a sensible and cost-effective way.

The cloning machine is, in effect, a box with a lid. Inside the box is a tray with prepared holes in which cuttings can be placed. The system works off a power pump that creates a fine mist inside the cloning machine. There is no need for the use of a growing medium as the cutting will root very quickly in the sealed, moist environment of the cloning machine.

This machine may be an expensive item initially, but in the long run, you are likely to find it was well worth the financial outlay.

Are there any serious plant diseases to keep an eye out for?

Watch out for root disease, rapid changes in the pH and PPM/EC as well as a rise in the temperature of the nutrient solution.

Do plants grow faster in the Deep Water Culture System?

Indeed, they do. The Deep Water Culture System is one of many hydroponically operating systems available. Plants can grow on average about 15% faster in most hydroponic systems as opposed to traditional soil gardening.

The best plants to grow in the Deep Water Culture System

The Deep Water Culture System is best suited to plants that require a lot of water and have a shorter life span, such as lettuce. This system is, however, not suitable for plants like tomatoes and brinjals as it offers little support for their height.

Please note, if you prefer a visual presentation of how a Deep Water Culture System works, please visit the "Epic Gardening Channel" by Kevin Espiritu on YouTube.

Are there any other tricks for successful hydroponic gardeners to use?

There are many ways to make your hydroponic system more efficient and to produce increased yields of crops. However, as you use the system of your choice and become familiar with the way in which it operates, you are very likely to experiment with a variety of different ways of encouraging your garden to produce more and better-quality crops. Remember, you may even decide to combine two or more methods, which may bring you greater success. According to Espiritu, one of the best ways to raise the level of production in your system is to cleverly engineer the humidity level of the root area, which

Gordon L. Atwell

will encourage your crops to fruit or flower more abundantly (Espiritu, 2019).

THE EBB AND FLOW SYSTEM

The third type of system you may wish to consider is the Ebb and Flow System which is similar in layout to the Wick System. An under-water pump that works off a pre-set timer floods the growing medium at regular, customized intervals to ensure optimum growth of plants.

The Ebb and Flow System, also called the Flood and Drain System, is quite popular with home hydroponic gardeners. The system, which operates either outdoors or in a closed environment, works off a timing device that allows nutrient-rich water to flow through the structure at set intervals to soak the roots well, and then it drains back into the reservoir. This system can be used for any type of plant that can be individually planted in separate containers or planted together in a single planting tray (D'Anna, 2020).

The Ebb and Flow System

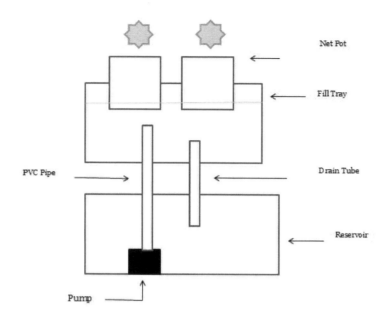

Requirements for the Ebb and Flow System

This is not as easy a system to erect as some of those previously mentioned in this text. However, once the Ebb and Flow System is up and running, it is very effective.

If the Ebb and Flow System is your choice for starting your hydroponic venture, then you will need to invest in a number of important items.

A Submersible Pump
A simple fountain or pond pump should do the trick. However, don't buy the cheapest one on the market as the pump is actually the crux of the system (Max, 2019).

A Timer
A good quality timer is essential to keep the rotation of nutri-

ent-rich water flowing into and out of the system.

A Reservoir
Any type of container that is suitable for holding water will suffice. The larger the system, the larger the reservoir needs to be.

Airline Tubing
Black air tubing for water transportation from the reservoir to the grow tray.

A Grow Tray
A good, solid grow tray that will support the weight of the pots you intend to use.

Net Pots
The number of net pots required will depend on what is to be grown.

Growing Medium
A good growing medium is vital for plant health. Choose a heavier variety to support pots so that they stay upright and don't float away. Perlite, stone wool, or gravel are good options.

Nutrients
Commercially available nutrients are readily available from garden outlets as well as online from the likes of Amazon.

pH Kit
A simple pool pH kit should be fine.

Overflow Pipe
A sturdy piece of pipe for draining water to return to the reservoir.

Good Quality Silicone Sealer
It is essential to use a good quality aquatic sealer to ensure there are no leaks in the hydroponic system.

Getting Started

- Fill the reservoir with water.
- Add the correct amount of nutrients according to the volume of water in the tank. See the instructions on the pack.
- Adjust the pH of the water. See the instructions on the pH kit.
- Drill a hole in the base of the fill tray to hold a length of PVC pipe that will carry water into the fill tank.
- Drill a second hole for the overflow pipe.
- Seal both holes well.
- Place the correct number of net pots filled with growing media and seedlings into the fill tray.
- Turn on the pump.

The Advantages of the Ebb and Flow System

- The system is dependable and inexpensive to erect.
- The flooding and draining action in this system encourages strong root growth.
- Water is recycled; therefore, none is wasted.
- Plants can be easily moved from one tray to another or replaced when necessary.
- This is a low-maintenance system because of the lack of moving parts.
- It is easy to change the growing medium if needed.
- The system is easy to operate.
- Plants grow almost twice as fast as in a traditional garden.
- The yield can be as much as 30% more than from a traditional system.
- No fungicides and pesticides are used.

- The system is easy to maintain.
- Good aeration of roots.
- Sturdy system to support heavier plants.
- The system can be used indoors or outdoors, making it more versatile.
- Good distribution of nutrients to roots.
- The Ebb and Flow System, although a somewhat more elaborate hydroponic method than those already discussed, is increasingly versatile and more adaptable (D'Anna, 2020).

The Disadvantages of the Ebb and Flow System

- Electrical or pump failure is perhaps the biggest potential hazard that will result in roots drying out in a very short space of time.
- A change in the nutrient level is also possible due to the continual recycling of the same water.
- The pH may also be adversely affected and will need to be checked regularly.

The Best Plants to Grow in the Ebb and Flow System

The versatility of this system allows you a wider choice for the plants that can be grown. The system is not suited to grow tubers such as potatoes. However, smaller plants including tomatoes, lettuce, peppers, and a variety of herbs including mint, oregano, and parsley should do well.

Cannabis can also be successfully grown using The Ebb and Flow System.

Once you have decided on the system that best suits your needs, you are well on your way to becoming a proficient hydroponic gardener. Good luck!

CHAPTER 3: HYDROPONICS VERSUS TRADITIONAL GARDENING

There are many enthusiastic gardeners worldwide who enjoy growing their own food and flowers. For the most part, gardening has been a traditional outdoor activity and has, therefore, been subjected to the challenges of seasonal and weather changes.

The hydroponic technique can, fortunately, be managed indoors and can, therefore, be successfully used to grow flowers, vegetables, and herbs throughout the year despite the season, weather, or even the terrain.

In this book, *Hydroponics For Beginners: The Ultimate Step-By-Step Guide To Building Your Own Hydroponic Garden System That Will Grow Organic Vegetables, Fruits, and Herbs*, you will discover many advantages to hydroponic gardening that make it a lucrative and rewarding way of growing a wide variety of crops.

With world population figures continuing to grow, natural resources are being put under greater pressure. Two of the most important considerations for choosing the hydroponic method of gardening may well be the optimal use of the "growing area" and the conservation of water resources.

THE ADVANTAGES OF THE HYDROPONIC SYSTEM

Hydroponic cultivations have a number of advantages over those of soil-based farming. Let's take a look at some of the benefits of this innovative and potentially lucrative way of growing plants.

Minimal Water Usage

There are many advantages to the hydroponic method of gardening that make for its success and long-term sustainability. Perhaps the most important of these is the fact that water containing nutrients continues to be recycled through a "closed" system. This ensures very little, if any, water is wasted as evaporation is dramatically reduced. A hydroponic farm uses approximately 10% of the volume of water used by a traditional farm with a similar yield.

With water conservation being high on the agenda of many world governments, hydroponics cultivation is a positively beneficial way in which water usage is minimized while simultaneously producing a large and healthy crop of vegetables, fruits, or herbs.

Increased Oxygen

Because the plants are suspended in water, their roots are exposed to increased amounts of oxygen, which as we all know, is vital for the life support of most living organisms. The plants grown in a hydroponic system respond particularly well to the increased oxygen supply and accordingly, give a high yield.

Better Temperature Regulation

Growing plants indoors makes it easier for farmers and gardeners to regulate the temperature and lighting in order to ensure optimum production. The chance of losing plants to inclement weather conditions is almost nil in a hydroponic system as opposed to outdoor gardening.

Less Land Required

Less land is required for hydroponic farming than for traditional farming. Every plant requires a specific amount of space in order to grow to maturity. A hydroponic garden can be grown horizontally or vertically depending on the availability of space and the type of plants to be cultivated. There can also be multiple levels of plants. Plant pots can be placed closer together thus using less space. This means the best utilization of space for high-density growth. A commercial hydroponic system makes use of as little as ⅕ of the land needed for a similar quota of plants cultivated on a traditional farm (Fitzpatrick, 2018).

Improved Yield of Food Per Square Foot

The yield ratio of plants grown in a hydroponic system is increased by a minimum of 30%, and the plants reach maturity much sooner than those in a traditional, soil-based garden. Hydroponically grown plants are more robust and grow faster; therefore, the turnover between planting and harvesting is greater.

Reduced Fossil Fuel Use Due to Flexible Locations

Hydroponic farmers can locate their farms closer to their marketplace, thus reducing the need for long-distance transport and by inference, cutting fuel costs.

Food is fresher as it has not been packed in cold storage for long-distance travel.

Less traveling means less fuel and lower costs to the hydroponic producer as well as a reduction in carbon emissions. This is a win-win situation all around.

Reduced Soil Erosion

Traditional farming often has a hugely negative impact on the soil, where vast tracts of land are laid waste through the effects of soil erosion. Since hydroponic farming doesn't use land or soil, there is no erosion.

Preservation of Precious Forests

Where traditional farming continues to encroach on forests leading to their destruction, hydroponics' gentle approach to growing foodstuffs poses no threats to nature.

More Versatile Options for Farming the Hydroponic Way

Traditional farming requires vast tracts of arable land for the successful cultivation of crops. The hydroponic methods of farming are so versatile that crops can be grown under any climatic conditions because they are housed under protective cover where temperature and humidity are controlled.

Aquaponics is the result of the combination of aquaculture and hydroponics to produce fish as well as fruits and vegetables under controlled conditions.

A Reduction in the Use of Toxic Chemicals

Unfortunately, traditional farming makes use of dangerous pesticides used to kill off unwanted bugs and herbicides that eradicate unwanted weeds. These toxic chemicals end up being washed further afield into rivers and watercourses from where they are carried far and wide, continuing their contamination of the environment as they go. The spin-off from this is not only water and air contamination but the poisoning of wildlife and irreparable damage to the natural ecosystems worldwide.

In hydroponics farming, the growth medium does not support the development of weeds, and most hydroponic farms are under the cover and protection of greenhouses. Therefore, the need for toxic chemicals is voided.

Control Over the Environment

Whereas the traditional gardener may struggle with the challenge of pests and plant diseases, the hydroponics gardener has greater control over the environment and, in turn, over the crops produced.

DISADVANTAGES TO THE HYDROPONIC SYSTEM

The hydroponic system comes with numerous benefits, but it also has its share of disadvantages.

Time Constraints

Time is always of the essence in any commercial or business enterprise. Hydroponic gardening takes a great deal more time than traditional gardening since constant monitoring of the nutrient and pH levels in the water, as well as humidity and temperature, are crucially important for successful hydroponic gardening. The rewards of the hydroponic method of plant production, however, outweigh those of traditional gardening.

The Initial Financial Outlay and the

High Cost of Infrastructure

The costs of setting up the infrastructure for a hydroponic garden are high. However, in the long term, these costs can be recouped fairly quickly when the yield from a well-managed system is prolific.

As with all projects, a great deal of planning is required for any success with farming, whether traditional in nature or hydroponically, to be forthcoming. Setting up the best infrastructure for a hydroponic garden can be costly and requires a sound knowledge of plants and how they interact with the environment.

Despite these snags, with hard work and attention to detail, hydroponic gardening can become a successful way of growing a wide variety of sustainable crops to feed the starving masses.

Unexpected Delays and Setbacks

The success of the hydroponic system is dependent on the recycling of water. In the event of a power outage or pump failure, the entire crop could be lost within hours. It is, therefore, essential to have a backup plan in place.

And, finally, as with any form of gardening, there are always the little critters waiting to pounce and chew up all your hard work. These come in the form of fungus, mold, or root rot when hydroponic systems are not managed well.

High Humidity

The increased humidity level in hydroponic farming may encourage the development of mildew and certain detrimental fungi that thrive under damp conditions. Added to these diseases are a number of pests, such as aphids, thrips, and spider mites that will challenge you for control over the delicious crops you are producing.

Lack of Sufficient Knowledge of the Physiology of Plants

Without a basic understanding of the physiology of plants and how each individual part works, it can be challenging to make the best choice of suitable plants for your hydroponic venture.

Here is a basic outline that may be of value. All plants are made up of three main parts, each of which plays an important role in the overall success of the plant's life.

Roots

The roots are made up of primary roots, secondary roots, and root hairs. Their function is to hold the plant steady in the growing medium and to absorb nutrients and water for the plant.

Stems

The stem holds the plant upright above ground level. It may divide into smaller parts called branches and ultimately into even smaller twigs. Some plant's stems are divided into nodes and internodes. Each node (the lump on the stem) has the potential to produce new shoots.

The stems carry water and nutrients from the roots to the leaves, flowers, and fruit.

Leaves

The leaves of each plant develop from shoots and are the "factories" where sunlight is trapped for the manufacture of chlorophyll through an amazing process called photosynthesis. Each leaf absorbs carbon dioxide from the air and uses solar energy to convert this gas, along with water, into carbohydrates. The carbohydrates are converted into glucose, which is processed further. Eventually, oxygen is formed and released from the stomata under each leaf.

This process of air-cleaning is vital for the survival of all life on earth. In your hydroponic garden, it has an opportunity to work at its best.

Inadequate Knowledge of the Requirements for Plants

A lack of understanding of what plants require in order to grow and flourish can affect the success of any garden. Plants, like all living things, are made from organic matter, which, in turn, consists of the following four basic elements, each of which is vital for survival:

- Oxygen,
- Nitrogen,
- Hydrogen, and
- Carbon.

Oxygen
Oxygen, the eighth element on the periodic table, is a non-metal element that has an oxidizing reaction with most other elements. It is essential for all life and, therefore, a vital component for the successful growth of crops in a hydroponic garden.

Nitrogen
Nitrogen, the seventh element, consists of two atoms that, when split, cause an explosion. Nitrogen is an essential element in the production of chlorophyll. It is also found in amino acids, which are part of the proteins vital to the growth and development of plant life.

Hydrogen
Hydrogen, the first element in the periodic table, is crucial to the life of all living organisms. When two atoms of hydrogen are added to one atom of oxygen, water is formed and, as you are aware, water is fundamental to life.

Carbon
Carbon, element number 6, is a non-metal element that binds with many other elements to create new compounds. It is also

a vital component for the perpetuation of plant and animal life.

Right, now that you have a basic idea of the comparison between hydroponic gardening and traditional farming, let's get down to the important task of understanding the real financial value of hydroponic gardening and farming.

CHAPTER 4: SUCCESSFUL PLANT CHOICES FOR YOUR HYDROPONIC GARDEN

Hydroponic gardening can be a successful way to grow almost any type of fruits, vegetables, and flowers. For the beginner hydroponic gardener, however, the choice of plants may initially be somewhat limited. Do not let this concern you because as you grow in confidence and hone your hydroponic gardening skills, you will venture into more complex options.

PLANT OPTIONS FOR YOUR GARDEN

Vegetables

Green, leafy vegetables such as spinach, swiss chard, lettuce, and kale are the most rewarding, successful, and the least complicated crops to start growing in your hydroponic garden. Their shallow root systems make these versatile plants suitable for growing in simpler hydroponic modes such as the Kratky and Dutch Bucket systems as well as the Ebb and Flow System and the Nutrient Film Technique System.

All of these vegetable varieties require less fuss than some other plant types, and their yield is relatively quick and prolific.

Added to the leafy green veggies you may have great success growing chives, garlic, leeks, onions, spring onions, and scallions, all of which are viable options as starter plants.

Herbs

Ideal herbs that are quick and easy for beginner gardeners to grow and which produce a good yield include basil, oregano, mint, and parsley.

Fruits

The choice of successful fruits best suited to beginner hydroponic gardeners includes strawberries, blueberries, a wide variety of peppers, cucumbers, and most tomato varieties, all of which are likely to produce a good harvest and produce a great sense of satisfaction for the gardener.

Cannabis

For those gardeners planning to grow this medicinal crop, be mindful of the importance of first checking the legal aspects of cultivating Cannabis in your town.

Cannabis is relatively easy to grow, and in the hydroponic system, it flourishes, producing an excellent yield in approximately half the amount of time it would take a crop of similar size to reach maturity in a traditional garden.

The plant is sturdy with a tough, strong stem that requires little or no support. The root system consists of a long taproot from which many fibrous roots protrude. The root system of any plant is of fundamental value to that plant's survival. It not only anchors the plant in the growing medium but also draws up water, oxygen, and nutrients for optimum growth.

To grow Cannabis, ensure your net pots are sturdy and of sufficient depth to support part of the stem. The roots will hang down into the water and, therefore, do not require support.

The most successful systems in which to grow Cannabis are:
- the Ebb and Flow System,
- the Deep Water Culture System (which may be one of the better options),
- the Wick System, and

Gordon L. Atwell

- the Drip System.

SOME OF THE HEALTHIEST FRUITS, VEGETABLES, AND HERBS TO GROW IN A HYDROPONIC SYSTEM

The general trend toward eating healthy, organic food is definitely increasing as people become more aware and better informed of the nutrient value of food produced in a hydroponic, eco-friendly farming system. Fresh fruits and vegetables that are grown under organic conditions are much sought after in the marketplaces of the world.

If you are an ardent and diligent gardener, your hydroponic growing system can produce some truly great quality crops with enormous health benefits to not only your family but also those consumers you supply.

Tomatoes

Tomatoes are classified as climbing plants that are easy to grow and can be trained to spread upward toward the roof of your enclosure. Tomato crops are particularly rewarding to grow as they not only produce fruits that have an attractive, vibrant red color but they can also render a prolific crop.

Tomatoes are fruits that are full of vitamin A and vitamin C, as well as folic acid. They are also rich in lycopene, a valuable carotenoid that not only gives the fruit its attractive color but is an important antioxidant. Regular intake of tomatoes in almost any form (fresh or processed) has been known to decrease the risk of certain chronic illnesses such as cardiovascular disease and certain types of cancer.

Lettuce

Lettuce is an uncomplicated, easy-to-grow, and fast-to-harvest vegetable that takes up relatively little space. The leaves can be picked on an ongoing basis for the entire life of the plant. This low-calorie vegetable is very much in demand as it contains phytonutrients that help to prevent certain diseases.

Iceberg lettuce, just one variety of many, contains rich sources of calcium, potassium, trace elements of iron, and the powerful antioxidant vitamin C that supports the immune system.

Cucumbers

This vine-like, water-loving fruit grows prolifically and can be trained to spiral upwards, thus saving space. The plants require some added support as the fruits can become quite heavy when they reach maturity.

Rich in micro-elements such as iron, calcium, zinc, magnesium, potassium, and vitamin C, vitamin B, and folic acid, cucumbers are a definite favorite among farmers and gardeners alike. Cucumbers assist with cleaning out the body and regulating cholesterol levels. They support the body's metabolism and are excellent anti-aging fruits.

Spring Onions

Spring onions are actually young onions that have not yet reached full maturity. They are a popular ingredient in salads and can be harvested every 3 to 4 weeks. They are full of antioxidants and have a very positive effect on the prevention of cellular tissue damage by reacting with free radicals to stop the harmful effects of these molecules on the body.

Spring onions are rich in vitamins A, B, C, and K and have a positive effect on the growth and development of healthy bones because they promote the absorption of calcium.

Peppers

Peppers are somewhat more challenging to grow as the plants will become increasingly productive if there is a slight drop in the daytime temperature and an equally slight rise in the temperature during the night. This will require careful monitoring by the hydroponic gardener to ensure the crop is well managed.

These low-calorie, colorful fruits are high in vitamin C and vitamin A, folic acid, fiber, and potassium. They are an excellent addition to any meal as they help to maintain good health because of their antioxidant value.

Spinach

Spinach is a fast-growing, abundant leafy vegetable rich in antioxidants. It is also a great source of protein; iron; vitamins A, C, K, and E; as well as minerals such as magnesium, copper, and zinc. Spinach is one of the best vegetables available for lowering cholesterol, and it also aids digestion in addition to having a positive effect on reducing the results of aging.

Strawberries

When correctly cared for, these vines are prolific, all-year-round bearers of delicious, bright red fruits that thrive in the damp conditions offered in a hydroponic garden.

Strawberries are a good choice of fruits for supporting the immune system as they are high in vitamin C and antioxidants. They have a positive effect on lowering blood pressure and cholesterol (D'Anna, 2020).

Blueberries

These popular, extremely healthy, and very delicious tiny fruits prefer an acidic medium in which to grow. They can make the most rewarding crop if the hydroponic gardener carefully controls the pH of the water and nutrients.

Blueberries are rich in antioxidants and rate very high on the scale of healthy foods because of their value in protecting the brain and nervous system.

Basil

Basil, a popular, prolific, and aromatic herb that is easy to grow in your hydroponic garden, not only adds flavor and fragrance to a meal but has great medicinal properties as well.

Basil is high in antioxidants and has a positive effect on slowing aging because it fights free radicals. It is also useful for reducing swelling and inflammation.

Coriander

Coriander is another healthy, fragrant, and prolific herb that is easy to grow under hydroponic conditions. It is rich in vitamins C and K and is a good source of protein and magnesium, iron, and fiber. It's many health attributes include relieving mouth ulcers, inflammation, and reducing high cholesterol.

Swiss Chard

This leafy green vegetable is usually cultivated in traditional gardens in the cooler seasons. However, when cultivated hydroponically, it can successfully be grown all year round, producing an abundant crop with each planting.

Swiss chard can be cooked or eaten raw in a salad. The leaves have a delicate, smooth texture and an appealing taste. The stalks of the young chard plant can also be eaten as they are deliciously crunchy and tender.

Swiss chard is packed with nutritional goodness in the form of vitamins A, C, and K. It is also a great source of magnesium, potassium, and plant fiber, which aids digestion.

Bok Choy

Bok choy is also known as Chinese Cabbage. This easy-to-cultivate, nutritious vegetable is rich in vitamins A, K, and C as well as foliate (Vitamin B-9), which plays an important role in early pregnancy. It can help to reduce the risks of potential defects in the infant's brain and spinal column.

This delicious and nourishing vegetable can be eaten raw or lightly stir-fried.

Chives

Chives, related to onion and garlic, are easy to grow. Under the right conditions, they are prolific producers of delicious, succulent, green stems that have a mild onion taste. These stems are usually chopped finely to add flavor to omelets, grilled steaks, and roast chicken.

Chives are very successful in a hydroponic system as each plant takes up very little space, so many plants can be grown together.

Oregano

Oregano is a popular herb used in a variety of dishes. It is also known as the "happiness herb" because its name is derived from the Greek word "garnos," which means "joy" (Brazier, n.d.).

Oregano, with its wonderful antioxidant, anti-inflammatory, and anti-bacterial properties, has a multitude of medicinal uses including the treatment of minor sores, muscle aches, asthma, and indigestion.

This prolific, easy-to-grow herb is part of the mint family. The fragrant leaves of the oregano plant can be used in salads or served with roast lamb. It can also be made into an herbal tea.

Oregano will be successful in most hydroponic systems and requires very little fuss. It will produce good yields all year round.

Parsley

Another popular herb that can be grown with great success in a hydroponic system is parsley. Low in calories and rich in a variety of vitamins, including vitamins K, A, and C, parsley is used to enhance the flavor of a variety of dishes.

It is thought that this simple herb may have great value for the health of your kidneys and heart. It may also have a positive effect on blood sugar levels. Parsley has anti-bacterial properties and can boost your immune system.

This bushy, soft-stemmed little herb grows with enthusiasm in most hydroponic systems to produce an abundant, year-round crop.

A Final Word of Caution

As you now realize, there is an abundance of fruit, herb, and vegetable options available to start growing in your new hydroponic garden. The more success you have with your crops, the greater your sense of satisfaction and the more enthusiastic you will be to expand your skills.

However, without dampening your avid enthusiasm, try not to diversify too quickly. It will be in your best interest to start small and learn the intricacies of the hydroponic system of your choice. As you master each setback, which I hope will be few, you will learn how to manage growing bigger and more challenging crops.

Good luck, fellow hydroponic gardening entrepreneur!

CHAPTER 5: THE VARIETY AND FLEXIBILITY OFFERED BY HYDROPONIC GARDENING

THE CHOICE OF MORE ADVANCED HYDROPONIC SYSTEMS

There is a wide variety of innovative hydroponic gardening or farming systems available. The choice is dependent on the space you have available, the scale on which you intend to grow crops, and ultimately, the type of crop you wish to cultivate.

If hydroponic gardening is your new venture, you will find the information in this chapter useful in helping you to decide on the system that will best suit your needs.

Let us take a good look at the options available to the more experienced gardener and take note of their advantages for you and your circumstances.

BUBBLEPONICS

Bubbleponics is essentially the same as the Deep Water Culture System, but with a single difference. In this system, germination and plant growth are assisted by feeding each individual plant from the top via a drip system (Espiritu, 2019).

The additional equipment you will require here will be:

- an extra water pump,
- a length of suitable hose,
- a tube, suspended above the plants, with suitable holes from which each drip line will flow, and
- a number of drip lines (depending on the number of pots to be watered).

ORGANIC GARDENING

The Bubbleponic System

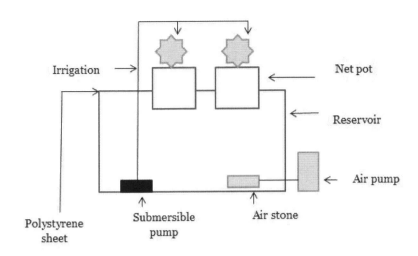

Requirements for the Bubbleponic System

This system is slightly more complicated than those discussed in Chapter 2 and might be more suited to an experienced hydroponic gardener

You will need the following items for this project:

Reservoir
For the storage of nutrient-rich water.

Submersible Pump
To circulate water through the system.

An Air Pump
To move oxygen through the system.

An Air Stone
To create oxygen for the plants.

Rubber Tubing

91

For transporting nutrients and water through the system.

Net Pots

To hold the plants you will grow.

Growing Media

Essential to support plants and hold nutrients.

pH Kit

Essential for keeping the acid level in the water at 6.5.

Polystyrene Sheet

To cover the reservoir.

Irrigation Tube

Suitable tubing for the irrigation line.

Getting Started

- Attach a suitable length of pipe or tubing to the submersible pump. The irrigation should be able to comfortably reach the plants.
- Place the submersible pump into the reservoir.
- Connect the air pump to the air stone.
- Place the air stone into the reservoir.
- Place the net pots containing growing medium and plants into ready-made holes in the polystyrene sheet. Ensure the base of the pots will be suspended in the water in the reservoir.
- Push the irrigation tube through a suitable hole in the polystyrene sheet, or attach it to the back of the reservoir.
- Fill the reservoir with water and the correct quantity of nutrients and acid as per instructions on the relevant packaging.
- Place the polystyrene sheet over the reservoir and turn on the pumps.

The Advantages of the Bubbleponic System

- This is an enclosed system from which very little water is lost.
- Growth is quick and steady. Plants should reach harvest within half the time they would take in a traditional garden.
- The system is easy to maintain.
- It is quick and simple to change plants, adjust growing medium, and harvest crops.

The Disadvantages of the Bubbleponic System

- The success of the entire system is dependent on the uninterrupted energy supply. In the event of a power disruption, the whole system will be adversely affected and the crops will be lost. Ensure there is a backup plan in the form of a fuel or solar-driven generator.

Questions About the Bubbleponic System

What are the best nutrients to use in the Bubbleponic System?

There are a number of good quality products on the market. You may, however, be happy to try the General Hydroponics Flora Series. This is a three-part nutrient that you will need to mix specifically to suit the growth stage of your plants (Espiritu, 2019).

Is a sterile reservoir necessary?

A sterile reservoir simply means one without algae. There are benefits to having some algae in the reservoir; however,

Gordon L. Atwell

you may experience some challenges when troublesome algae make their debut in your tank.

DRIP SYSTEM

The Drip System, first developed in Israel where it was used for outdoor crop production, is one of the most popular and viably active hydroponic systems that makes use of a pump to distribute water to all the plants in the system (Thu, n.d.).

As the name implies, nutrient-rich water is drip-fed to the individual plants via a series of tubes. This is a highly water-efficient system as water is dripped through a network of pipes that feed the plants at a slow but steady rate.

The Drip System is eco-friendly in that there is no wastage of water, which has become one of the world's most precious commodities. All excess water is caught and recycled via an overflow pipe to the reservoir from where it will be re-pumped into the system.

The Drip System

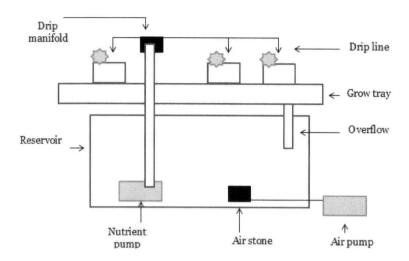

How the Drip System works

- Net pots filled with the growing medium are placed in a grow tray, either side by side in a row or groups, depending on the size of the tray and the crops to be grown.
- The grow tray is suspended above the reservoir which can be a tank or bucket.
- One end of a main-line, PVC tube is connected to a submersible water pump that supplies the pressure to push the water through the system. In some instances, water can be moved through the system without using a pump. This then occurs through the use of gravity.
- The other end of the main-line PVC tube is connected to a drip manifold.
- Several smaller drip pipes, called "drip emitters," are also connected to the drip manifold (Max, 2019).

ORGANIC GARDENING

- Each of the drip emitters is suspended directly above a plant.
- Water is delivered to each plant in a controlled manner.

Variations to the Drip System

The Drip System is highly versatile and can be set up in any number of configurations for maximum usage of water. The two main ways in which this can be done are mentioned below.

Recirculating/Recovery System

All the excess water that drips through the growing medium in each pot is collected and returned to the reservoir for re-use. In this way, water and nutrients are not wasted.

However, each time water returns to the reservoir, it dilutes the pH and nutrient levels. It is, therefore, important to check these levels regularly and adjust them when necessary.

This type of system works well on a small, home-based scale where it is easier to monitor than in a large commercial enterprise.

The Non-Recovery/Non-Circulating System

All excess water is allowed to run off without being collected for recirculation. Unfortunately, this is a wasteful way of irrigating the plants. However, in large commercial enterprises where this method is used, timing devices accurately adjust the amount of water that is dripped out at regular intervals. In this way, minimal water wastage is ensured.

The Advantages of the Drip System

- The biggest advantage of this system is the controlled manner of the water supply.

- There is little or no wastage of water.
- The system is viable for usage with gravity as well as electricity. In instances where there is a power cut, the system can continue effectively if it has been designed to use gravity flow as a backup.
- There is a high degree of accuracy in a well-designed system.
- This system lends itself to being highly mechanized (Max, 2019).
- The system works well for vertically placed grow trays as the water sprayed out above the first plant at the top will filter down to the plants below. Plants in horizontal trays are watered directly from the drip tube.
- A flexible system with a wide variety of options.
- Low maintenance.
- Affordable.

The Disadvantages of the Drip System

- The system requires careful initial installation.
- If left uncontrolled, plants can receive excessive water and end up being swamped (Max, 2019).
- The system might be a little too complicated for the smaller growing operation.
- If the non-recovery system is used, there will be a lot of wastage of water, which can be costly.

Getting Started

Because of the versatility of the Drip System, you may decide to use more or fewer drip trays depending on the space available and the plants you decide to cultivate. The grow trays can be many or few.

Drip Emitters

Sufficient drip emitters will be required to ensure each plant will be individually watered.

You may decide to simply poke holes in the tubing, thus avoiding the necessity for drip emitters. However, you will need to measure the distance between the holes to ensure each hole will be above a pot.

Thin Rubber Tubing

This tubing is attached to each drip emitter and carries water to the plants.

Thicker PVC Tubing

The thicker tubing carries water from the reservoir to the emitters. The number of tubes required will depend on the size of the setup.

Water Pump

A submersible water pump is required to create sufficient pressure to circulate the water throughout the entire system.

Should you decide not to make use of a pump and use a gravity feed system instead, the layout of your system will change. The reservoir will need to be placed above the plants to allow for the water to drip out slowly. A special valve is required that will be opened and closed by a timing device.

A Draining Tray/Grow Tray

All the net pots are placed on a draining tray to ensure a single platform for collecting the run-off water. Using a draining tray excludes the necessity for individual draining pipes from each plant pot.

If you decide to go with the gravity feed method, make sure your drip tray is placed at a slight angle to allow water to run back into the reservoir. Obviously, the angle of the tray should not interfere with the stability of the pots.

Nutrient Pump
This is an electrically operated submersible pump that will circulate the nutrients through the system.

Drip Manifold
The drip manifold holds the tubing in place over each plant.

Reservoir
The reservoir can be any large, sturdy container that will hold sufficient nutrient-enriched water.

Net Pots
You will need as many net pots or other suitable containers for the number of plants you have. Any other types of non-toxic plastic planters can be used, provided they have sufficient small holes for adequate drainage.

A Garden Timer
This is attached to the pump and will switch on and off as programmed.

Aquarium Grade Silicone Sealer
This is important to ensure all the necessary joints and connections between pipes and PVC tubing are well-sealed.

Hydroponic Growing Medium
There is a wide variety of growing media to choose from. Coconut coir works quite well in the Drip System.

A Power Drill, Hacksaw, and Clamps
General tools required for the task of setting up your new Drip System.

Plants Best Suited for the Drip System

Because of its versatility, the Drip System works well for the following plants:

- lettuces,
- onions, leeks, and radishes,
- peas, tomatoes, strawberries, and cucumbers, and
- melons.

The Drip System works particularly well for larger plants because the timer can be set to produce a specific amount of water for the needs of individual plants.

The larger the plants you grow, the denser the growing medium should be to ensure water is retained around the roots for a longer period.

The gravity feed Drip System works very well in conjunction with the Vertical System, which is not only a great way to maximize water usage but also saves space and allows for more plants to be grown per square foot.

KRATKY METHOD

The Kratky Method is a passive hydroponic system that does not require a pump or electricity. Plants are placed into a raft which is then placed over a container that has a solution of water and nutrients. The raft effectively seals the container allowing just the roots of the plant to hang into the nutrient-rich water (McKee, 2017).

Over a period of time, the water is depleted as the plant grows. The roots lengthen as the water is used. This creates an air pocket for the roots so they don't drown.

Once the plant is ready to harvest, the water and nutrients can be replenished and a new plant can be placed into the raft. This process can be repeated up to 5 times before the container needs to be thoroughly cleaned for the start of the next 5 cycles.

The system is simple and ideal for home use.

The best plant to begin with is lettuce. Suitable nutrients containing calcium nitrate and magnesium sulfate are ideal for this crop. For the best results, follow the instructions on the containers.

As the plant begins to grow, the level of the nutrient-rich water drops, allowing increased air into the system. The excess of oxygen is hugely beneficial to the plant, promoting its speedy and healthy growth.

The versatility of the Kratky System lends itself to be a worthwhile, easy-to-manage home hydroponic option.

The Kratky Method

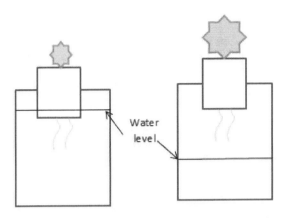

Growth after 30 days

Requirements for Building the Kratky Hydroponic Method

For the Kratky Hydroponic Method to be installed, you will require the following equipment:

Reservoir
A suitable container that will hold sufficient water enriched with nutrients to grow the number of plants you have in mind.

Grow Tray/Lid
An airtight tray that fits across the top of the water container, with holes to hold the individual plants.

Net Pots
A number of net pots depending on the number of plants you have.

Suitable Area
A suitable place to put all your equipment. This may be in

the form of a hothouse, an outdoor dome, or a specific room where you can grow your plants.

Light

Remember, natural sunlight is generally used.

Seeds or Seedlings

Whichever seeds you choose to grow should be suited to the Kratky Method of gardening.

Nutrients

As previously discussed, a variety of good quality nutrients are available from online stores or garden outlets. Read the instructions carefully to ensure you offer your plants the best opportunity for successful growth.

Setting up the Kratky Method of Gardening

- The container you require will need to "fit" the purpose for which you want to use it. A tomato plant will need a bigger/deeper container than a lettuce plant.
- Fill the container with a water and nutrient solution.
- Check the pH and ensure this is correct for the plant type you wish to grow.
- Make a hole in the lid of the container, just big enough for the net pot to fit securely. Place the lid onto the container and check that the base of the pot is just in the water.
- The lid plays a vital role in the Kratky Method as it seals the container thus protecting the contents from contamination. It traps air in the container between its underside and the surface of the water. The air becomes moist and helps to keep the upper area of the root damp. The lid also acts as a support for the pot as well as the plant.
- Ensure the pot has sufficient light, although it does not require direct sunlight.
- As the plant grows, it draws water from the container.

Once the water in the container is almost finished, the plant should be ready to be harvested.

Plants Best Suited for the Kratky Method

For the most part, smaller, light-weight plants work well. However, larger varieties are not excluded. Depending on the plants you wish to grow, you will need to adjust the size of the container and pot accordingly. The larger the plant, the greater the air space should be (McKee, 2017).

Lettuce, spinach, herbs, and some varieties of smaller tomatoes should work well.

The Advantages of the Kratky Method

The Kratky Method of hydroponics is specifically aimed at gardening in smaller, portable containers (McKee, 2017).

It was developed by Bernard A. Kratky from the University of Hawaii and is a simple, passive method of growing fresh produce on a fairly small scale. It requires no electricity for a pump, so it is an easy and inexpensive method to operate.

- Any kind of container can be used.
- Trays can be made from polystyrene.
- Easy to maintain.
- No strict temperature control required.
- Natural sunlight.

The Disadvantages of the Kratky Method

- The Kratky Method is more difficult to control when it is operated outdoors.
- Exposure to rainwater can seriously undermine the nu-

trient and pH levels in the water, which will, in turn, have a disastrous effect on their growth.
- The larger the plants get, the slower their growth. These plants will benefit from added oxygen.
- Stagnant water can become a serious problem in the Kratky system. A rise in the water temperature will lead to root rot and will attract an array of unwanted pests.
- The Kratky Method requires good quality water to start the system going. The pH must be correct for the duration of the plant's life.
- Fluctuations in external temperature adversely affect the Kratky System. Insulation of some sort will help to keep the water temperature consistent. This should be between 65° and 80° F (18° - 25° C).

DUTCH BUCKET

The Dutch Bucket System is a useful, home-styled hydroponic system that can cater to larger varieties of plants. As the name implies, the Dutch Bucket System uses buckets, one or more, depending on how big you need your system to be. The Dutch Bucket System operates on the same principle as the Ebb and Flow System with one main difference: A bucket is used in place of the tray.

Although this is an active system requiring electricity and a pump, the possibility of turning it into a gravity feed system could work as well (Dutch Bucket/Bato Bucket Hydroponic System, 2019).

The Dutch Bucket System

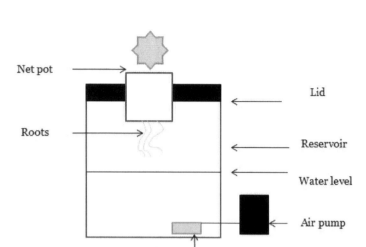

How the Dutch Bucket System Works

- A large bucket that acts as the reservoir is filled to about ⅓ of its capacity with the nutrient-enriched water and is fitted with a pump.
- A single smaller bucket or container filled with the growing medium of your choice and holding a single plant is placed into the prepared hole in the polystyrene lid of the reservoir bucket.
- Each reservoir bucket only holds a single plant.
- The pump is connected to an air stone.
- The air stone is placed in the bucket.
- When the bucket is securely sealed by the polystyrene lid and the pump is turned on, the water begins to bubble creating moist air around the roots of the plant.

The Advantages of the Dutch Bucket System

- The system can accommodate larger, bushy plants.
- This is a great space-saving hydroponic system.
- The system is sufficiently flexible to accommodate a number of buckets.
- The layout of buckets is also flexible in that they can be placed higher or lower in the growing area, depending on the space available.
- Pest management is easier in the Dutch Bucket System. If one bucket becomes contaminated, it can be replaced without upsetting the entire system.
- The closed, recirculating system saves water and nutrients.
- The system does not necessarily require an electric pump as it can work on gravity alone if structured to do so.
- If the pump is used, it can run indefinitely without flooding the buckets.
- Plants grow twice as fast in the Dutch Bucket System as they would in a traditional farming system because their roots are constantly exposed to nutrient-rich moisture.
- There is no chance of plants "drowning" in the Dutch Bucket System.
- The system can be operated off a timer, making it more efficient and less labor-intensive.
- The Dutch Bucket System is great for beginner hydroponic gardeners.

The Disadvantages of the Dutch Bucket System

- The system requires constant care, so it is time-consuming.

- If there is contamination in the reservoir, the entire system has to shut down. All equipment needs to be sterilized and plants need to be destroyed. In effect, if this ever happens, you have to start from scratch, which is a costly business.
- The grower needs some knowledge of hydroponic culture in order to make the Dutch Bucket System work to its best advantage.
- The nutrient level in the re-circulated water can drop, so it should be checked regularly.
- The pH levels can also change for the same reason, so it should also be closely monitored.
- Pump failure can lead to crop decimation. If a pump is used in your Dutch Bucket System, consider investing in a generator or a solar-powered unit.

Which Growing Medium Is Best for This System?

Because the Dutch Bucket System supports larger plants, the correct medium for this growing success must be chosen with care. The growing medium should hold sufficient water for the larger plants and be eco-friendly and sustainable. Available products include perlite, vermiculite, and coconut coir.

These examples of growing media can be used in isolation or they could be mixed in equal proportions to lend better plant stability.

Plants That Are Best Suited to the Dutch Bucket System

A variety of plants grow well in the Dutch Bucket System.

Climbers
Climbing plants such as cucumbers, pole beans, zucchinis, and tomatoes make excellent crops in this system. Remember

that climbing plants may require added support for their continued success and survival.

Root Vegetables

Root vegetables such as potatoes, beets, and sweet potatoes do well in the Dutch Bucket System because of the depth of the buckets and the extra support they offer the plants.

Capsicum and Chilies

Bell peppers and chilies are successful crops to grow in this system. They reach their harvest level within half the time of those planted in soil. Their yield is also higher.

Leafy Vegetables

Leafy green vegetable varieties such as broccoli, spinach, swiss chard, and lettuce are successful crops to consider if you are using the Dutch Bucket System.

CHAPTER 6: ADVANCED TECHNIQUES FOR ENTHUSIASTIC HYDROPONIC GARDENERS

The more interested you are in hydroponic gardening, the more encouraged you may become to try your hand at other advanced techniques in hydroponics.

Once you have gained experience with a simpler method, you will have a greater understanding of the hydroponic process and its successes, as well as the potential pitfalls.

This section gives you the opportunity to discover more about this economically viable and pleasurable gardening technique.

THE NUTRIENT FILM TECHNIQUE

The Nutrient Film Technique (NFT) funnels nutrient-rich water from the reservoir through shallow pipes past the exposed roots of the plants. This process uses recirculating water (D'Anna, 2019).

The Nutrient Film Technique

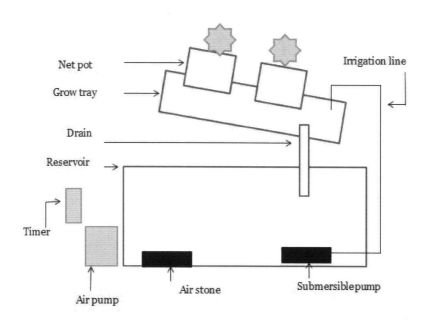

Similar to the Ebb and Flow System, the Nutrient Film Technique System uses recycled nutrient-rich water that constantly flows in a thin layer over the area of the root submerged below water level. The upper area of the root remains dry and exposed to oxygen in the air. This process uses a gravitational system, ensuring the roots are not soaked in water. It is most suited to light-weight, fast-growing plants. Vine plants, such as tomatoes, will require good support in this system.

The Nutrient Film System uses PVC tubes with holes drilled in it for plants. It is important to note the holes in the tubes do not go right through the PVC tubing because the plant is supported in the hole and where the water runs past its roots.

The benefits of the Nutrient Film Technique

This popular and versatile hydroponic design can have as many additional channels as you have space for, thus increasing your yield capabilities without much effort. The benefits for the Nutrient Film Technique include:

- Low cost of installation.
- Low maintenance.
- Uses less growing media.
- Works in a closed system so less water is needed.
- There is less chance of contamination in the water.
- Constantly moving water does not encourage the build-up of salts around roots.
- The modular structure is easy to expand when necessary.

The disadvantages of the Nutrient Film System

- Excessive root growth can block the channels.
- Pump failure can decimate the entire crop within hours.
- This system does not cater for plants with taproots.
- Plants requiring support do not do well in this system.

What You Need to Build a Nutrient Film System

Reservoir
A suitable container to use as a reservoir.

Air Pump
An air pump is essential to pump sufficient oxygenated air through.

Available from Amazon at a cost of between $24 - $30

Air Stone
An air stone to oxygenate the water.

Available at Amazon at a cost of around $20 - $25

Airline Tubing

Airline tubing to connect the pump to the air stone. Black air tubing is best as the transparent type attracts algae.

Available at Amazon for between $8 - $10

Water Pump

Water pump to pump nutrient-rich water through the system.

The Waterfall Pump available from Takealot at a cost of between $20 - $25

Nutrient Film Tubing/PVC Pipes

NFT channels or PVC pipes to transport water through the system.

These are available at your local gardening outlet or suitable online stores.

Net Pots

A variety of net pots are available from your local gardening outlet or online store. You may, however, use any suitable non-toxic plastic container with holes cut in the bottom.

Growing Medium

A variety of different types of growing mediums are available from your local garden outlet or may be purchased online.

Hydroponic Nutrients

These are available from a garden outlet or suitable online stores.

Getting Started

- A good quality reservoir is essential for the Nutrient Film System. It is placed beneath the channel structure to ensure nutrient-enriched water is pumped up through

- the entire system and eventually returned to the reservoir.
- A series of flat trays (½ rounds of PVC piping can be used) with polystyrene covers are erected above the reservoir and linked with tubing to ensure the water flows from tray to tray.
- Net pots with sufficient growing medium to hold the seedlings in place are suspended into the channels. The roots grow through the net pot and hang into the water as it passes through the channels.
- Take care to control the environment by monitoring air temperature, water temperature, humidity levels, and airflow. A water temperature between 65 - 68° F (18 - 20° C) is ideal for plant production.
- Decide how best to start your plants. Most growers use Rockwool cubes or Rapid Rooter plugs.
- Keep the nutrient solution calibrated so that you can make adjustments where necessary.
- Monitor the pH and maintain levels between 5.8 and 6.3. A standard pH kit should be sufficient for this task.
- Change the water in the reservoir weekly.
- Keep light out of the reservoir and the channels to avoid algae growth.
- Keep the environment spotlessly clean to avoid contamination of infestations of unwanted "critters."
- Monitor your nutrients and check their impact on the plants. Adjust the dosage as required. Start off with less of the nutrients and gradually add more if needed.
- Check root health and eradicate any plants with unhealthy roots (root rot).

The Advantages of the Nutrient Film Technique

- This is a fairly easy system to establish.
- Good quality crops are produced when the system runs

well.
- Less chance of water contamination due to the closed system.
- Transplanting seedlings is easier.
- Larger crops can be accommodated.
- Fewer nutrients are required.
- Better utilization of space because of the tiered system.

The Disadvantages of the Nutrient Film Technique

- Challenges in keeping the pH levels consistent.
- The danger of light infiltrating the reservoir.
- Potential for root rot to develop.
- Potential for roots to clog up the channels.
- Pump failure can cause total loss of crop.
- The system requires constant vigilance.

THE VERTICAL GARDEN

The increased concentration of constructions in urban areas has used up vast tracts of land that could have been utilized for horizontal gardening and farming. The far-reaching and devastating effects of deforestation and the destruction of the natural vegetation on the environment and humanity as a whole have been a source of great concern for many years.

Not only have the aesthetics of our world been destroyed, but so too, the opportunity for the continued natural reproductive functions of our flora and fauna. Added to this is the huge negative impact on the continued depletion of the protection of life-giving ozone.

As we already know, hydroponics is a soilless method of gardening with many possibilities for personal creativity and design. Vertical gardens are among those that have been developed as a result of the denuding of natural vegetation in areas where living complexes, buildings, and office blocks have been erected all in the name of progress (Horticulture: Landscaping: Vertical Gardening, n.d.).

In an attempt to improve the aesthetics of buildings and to bring some form of natural plant-life back into our concrete jungles, landscapers and architects have begun to work hand-in-hand to find solutions to the challenge of our diminishing natural habitat.

A number of buildings now boast of "wall-gardens" or huge, eye-catching vertical gardens that adorn otherwise empty spaces offering humanity the opportunity to witness and admire some of the beautiful flora that would otherwise never be seen. Many of these vertical or hanging garden structures are hydroponically operated.

So, let us take a look at what it means to garden in a vertical dimension as opposed to the traditional horizontal format.

Vertical Hydroponic Cultivation

Initially, hydroponic gardens were laid in a horizontal structure, simply because traditional gardening is the same. However, as time progressed and gardeners became more innovative due to space constraints, the vertical hydroponic concept began to take shape (Horticulture: Landscaping: Vertical Gardening, n.d.).

Vertical gardening structures are, in fact, an ingenious method for saving space while at the same time increasing the number of plants per square foot. In fact, the theory of vertical gardening may have developed out of the same concept of high-rise buildings. These structures take up relatively limited ground space compared to the number of people that can be housed within their concrete and steel walls.

The Vertical Garden

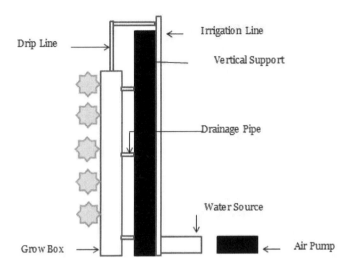

The vertical system of cultivating plants is a brilliant innovative method for small-space, big-yield gardening. It increases the vegetation surface area while simultaneously having a positive effect on the reduction of environmental pollution.

These gardens improve not only the aesthetics of the environment but enrich and enhance the green surroundings. The added value of vertical gardens on buildings effectively insulates the walls, cooling these during the hot months but absorbing CO_2 and hot gases from the air. In return, the plants release O_2 into the air, which is a vital element for sustaining life on planet earth.

The vertical hydroponic garden is a particularly successful model for crop production. It's capacity to hold many more plants than most other systems results in it being a cost-effective way to farm. Productivity increases exponentially the more plants that grow in the vertical system.

A simpler form of vertical gardening has been in evidence for many years in the form of growing vines on a trellis or over a pergola. It has now developed into a popular method among many hydroponic gardeners and farmers.

Requirements for a Vertical Garden

Support Structure
As all vertical gardens require firm support to keep them upright, your first decision is going to include how best to create a suitable frame.

Weightless Growing Medium
Thinking of the potential weight that the structure you have created above has to support, choose a weightless medium for growing your plants. The medium should be fairly porous so as not to clog up the system. Perlite, vermiculite, or cocopeat are potential choices.

Effective Watering System
The vertical garden requires a good and continuous supply of nutrient-rich water that will drain through the vertical system and be replenished on a regular basis. This irrigation system should be simple yet effective. It should operate at a maximum water-saving level. A drip system is usually the most effective for keeping the roots moist. However, Fogponics may work well depending on the situation of the vertical garden.

pH Kit
As with hydroponic systems, it is essential to maintain a balanced pH of between 6.5 and 8.5.

Timer

A reliable timer is essential to operate the watering system. This will, of course, rely on an electrical supply point. Because the water system is of fundamental value to the success of the crop, without power to operate the timer, the entire system could fail. It may be worth investing in a generator as a standby in the event of a power cut.

Irrigation Line

A light-weight rubber tube of sufficient length should do the trick as an irrigation line. This line should run from the pump to the full height of the vertical system from where it will operate as a drip system to irrigate the plants.

An Air Pump

An air pump is vital for pushing the nutrient-enriched water through the system.

Drainage

Adequate drainage of excess fluid is essential to avoid wastage of water.

Recycling Tank or Water Source/Reservoir

A suitable source of good quality water is essential for any type of successful gardening. The water in the vertical system will drain through the grow-box and collect in the reservoir to avoid wastage.

Vertical Grow-Box

A vertical grow-box structured to suit the available space and the type of plants intended to be cultivated.

Lights

A warm, sunny space is required for plants to thrive. If you are working indoors, then you may require an appropriate light.

There are three main types of lights suitable for the support of plant growth in most hydroponic systems: the compact fluorescent light (CFL), the high-intensity discharge light (HID), and the light-emitting diode (LED).

For more information on this subject, please visit the useful website mentioned here: https://heavy.com/garden/2015/09/best-full-spectrum-grow-lights-hydroponics-for-sale-reviews-bulbs-cannabis-marijuana/

Plants/Crops

The crops best suited for the vertical hydroponic system should be fairly light-weight and fast-growing.

The Advantages of the Vertical System

- It saves a great deal of space.
- This system is a fairly cost-effective farming method.
- Indoor vertical farming increases the area for growing crops by allowing for an increased number of crops that can be cultivated per square foot.
- The system offers a good return on investment.
- The economical use of water means there is little or no wastage of this precious commodity.
- The versatility of this system is ideal for use with a variety of other hydroponic methods. Fogponics may be one of the most successful methods to consider.
- The vertical system reduces CO_2 levels and increases O_2 output.
- It is an energy-efficient system.
- The vertical system is relatively easy to operate and maintain.

The Disadvantages of the Vertical System

- The farmer will require some knowledge of how best to erect a secure structure.
- The system requires an electric pump for the adequate circulation of water.
- The system requires adequate lighting for crop growth.
- Any dead plant material should be removed as soon as it is noticed to avoid clogging the system.
- Regular checks on the nutrient and pH levels are essential as these will fluctuate due to the recycled water.
- Regularly check that all crops are receiving sufficient nutrients.
- The spread of disease or contaminants is easier in the vertical system. Keep the area spotless and immediately

remove any suspect plants.
- Don't make the structure higher than you can comfortably reach.

Types of Vertical Gardens

Fortunately, there is an endless supply of ideas for vertical gardens. You can be as creative as you wish in creating your own masterpiece.

Hanging Pots
These pots can be attractively arranged against a supportive backdrop where the plants will receive sufficient light and water to sustain their growth.

Tiered Gutters
Repurposed gutters make very satisfactory containers for plants.

Trellis
The trellis system for growing vines is a useful vertical system. This can be the wooden variety or the plastic "gardening cloth" type.

Tower Pots
There are a variety of different types available. Homemade versions can be quite innovative. Tower pots consist of a number of different sized pots that fit one on top of the next, with the largest one at the bottom of the stack and the smallest on top. Irrigating the pots from the top ensures all the plants throughout the system will receive water via drainage.

Tower pot

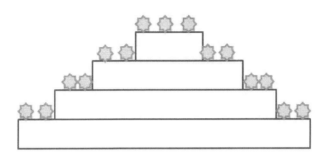

Vertical Trays
Trays of almost any variety can suffice for vertical gardening. These can be made from wood, plastic, metal, or bark.

Bottles
Plastic bottles make an interesting and inexpensive garden display when hung at different angles against a wall.

Free-Standing Tiered Type
This type of tiered garden is generally quite small and makes a good starter-garden for someone wanting to experiment with vertical gardening techniques. The structure can be made from wood, plastic, or non-corrosive metal.

Free Standing Tier Garden

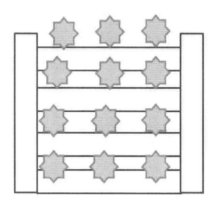

Beam Garden

A series of discarded wooden beams make a cleverly designed vertical garden. Each beam requires several holes drilled along its length into which plants will be placed. The beams are then turned into a vertical position and secured in place.

The Beam Garden

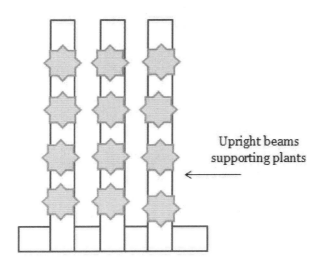

Stair Garden

This type of garden is built on a series of steps, each of which has a plant box. The tiered effect of this type of hydroponic structure can be most aesthetically pleasing.

THE AEROPONICS SYSTEM

Aeroponics is another eco-friendly hydroponic system for growing crops in which roots are exposed to the air and are sprayed regularly with nutrient-enriched water to keep them moist. There is no growing medium required. An aeroponic system is best suited to plants with non-woody stems, which makes it easy to cut them for cloning purposes (Barth, 2018).

The Process of Aeroponics

Seedlings are placed at regular intervals in fairly thick strips of polystyrene and then suspended under lights and over a water spraying system. The plants remain in place until harvest is complete. This excludes the need to transplant seedlings when they grow bigger.

The Aeroponic System

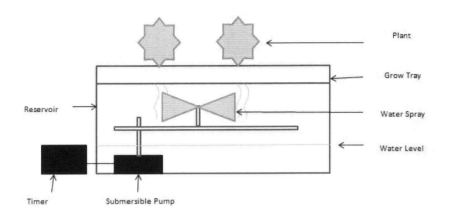

The Advantages of Aeroponics

- The exposure of the roots increases the oxygen they can absorb.
- Water is sparingly used. There is a saving of up to 95% of the water in the Aeroponic system.
- Aeroponics requires no growing medium.
- The system is highly eco-friendly.
- Aeroponics is a totally enclosed system; therefore, there is no waste run-off.
- Equipment is regularly sterilized to keep it spotless; therefore, no chemicals are required for cleaning purposes or for treating pest infestations.

The Disadvantages of the Aeroponic System

- It requires good knowledge of the hydroponic growing system.

- Requires careful monitoring to ensure temperature and nutrient concentration are absolutely "spot-on."
- The system is easily affected by the slightest change, so an entire crop can be quickly lost.
- Pump failure will lead to the almost immediate death of the fragile root systems.
- The water misters need regular cleaning to stop them from clogging up.
- Energy-intense lighting works best for aeroponic systems; therefore, potential power failures are a huge hazard.

Setting Up an Aeroponic System

A high-quality aeroponic system can be expensive. The do-it-yourself option is available but may not work as efficiently as the real thing (Barth, 2018).

The equipment you will require for this system includes:
- a good quality, non-toxic, solid plastic bin with holes drilled for each plant,
- a tank for the nutrient solution,
- towers or trays, depending on whether the system works vertically or horizontally,
- a pump to spray the nutrient-rich water onto the roots,
- pressure misters, either of a low or high-pressure variety,
- net pots,
- tubing and supports, and
- a timer for the spray function.

What Can Grow in the Aeroponic System?

Basically, most of the same fruits and vegetables that are grown in a standard hydroponic system can grow in the aeroponic system. These include leafy green vegetables, strawberries, blueberries, peppers, cucumbers, and tomatoes. This system is unsuitable for root vegetables (Barth, 2018).

FOGPONICS

What exactly is "Fogponics"? Fogponics is an innovative, highly specialized, yet easy-to-operate method of hydroponic gardening. As with all hydroponic systems, Fogponics relies essentially on the water in order to function, but as the name implies, it functions in a "foggy" environment.

Similar to Aeroponics in most other aspects, Fogponics also operates without a growing medium. The difference between Fogponics and other systems is that the plants' roots are directly exposed to a fine, nutrient-rich, oxygen laden mist of water droplets from which they absorb their food.

Now we understand already that oxygen plays a vital role in the plant's life. Not only is this essential element absorbed through the roots, but it is also released from the leaves as a by-product of photosynthesis.

Oxygen assists the roots in breaking down the nutrient-rich component in the fine mist, thus enabling them to absorb their food more easily. The plant responds by growing quicker than it would do if the nutrients had to be separated from the medium first before absorption could occur.

So, the result of exposing the plant's roots directly to the nutrient-laden mist ensures a faster turnaround time from planting to harvesting. This, of course, makes perfect economic sense.

To further improve the yield in the Fogponic system, the number of plants can be substantially increased in the available space. Altogether, Fogponics appears to be the "mecca" of the future success of hydroponic gardening (Elliott, 2016).

Let's Take a Closer Look at the Process of Fogponics

In the Fogponic system, plants are suspended in their growbox where they are exposed to consistent spraying by a fine fog-like mist of nutrient-enriched water. The droplets in the fog are between 5-30 μm and are, therefore, small enough to be readily absorbed by the roots.

However, Fogponics operates by exposing the entire plant to this fine cloud of water vapor, thus enabling the leaves and stems to benefit as well. The result of this massive dose of nutrients to the entire plant can only mean one thing. Yes, you guessed it. Faster, more prolific plant growth.

Plants grown in this system are not only healthier and more robust but reach their harvest potential sooner.

The Advantages of Fogponics Versus Aeroponics

Although neither system makes use of a growth medium, both are viable producers of healthy, robust plants.

In the Aeroponic system, plants are suspended in a growthbox and exposed to regular spraying with nutrient-enriched water. The Fogponic system clouds the entire plant from leaf to root in a nutrient-rich mist.

Both systems operate more efficiently off a timer. This ensures a regular supply of nutrients throughout the day and night.

Both systems are operated from indoors. That is, they are housed under some sort of roofing as in a dome or greenhouse.

Both systems make use of lighting to encourage photosynthesis and, ultimately, plant growth.

The conservative use of water in both systems ensures there is no wastage of this precious commodity.

Both the Aeroponic and Fogponic systems utilize space economically, thus ensuring more plants can be grown per square foot.

There is less chance for errors in feeding the plants in both systems. Both the spraying system in Aeroponics and the misting method in Fogponics ensure the nutrients are delivered to the plants. The plants, in turn, absorb and utilize the correct amount of nutrients with each delivery of water.

Both systems are easy to operate and require minimum fuss once they are up and running.

The Disadvantages of Fogponics Versus Aeroponics

As with any hydroponic system, there are always potentially harmful aspects to keep in mind. To be forewarned is to be forearmed, as the saying goes.

Under normal circumstances, both the Fogponic and Aeroponic systems will run indefinitely, delivering nutrient-rich mist to the plant. There will, however, come a point where glitches begin to make themselves known. As with any challenges, as soon as you become aware of these, you need to act immediately in order not to jeopardize your entire crop.

Look out for the blocked-nozzle-syndrome, which is more likely to occur in the Aeroponic system. This problem can creep up unexpectedly and is the result of a build-up of a solid nutrient scale in the spray nozzle. Consequently, the required amount of spray that should be generated will drop and the health and growth of the plants will be adversely affected. The misting system in Fogponics is less likely to suffer the same issue; however, you should remain alert for any changes.

Keep a watchful eye on the area covered by the mist. If any plants fall outside the nutrient-rich spray or fog, sometimes called a void area, those plants will, of course, die.

Another challenge to be aware of is that of overgrown roots in both the Aeroponic and Fogponic systems. Sometimes roots become so intermeshed that the nutrients cannot reach the entire root system. Sections of the roots may then begin to deteriorate, causing the death of the plant.

Both systems rely on electricity for the generation of spray and mist. In the event of a power failure or motor malfunction, the entire crop could be destroyed. If you are farming with one of these hydroponic methods, consider investing in a generator or some sort of solar-powered device as a good standby in an emergency.

Both the Aeroponic and Fogponic systems are considered advanced hydroponic techniques and, therefore, because they are more refined, they require an in-depth knowledge of the hydroponic process as well as an understanding of how to maximize the advantages of the system (Elliot, 2016).

Gordon L. Atwell

New Designs in Grow-Boxes

The design of grow-boxes has begun to develop along interesting and in many cases, more scientifically governed lines. The emphasis is now to create a grow-box that will house as many plants as possible in order to substantially increase the yield. This makes the Fogponic and Aeroponic methods of hydroponic farming far less labor-intensive and more economical to operate. A win-win result for sure! Perhaps these two methods will vie for the future "number one slot" in the field of hydroponic gardening.

CHAPTER 7: CHALLENGES HYDROPONIC GARDENERS MAY FACE FROM TIME TO TIME

Hydroponic gardening, like any traditional gardening and farming, brings with it a host of challenges. Just when you thought your hydroponic system was flourishing and producing an abundance of healthy crops, you face the serious setback of a "critter infestation." There are ways and means of ridding your system of these unwanted little visitors, so before you go into panic-mode, read on to discover the weaponry at your disposal.

COMMON PESTS AND HOW TO ERADICATE THEM

There are five common pests that have a preference for hydronic crops. If you learn to identify these unwanted guests, you are well on your way to ridding your garden of them.

Spider Mites

An infestation of spider mites is one of the most common problems in a hydroponic garden. These mini-spiders are prolific breeders that cause irreparable damage to plants by sucking them dry. They initially go unnoticed because they are difficult to see with the naked eye. The first sign of their presence will be a fine, almost undetectable webby structure on the underside of the plant's leaves that will shortly be followed by yellowing and wilting. Damaged plants seldom survive and an entire crop can be wiped out in one go by these seemingly inconsequential bugs.

Their favorite crops are beans, peas, strawberries, eggplant, melons, and tomatoes, but they will damage other crops as well. Spider mites are a more common problem during the hot season.

These tiny bugs are wind-borne across vast areas of land. Their life cycle from egg to fertile adult takes about five days. A single female can lay up to 300 eggs. It's no wonder that these critters multiply faster than you can imagine.

Keep your eyes peeled for the webs, and if you suspect you may have a plague of spider mites, run a tissue over the underside of a few stricken leaves. Red smears on the tissue are a clear indication that spider mites have taken up residence in your beautiful garden. Act fast! See the options listed in the next section.

Thrips

Thrips, like spider mites, are sapsuckers. These tiny, winged insects often go undetected until they have caused irreversible damage to your crops. If leaves develop tiny, metallic black dots and begin to turn yellow, thrips may be the culprit.

However, some species of thrips are insectivores because they eat other harmful insects, so it's better to keep the population of these pests down rather than to eradicate them entirely.

Aphids

These tiny, soft-bodied, pear-shaped insect pests can be green, gray, or black and are also sapsuckers that quickly destroy valuable crops. Because ants drink the moisture that forms at the base of the aphid's abdomen, where there are large colonies of ants, aphids will be found as well.

There are a number of different species of these small pests, each of which has its own special taste for a specific type of plant food.

Aphids usually congregate in substantial numbers on the underside of leaves. Their presence will be discovered when leaves begin to turn yellow and become distorted.

Aphids are good transmitters of diseases between plants and should, therefore, not be encouraged in your garden.

Fungus Gnats (Fruit Flies)

These small flies are attracted to fruit and the damp soil in indoor plants where the female lays her eggs. The life cycle of these insects is about 14 days from egg to fertile adult.

Although the adult insect is not harmful, the larvae of the fungus gnat are because not only do they chew through these life-giving appendages, but the destruction they cause also causes the roots to be susceptible to bacterial infection.

As the roots lose their ability to draw up moisture for the plants, the plant's lower leaves begin to yellow and drop off. Gradually, the plant begins to die due to lack of water and adequate nutrients (10 Most Common Hydroponic Plant Pests and Diseases, 2019).

Whiteflies

The hydroponic world seems overrun by "vampire critters"! Whiteflies are yet another example of sapsuckers!

These tiny pests are more moth-like in appearance and are difficult to eradicate.

Whiteflies are not at all fussy about their menu, and a wide variety of crops fall well within their gustatory delights. They invade plants and steadily suck out the plant's nutrients, leaving it to wither and eventually die.

The tobacco whitefly and the glasshouse whitefly are the most common varieties that create problems for hydroponic gardeners. The life cycle of the whitefly can range between 15 to 40 days. The warmer the temperature, the faster the incubation of these pests.

The larvae are actually the sapsuckers. As they feed on the underside of leaves, they secrete a toxin into the phloem which poisons the entire plant.

The nymphs also excrete a sugary substance that encourages the growth of "sooty mold" on the leaves.

The third problem with these awful critters is that they carry a variety of viruses that can spread to a vast number of plants in your hydroponic garden in a very short time (Whitefly Damage and Control, n.d.).

SUITABLE WAYS TO RID YOUR GARDEN OF THESE PESTS

Spider Mite Control

- Control of bugs is essential for the survival of your crops. However, pesticides generally wipe out all the good critters too, which means that spider mites have fewer enemies and can continue to multiply with abandon.
- The use of eco-friendly, natural, and organic methods is recommended.
- For the treatment of spider mite infestations, prune the affected plants and, where necessary, remove the entire plant to avoid the problem spreading. Make sure to destroy all infected plants by burning, if this is allowed in your area, or by disposing of plants in the garbage system. Do not throw affected plants onto the compost as this will simply cause the infestation to increase the following season.
- Import beneficial bugs like lady beetles and lacewings.
- Wash plants down with blasts of water.
- A useful, natural, organic insecticide like "Nuke Em" could be very beneficial (Spider Mites SUCK!, 2020).
- "BotaniGard ES" used weekly is a useful insecticide for a variety of unwanted plant pests.

ORGANIC GARDENING

- For more information, please visit: Spider Mites SUCK! at https://www.planetnatural.com/pest-problem-solver/houseplant-pests/spider-mite-control/

Thrips

- Not all thrips are bad. To the layman, it is almost impossible to tell one species of thrips from another as they all look much alike. It is difficult, therefore, to know which variety is harmful and which is not.
- The best option to cut down the population of thrips is to use insecticidal soap or neem oil (Controlling Thrips, 2018).
- Severe pruning is also beneficial for getting rid of thrips.
- To avoid further infestations, disposal of infected plants should be done via the garbage outlet rather than the compost.

Aphids

- Water blasts can dislodge these tiny bugs and some will be drowned.
- A more lasting method of getting rid of aphids is to spray them with a solution of liquid soap in the proportions 1 part soap to 10 parts water.
- Dusting with household flour has been known to be beneficial in getting rid of Aphids.
- Neem oil is also a good option. Make sure you read the instructions before applying this product.
- Introduce beneficial insects such as lady beetles.
- Garlic, chives, and catnip repel aphids, according to the Old Farmer's Almanac, 2020.

Fungus Gnats

- Because fungus gnat adults are attracted to yellow, placing sticky yellow cards strategically around the plants will trap these insects.
- Cider vinegar traps also work well: In a suitable, shallow container, mix equal parts of cider vinegar and water and place the trap close to the infestation.
- Placing a layer of dry sand around the plants also helps to stop the adult fungus gnat from burrowing into moist soil.
- For more information, please visit Old Farmer's Almanac at https://www.almanac.com/pest/fungus-gnats

Whiteflies

Biological Control

Biological warfare on these unwanted members of the insect population can be waged by introducing the *Delphastus catalinae beetle*. There are also tiny wasps from the Aphelinae family that use the whitefly larvae as hosts for their eggs (Whitefly Damage and Control, n.d.).

A third biological way to fight whiteflies is to introduce the *Verticillium lecanii fungus,* which infects the whitefly and eventually annihilates it (Whitefly Damage and Control, n.d.).

Cultural Control

Remove all weeds from the area near your hydroponic garden site, as these are the breeding grounds for whitefly.

Phytosanitary Treatment

In serious cases of whitefly infestation, treating your crop seeds with a suitable insecticide may prove useful. *Rhino Skin,* a potentially useful, non-toxic insecticide containing potassium silicate, effectively coats the plant thus protecting the leaves from the onslaught of would-be invaders.

PLANT DISEASES COMMON TO HYDROPONIC GARDENS

Powdery Mildew

This highly dangerous, wind-spread disease presents as a powdery coating on the plant and will, in a fairly short space of time after stunting plant growth and changing the leaves to a sickly yellow, kill the plant completely.

Downy Mildew

Downy mildew develops on the underside of leaves, especially those of the spinach family. Although downy mildew is more of a gray color than the powdery mildew, it is difficult to distinguish one from another.

There are a number of ways to protect your plants against these two diseases.

- Always ensure scrupulous cleanliness in your hydroponic garden. Wear gloves when working with diseased plants, and ensure you change gloves and clothing when

moving into another area of your garden. This will help to stop the spread of disease.
- Drip watering your plants will avoid the leaves being continually soaked and thus encouraging the growth of mildew.
- Rotate your crops each season to avoid similar diseases attacking the same crops.
- Fungicides should be used when all other avenues have been exhausted. Always read instructions carefully to ensure the correct dilutions are used.

Gray Mold

This fungal disease is easy to spot. Although the disease affects all parts of the plant, fruits, particularly strawberries and grapes, develop a gray, furry mold over the entire surface of the fruit.

The disease is more prevalent in moist areas where it begins to thrive and quickly spread. Although it attacks all plants, those that are already compromised by damage of some sort are generally the first to fall prey to gray mold.

Protecting Your Plants Against Gray Mold:
- Cleanliness in your hothouse area is essential. Destroy all damaged and diseased plants with great care so as to avoid contaminating the rest of your crop.
- Handle your plants with care. Damaged plants are more susceptible to disease.
- Ensure your plants are sufficiently well spaced to allow for a free flow of air.
- Allow time between watering sessions for plants to dry out a little.
- Avoid watering late in the afternoon so that plants don't remain damp throughout the night.
- Keep the areas between your plants clean and free from

dead leaf build-up which is a good place for mold to start.

Root Rot

Root rot is a common, challenging disease that is linked to an excess of moisture around the root base of the plants. Where there is too much water, there is insufficient oxygen.

Protecting your plants from root rot is not an easy task.

- Firstly, don't overwater the plants.
- Ensure the pots have good drainage and that there are no areas where water puddles for long periods.
- One of the best solutions, although not the most cost-effective, is to remove the plant from the soil, wash the roots under cold running water, and cut away all the damaged roots. Now, disinfect the shears and snip away about ⅓ of the foliage before repotting the plant in the freshly growing medium in a new pot.

Iron Deficiency

An iron deficiency in your plants results in a shortage of chlorophyll, which will be noticeable by yellow leaves with green veins called leaf chlorosis. If left untreated, plants will eventually die (Leaf Chlorosis And Iron For Plants: What Does Iron Do For Plants, 2018).

The best solutions to medicate your plants in the case of an iron deficiency will be:

- Adjust the pH of your soil. The ideal pH should be between 5.8 and 6.2.
- Check the clay content of the soil. Excessive clay interferes with the absorption of nutrients. Add more organic material to the soil.

- If the soil is too compacted and damp, improve drainage by allowing excess water to flow away from the plant's roots and turn the soil lightly to loosen it.
- Reduce the amount of phosphorus in the soil. Check the percentage of phosphorus in the fertilizer you are using and adjust this accordingly.

SOLUTIONS TO STEER YOUR GARDEN BACK TO VIBRANT HEALTH

Cleanliness Is the New Buzzword

As the saying "cleanliness is next to godliness" goes, keeping your clothing, shoes, gloves, and gardening tools spotlessly clean and disinfected will go a long way in supporting plant health in your hydroponic garden.

Sensible and careful disposal of waste, dead and decaying plant material, as well as infected material, is of paramount importance. Remember, many plant diseases are wind-borne.

Make sure your hydroponic system is well insulated and avoid bringing in plants from unknown sources. Ensure all plants are regularly checked for disease, pests, or damage. Keep the area clean, well swept, and washed down to avoid dust and contaminants infiltrating your system. And above all, remember that clean plants mean good health, not only for the individual plant but for the entire crop.

THE VALUE OF USING GOOD QUALITY PRODUCTS

Hydroponic gardening is not as inexpensive a gardening system as you may have at first believed. Although you can start out fairly simply and cost-effectively, gradually as your system develops, you will realize that there are some shortcuts you should avoid at all costs. Among these is the very real and important aspect of using the best quality products that you can afford.

Nutrients

Because hydroponic gardening is a soilless method of growing plants, the nutrients essential for plant growth that would have been available in the soil need to be provided by the gardener.

There is a wide variety of nutrients on the market, and for the beginner hydroponic gardener, it can be confusing to make the right choice.

Here are some tips on how to make the best choice.

- Start with a water test of alkalinity, electrical conductivity, and the presence of essential elements such as phosphorus, magnesium, zinc, boron, chloride, and nickel, to name a few.

- Water alkalinity is vital for the successful growth of your plants and will also determine the amount of acid required to balance the pH.
- The electrical conductivity of the water gives you a good idea of not only the presence of essential elements but also the sodium level in the water. The electrical conductivity results will enable you to decide between using an open or closed irrigation system.
- Filtering the water from its source, via a process of reverse osmosis, is often a good although an expensive option to consider.
- Nutrients play a vital role in the success of your hydroponic garden.

For more information on the best available products, please visit https://www.greenandvibrant.com/best-hydroponic-nutrients

pH Solution

The pH level of your water will depend on the level of alkalinity, discussed above. The best pH level is between 5.8 and 6.2. A favorable pH level enables the plants to absorb their quota of micronutrients from the nutrient-enriched water and thus produce their best crop (Stephens, 2019).

Growing Media

Again, there is a variety to choose from, and depending on your choice of crops, some media will be more successful than others.

Perlite, Rockwool, and coco coir are popular for beginner hydroponic gardeners to use as none of these media have a detrimental effect on the pH.

Temperature

Temperature plays a vital role in the success of your hydroponic culture. Ideally, it should be between 65° F and 68° F (18 - 20° C).

As the temperature increases, water evaporates quickly and a build-up of mineral salts results (Stephens, 2019).

For more information on this topic, please visit https://thehydroponicsplanet.com/learn-how-to-keep-ph-stable-in-hydroponics/

Tools and Equipment

All tools and equipment should be kept spotlessly clean and disinfected.

Essential tools that every hydroponic gardener should have are:

Scissors and Shears
A few good, sharp pairs of scissors or shears of different sizes for trimming, harvesting, or removing damaged parts of the plant are essential to avoid "ragged cutting" and plant damage (Simple, Must-have Tools for Indoor Gardening, n.d.).

Spray Bottles
A variety of spray bottles, each for a different purpose, is useful for direct, controlled spraying of specific areas. You will need to mix nutrients and fungicides so ensure each bottle is clearly labeled to avoid confusion.

Measuring Cups
Measuring cups are an essential piece of equipment for accurate measuring of nutrients, pH, and the like. Syringes and

measuring cups and spoons are good for small quantities.

Accuracy is paramount to the production of successful crops in the hydroponic garden.

Buckets

A variety of different sized buckets will prove useful for mixing and as growing pots as well as general transport of growing media and waste.

Brushes

A number of different sized brushes are useful for cleaning out your hydroponic system, clearing clogged areas, and general maintenance of pots, grow trays, and the like.

Brushes are great tools for cleaning out small areas and sweeping up fallen leaves and debris that can build up around your plants.

Remember to keep all your tools and equipment in tip-top condition so as to avoid the development of unwanted diseases (5 Simple, Must-have Tools for Indoor Gardening, n.d.).

SUPPORT FOR GETTING YOUR SYSTEM BACK ON TRACK

Among the many supplements available to hydroponic gardeners are the following that may prove very useful when you are starting out.

Rhino Skin

As previously mentioned, Rhino Skin is a dissolvable mixture of potassium silicate that reinforces the plants' ability to withstand disease, drought, and stress. The silicon effectively fills the gaps in between plant cells making the plant sturdier and more resistant to potential damage.

The Importance of Calcium and Magnesium

If your plants are showing signs of stunted growth and wilting leaves, they may require added nutrients. Sensi Cal-Mag Xtra is essential for balancing the calcium and magnesium levels in your plants.

Plants Come Alive with "Revive"

If you experience serious concerns about the health of your crops, Revive may be the best solution for wilting, "sad" crops.

OTHER POTENTIAL CHALLENGES TO HYDROPONIC GARDENING

So, now that we have talked briefly about the challenges of pests and potential disease and how best to counteract these, you may be thinking you are on the "home straight" and there is little else to stand in the way of you setting up and developing a viable, hydroponic crop.

There are a number of other potential challenges you should be aware of to ensure you have as much knowledge as possible to begin your exciting venture (Meerasaivu, 2019).

The Growth of Algae

Algae is more of a challenge for the aquaponic gardener. In small amounts, it is not harmful; however, if allowed to increase, it can quickly become a serious problem. Excess algae use up the oxygen your plants require for optimum growth, and it also causes fluctuations in the pH levels.

This is of particular concern in an aquaponic system as less oxygen is released at night, and the fish will begin to die.

Suggestions to Resolve the Problem of Algae

- To counteract algae growth, keep the temperature range consistent and make sure the phosphorus levels don't rise.
- Shading your fish tank will help to cut the light factor, which encourages algae growth.
- Filter the water to clear the algae.
- The use of ultraviolet light can slow algae growth.
- Use opaque glass for the tank.
- Ensure the tank has a well-fitting lid.
- Any holes required in the lid or tank for tubing should be just big enough to support the tube and be well-sealed around the edges.
- Humic acid can be used to darken the water and slow algae growth (Storey, 2019).

Leaks in the Hydroponic System

Leaking joints and valves can cause a real headache. Not only can leaks cause severe water loss, but water levels will also be affected and, in turn, the well-being of plants is jeopardized.

Leaks are more prevalent in high-pressure systems. They can also occur as a result of a tube or drip emitter having moved slightly.

Suggestions to Resolve the Problem of Leakages

- Test the system with water before you start.
- Make sure the reservoir is sufficiently strong to hold the volume of water for which it is intended.
- Check all seals and valves.
- Ensure the piping and tubing is large enough to carry the volume of water required.
- Design your hydroponic system around the use of a low-pressure pump.
- Use a good quality non-toxic aqua silicone sealer (Meer-

asaivu, 2019).

Clogs

Blockages are a fairly common problem in a hydroponic system. These can be as a result of tiny particles of nutrients and a build-up of salts clogging the drips and sprays.

Over-active roots can also cause blockages.

Suggestions to Resolve the Problem of Leakages
- Regular checking of equipment is essential.
- Detangle root systems and trim if necessary.
- Make sure containers are sufficiently large to allow space for the roots to grow unhindered.

Easy Cleaning Solutions

When designing your hydroponic system, bear in mind the importance of having to clean it out on a regular basis. Plan easy access to all parts of the system. Make holes large enough for a small brush to reach into, and try to avoid sharp bends in the tubing.

The system should be easy to empty and wash out between uses. It should not take long to adjust the nutrient solution while the system is in operation.

Remember, time is money, so plan your system accordingly.

Unpredictable Issues

Your hydroponic system will need to have nutrient and pH levels checked daily. If you use a drip system, drip emitters need to be checked at least four times a day. Spray nozzles should be checked at least four times a day. Loss of nutrients to your plants will be fatal within an hour.

Check the pump system and ensure you have a backup in the event of a power outage.

The least temperamental systems to operate that require checking once a day are the Deep Water Culture System and the Nutrient Film Technique (Common Hydroponic System Problems, n.d.).

The Dangers of Recycling Materials

Recycling used materials in your hydroponic system is not recommended. Understandably, you will not want to incur unnecessary costs. Most of the large equipment items such as tanks, tubs, net pots, tubing, and grow trays are perfectly fine for re-use. Obviously, these need to be thoroughly cleaned after each use.

One of the costly items that has to be replaced for each new use is the growing medium. Under no circumstances should you attempt to re-use the old medium.

For further information visit Common Hydroponic System Problems at https://www.jasons-indoor-guide-to-organic-and-hydroponics-gardening.com/hydroponic-system.html

STAY ALERT!

The best advice for any new hydroponic gardener is to be watchful and take note of any changes in the growth and development of your crops and to then act swiftly to avoid disaster.

CHAPTER 8: STARTING YOUR OWN HYDROPONIC GARDEN

Hydroponic gardening can be a very rewarding hobby to pursue or it can develop into a good source of income depending on your long-term goals.

Because there is no soil used in the hydroponic system, it is a relatively "clean" type of gardening practice, which might appeal to a lot of gardeners who feel they are up for a new challenge in their field.

WHAT QUALIFICATIONS DO I NEED TO START?

Although there are some basic requirements for successful hydroponic techniques, anyone with a keen interest in gardening, a love for plants, an appreciation of enjoying the fruits of your labor, and a good dose of enthusiasm can start this innovative and rewarding type of plant cultivation.

Many of the requirements for this method of gardening are based on common sense and a knowledge of good gardening practices. Much like you, all plants need water and air to survive. They also require nutrients and a safe, warm place to grow.

SO HOW DO I GET STARTED?

To begin your gardening venture, you will require the following items:

- a hydroponics system of your choice (there are many different ones to choose from),
- hydroponic nutrients (available from a variety of outlets),
- suitable hydroponics growing medium (also available from a specific store that caters for gardeners),
- a light source (available from a reputed dealer),
- lots of time, and of course,
- plants, the variety of which is enormous.

WHICH HYDROPONIC SYSTEM CAN I USE?

A hydroponic system is a structure that holds water and nutrients that support the growth of the plants you choose to grow. There are two kinds of systems:

- a solution culture system where the roots grow straight into the nutrient-rich water, such as in the Kratky Method, and
- an aggregate culture system in which the roots grow in a hydroponic medium, such as in the Ebb and Flow System.

Kit Systems

A number of hydroponic "kits" are available for beginner gardeners from a variety of commercial outlets. These do-it-yourself projects can be very useful for those gardeners who have limited DIY skills or who cannot easily source suitable materials to build their system from scratch. For more information visit the following websites:

- https://www.amazon.com/slp/Best-Hydroponics-Systems/8b75vd252xx938n
- https://www.amazon.com/Foody-Vertical-Garden-Hydroponic-Growing/dp/B012UEB6X8

Building Your Own System

You could, of course, build your own system, depending on how handy you are with DIY projects and if you have the materials you require for your project.

In order to design and build your own versatile hydroponic system, you can be as creative as you wish. That's the beauty of working with this method of gardening.

First, decide where you will construct your garden. Will you work indoors or out? You will require sufficient space to set up a system of your choice. As a beginner, it is advisable to start small and simple, and as you gain confidence and experience, branch out into a more complex and challenging technique.

Remember that although there are some basic rules for good gardening practice, your hydroponic plant cultivating system will most likely become a very personalized structure.

BUILD A BASIC, EASY-TO-OPERATE HYDROPONIC SYSTEM

The Kratky Bucket Method

This passive method is great for beginners as it requires no moving parts, pumps, or other complicated electrical mechanisms.

A basic plan that you may find of value has been included here. Remember, your container need not have exactly the same dimensions as those given.

Requirements
- One large, non-toxic plastic bucket or a glass container with a well-fitting lid. If you construct your own glass container, ensure the edges line up properly and seal them well with a high-quality, clear aquarium silicone sealer.
- One or two net pots. The number of net pots you use will depend on the size of the container as well as the pots. Don't try to fit too many pots into the system. You may find 1 or 2 sufficient for your needs.

- Growing medium such as "hydroton" or perlite (Pulsipher, 2019).
- The best plants to use in this solution culture system include those with a shallow root system such as spinach, lettuce, and a variety of herbs.
- Hydroponic nutrients.
- pH kit.

Assembling the Kratky Bucket System
- Choose a suitable, warm, sheltered, sunny spot for your container. This can be indoors or outside.
- Wash the container and net pots well.
- Measure the circumference of the neck of the net pot.
- Carefully cut a hole of the same size in the lid of the container. The net pot should fit snugly into the hole and not slip through.
- Place the plant into the net pot and fill the pot with the growing medium of your choice.
- Fill the container about ¾ with water. Mix in the required amount of nutrients, as per instructions on the bottle.
- Test the acidity level of the water using the pH kit. Adjust the level accordingly by adding acid until the correct color on the chart is achieved.
- Seal the container and carefully place the pot into the hole in the lid.
- Leave the container for about 30 days, checking on the plant from time-to-time, without opening the container.
- Your plant should be ready for harvesting (Youst, 2019).

Gordon L. Atwell

The Kratky Bucket Method

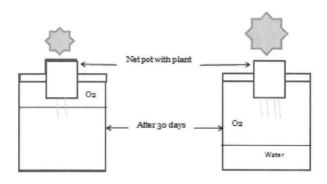

Suggested dimensions for both buckets

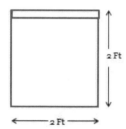

The Simple Bucket System

This is another simple, passive method suitable for beginner gardeners. Below, please find a basic plan that you may find useful. You can make use of any kind of container. However, if you intend on growing tomatoes, beets, or peppers, you will do well to choose a deeper container.

Requirements
- One large, non-toxic plastic bucket or plant pot.
- Draining tray.
- Growing medium such as vermiculite or perlite.
- Plant.

- Hydroponic nutrient mix.

Assembling the Simple Bucket System
- Choose a suitable, sheltered sunny spot for your container. This can be indoors or outside.
- Wash the container well.
- Drill about 4 - 6 small drainage holes into the base of the container.
- Half fill the container with the growing medium, place the plant into the container and add a little more growing medium until the container is about ¾ full.
- Place the container on the draining tray.
- Water daily with about 1 cup (250 ml) of nutrient-rich solution.

Gordon L. Atwell

The Simple Bucket System

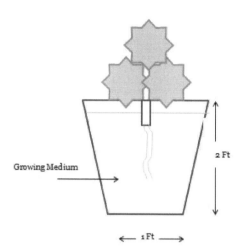

The NFT System

The Nutrient Film Technique System is a little more complex than the previous examples. This is what is termed a "closed system," in which water from the reservoir is recycled through the system by a pump.

Requirements
- 4 inch (10 cm) PVC pipe cut into three lengths of 4 ft (1.2 m) each.
- Two pipe-ends to seal off each pipe.
- A solid frame. This could be an old table or a wooden frame specifically made for this project.
- A container that will hold at least 10 gallons (20 liters) of nutrient-enriched water.
- A number of net pots with the growing medium of your choice.

- 12 - 15 ft (3.5 - 4.5 m) irrigation tubing about 1 ½ inch (4 cm) in diameter.
- Plants of your choice.
- Hydroponic nutrient mix.
- pH kit.
- Water pump.
- Lights.

Assembling the NFT System
- Choose a suitable, sheltered, sunny spot for your container. This can be indoors or outside. If the system is indoors, you will require lights.
- Cut the PVC pipe into three lengths of 4 ft (1.2 m) each. You can cut more lengths if there is sufficient space in your frame.
- Wash the PVC pipes, reservoir, and net pots well.
- Drill holes sufficiently large enough for a net pot to fit snugly into. These holes DO NOT go right through the PVC pipe.
- Seal the ends of the PVC pipe with pipe ends and silicone these well to stop leaks.
- Measure the distance between each PVC pipe and make a hole to match in the irrigation tube. This will allow water to flow through the entire system.
- Drill holes into the sides of each PVC pipe large enough to thread the irrigation tubing through. Make sure each hole in the irrigation pipe lies inside a PVC pipe. Seal all the joins well.
- Attach the irrigation tube to the pump.
- Connect the pump to the reservoir.
- Fill the reservoir with nutrient-rich water and check the pH level.
- Prepare the plants and place each net pot into one of the holes in the PVC pipe. You should cater for between 20 - 40 plants in this system.

The Nutrient Film Technique System

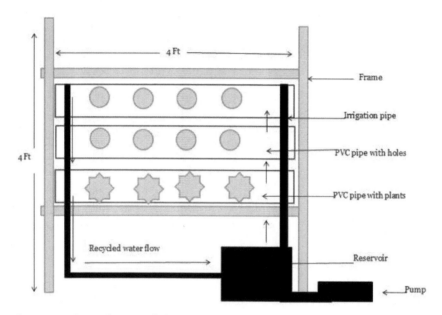

These are just three of the many examples you can use for your project. As mentioned previously in Chapters 2 and 4, you will find other potential options that may be more appealing to your adventurous spirit.

Whichever method you choose, let your enthusiasm and creativity flow as you discover the enjoyment and rewards of this pleasurable and lucrative, eco-friendly way of gardening.

Enjoy the experience and good luck.

CONCLUSION

With worldwide food shortages constantly growing due to a variety of unexpected and unprecedented natural calamities, there is a definite move toward communities learning the required skills for planting viable crops that will deliver good quality, regular harvests to feed the starving masses.

According to Mark Bittman, in his article on "How to Feed the World," "It's been 50 years since President John F. Kennedy spoke of ending world hunger," and still the problem persists and has, in fact, dramatically worsened since his speech at the World Food Congress in 1963. Currently, the commercial prototype for food production is failing dismally to generate sufficient viable crops to break the hunger cycle.

Added to this is the challenge of the increase in the number of people either ingesting the incorrect foods or eating too much at one sitting. The increase in obesity among the American population is alarming and is indicative of the fact that populations are governed by the media and its powerful ability to persuade the masses that fast foods are the way to eat.

That may well be one point of view; however, the very real challenge of degradation of natural resources, either through human's decimation of forests and water sources or by natural disasters, is far more prevalent and of greater concern.

According to Bittman, in his article on "How to Feed the World," "high-yielding varieties of any major commercial monoculture crop will produce more per acre than peasant-bred varieties of the same crop. But by diversifying crops, mixing plants and animals, planting trees which provide not only fruit but shelter for birds, shade, fertility through nutrient recycling, and more—small landholders can produce not only more food, but also a wider variety of crops with fewer resources and lower transportation costs." All-in-all, this results in a lower carbon footprint, while providing greater food security, maintaining improved biodiversity, and better and more innovative opportunities to withstand the damaging effects of climate change (Bittman, M.).

If indeed, more people could be encouraged to grow hydroponically cultivated crops, the likelihood of challenging the ongoing war against the worldwide food shortage could prove successful in substantially reducing the percentage of starving people within the next decade.

THE NEED FOR PROGRESSIVE AND INVENTIVE AGRICULTURE

The United Nations (UN) calculated that by 2050, the global population is expected to reach close to 10 billion people. Shockingly, in 2019, just under 125 million people were confronted by severe food shortages as a result of unprecedented changes in climatic conditions, resulting in crop damage from flooding and drought (Bills, 2019).

According to Braden Bills, "Given that hydroponics can grow food in a controlled environment, with less water, and in higher yields, the Food and Agriculture Organization of the United Nations has been implementing hydroponic farming in areas of the world that suffer from food shortages" (Hydroponics: The power of water to grow food).

Many agricultural projects have been set up worldwide in an attempt to teach people to become self-sufficient at providing good, nourishing food for themselves and their families.

The more people like you and I who learn about the value of hydroponic gardening, the better prepared they will be to help stem the tide of famine that threatens so many countries.

Now you have a good idea of what hydroponic gardening is all about and what an amazing opportunity it gives you to be able to grow your own produce and beautiful flowers from the comfort of your home, while at the same time affording you the chance to develop your creative gardening skills without getting yourself all muddy.

Once you have established the gardening method of your choice, you are most likely going to find it so rewarding that you will wonder why it has taken you so long to get started.

FROM BASICS TO SUCCESSFUL GARDENING AND GOOD FOOD

From cultivating flowers like Phalaenopsis orchids, roses, gladioli, lilies, lupins, and pansies to name but a few varieties, to growing vegetables and fruit for your family, friends, and perhaps the neighborhood farmers market, the opportunities to showcase your skills are limitless.

Being the creative individual you are, perhaps you will find further possibilities to branch out into the culinary world of preserves, salsas, relishes, fruit jellies, and the like. If this idea appeals to you, get your garden started, and with your goal in mind, push forward to success and personal satisfaction.

To help you get started, here is a recipe that's perfect for surprising your guests who are arriving to watch the Big Game. It's a quick, easy, delicious, meatless recipe. Most of the fresh ingredients could well be supplied from your hydroponic garden!

AMAZING VEGGIE TORTILLAS

Ingredients

½ cup (200g) mushrooms, washed and chopped

4 tablespoons (56g) chopped almonds

2 tablespoons soy sauce

1 tablespoon rice wine

1 teaspoon sesame seeds

½ tablespoon sesame oil

1 teaspoon brown sugar

2 spring onions, sliced very fine

½ a medium-sized cucumber, finely diced

½ a butter or gen lettuce, roughly chopped

4-5 tablespoons hoisin sauce

Salt and pepper to taste

Sprigs of parsley

6 tortillas

Method

1. In a large bowl toss all the ingredients well.
2. Scoop a generous portion into each tortilla and roll.
3. Serve with sprigs of parsley and your favorite wine.

This is just one example of the delicious meals that you can make using your hydroponic vegetables. Now that you've learned how to build your own hydroponic garden and what delicious fruits and vegetables you can grow, it's time to get started!

REFERENCES

Avoiding Downy Mildew in Spinach: A Grower's Guide. (n.d.). Retrieved from https://www.highmowingseeds.com/blog/avoiding-downy-mildew-in-spinach-a-growers-guide/

Barth, B. (2018, July 26). How Does Aeroponics Work? Retrieved from https://modernfarmer.com/2018/07/how-does-aeroponics-work/

Benefits of Hydroponics. (n.d.). Retrieved from https://greenourplanet.org/benefits-of-hydroponics/

Bittman, M. (2013, October 14). How to Feed the World. Retrieved from https://www.nytimes.com/2013/10/15/opinion/how-to-feed-the-world.html

Braden Bills. (2019, October 4). Hydroponics: The power of water to grow food. Retrieved from http://sitn.hms.harvard.edu/flash/2019/hydroponics-the-power-of-water-to-grow-food/

Brazier, Y. (n.d.). Oregano: Health benefits, uses, and side effects. Retrieved from https://www.medicalnewstoday.com/articles/266259.php

Common Hydroponic System Problems. (n.d.). Retrieved from https://www.jasons-indoor-guide-to-organic-and-hydroponics-gardening.com/hydroponic-system.html

Controlling Thrips – How To Get Rid Of Thrips. (2018, April 5). Retrieved from https://www.gardeningknowhow.com/plant-problems/pests/insects/controlling-thrips.htm

D'Anna, C. (2019, April 21). Learn How to

Use the Nutrient Film Technique in Hydroponics. Retrieved from https://www.thespruce.com/hydroponic-gardens-nutrient-film-technique-1939220

D'Anna, C. (2020, January 6). Hydroponics For Beginners - The Definitive Guide. Retrieved from https://www.greenandvibrant.com/hydroponic-gardening

Dutch Bucket / Bato Bucket Hydroponic System. (2019, January 6). Retrieved December 26, 2020, from https://www.greenandvibrant.com/dutch-bucket

Elliott, S. (2016, December 27). Figuring Out Fogponics. Retrieved from https://www.maximumyield.com/figuring-out-fogponics/2/1361

Espiritu Founder, K., & Teodoro Researcher, C. (2019, October 3). History of Hydroponics: When Was Hydroponics Invented? Retrieved from https://www.epicgardening.com/history-of-hydroponics/

Fitzpatrick, H. (2018, August 25). 5 Environmental Benefits of Hydroponic Growing (Explained in Detail). Retrieved from https://get-green-now.com/hydroponics-environmental-benefits/

Horticulture: Landscaping: Vertical Gardening. (n.d.). Retrieved from http://agritech.tnau.ac.in/horticulture/horti_Landscaping_vertical gardening.html

Leaf Chlorosis And Iron For Plants: What Does Iron Do For Plants. (2018, May 8). Retrieved from https://www.gardeningknowhow.com/plant-problems/environmental/leaf-chlorosis-and-iron.htm

Max. (2019, January, 6). Ebb & Flow (Flood and Drain) Hydroponic System. Retrieved from https://www.greenandvibrant.com/ebb-and-flow-hydroponics

McKee, S. (2017, March 6). The Kratky Method is a Simple and Fun Way to Grow. Retrieved from https://

www.maximumyield.com/the-kratky-method-is-a-simple-and-fun-way-to-grow/2/2996

Meerasaivu, M. (2019, September 26). 15 Common Problems With Hydroponics (And How To Fix Them). Retrieved from https://smartgardenguide.com/problems-with-hydroponics/

Oder, T. (2020, January 31). How to start your own hydroponic garden. Retrieved from https://www.mnn.com/your-home/organic-farming-gardening/stories/how-to-start-your-own-hydroponic-garden

Old Farmer's Almanac. (n.d.). Aphids. Retrieved from https://www.almanac.com/pest/aphids

Pulsipher, K. (2019, March 10). What Is The Best Growing Medium For Hydroponics? Retrieved from https://smartgardenguide.com/best-growing-medium-for-hydroponics/

Shiffler, A (2018, February 16). 10 Companies Using Hydroponics Technology to Disrupt the Agriculture Industry. Retrieved from https://www.disruptordaily.com/10-companies-using-hydroponics-technology-disrupt-agriculture-industry/

Spider Mites SUCK! (n.d.). Retrieved from https://www.planetnatural.com/pest-problem-solver/houseplant-pests/spider-mite-control/

Stephens, O. (2019, September 30). Learn How to Keep pH Stable in Hydroponics. Retrieved from https://thehydroponicsplanet.com/learn-how-to-keep-ph-stable-in-hydroponics/

Storey, A., Aliyev, A., & Godfrey, M. (2019, January 16). How to Manage Algae in Aquaponics and Hydroponics. Retrieved from https://university.upstartfarmers.com/blog/manage-algae-aquaponics-hydroponics

Sysadmin. (1970, January 1). William Frederick Gericke (b.

1882). Retrieved from https://siarchives.si.edu/collections/siris_arc_383352

Thu, M. (2019, November 4). Hydroponics For Beginners - The Definitive Guide. Retrieved from https://www.greenandvibrant.com/hydroponic-gardening

Whitefly Damage and Control. (n.d.). Retrieved from http://www.cannagardening.com/whitefly_damage_and_control

Youst, B., Youst, B., Lauenroth, M., Lauenroth, M., Lauenroth, M., & Lauenroth, M. (2019, March 14). How To Start Growing With The Kratky Method. Retrieved from https://university.upstartfarmers.com/blog/kratky-method

5 Simple, Must-have Tools for Indoor Gardening. (n.d.). Retrieved from http://www.saferbrand.com/articles/gardening-tools-hydroponics

10 Most Common Hydroponic Plant Pests and Diseases (Plus, How To Fight Them!). (2019, June 18). Retrieved from https://www.advancednutrients.com/articles/hydroponics-plants-pests-and-diseases/

AQUAPONICS FOR BEGINNERS

The Ultimate Step-by-Step Guide to Building Your Own Aquaponics Garden System That Will Grow Organic Vegetables, Fruits, Herbs and Raising Fish

GORDON L. ATWELL

INTRODUCTION

"Climate change is destroying our path to sustainability. Ours is a world of looming challenges and increasingly limited resources. Sustainable development offers the best chance to adjust our course." ~Ban K-moon

Aquaponics has been around for a number of centuries already, practiced in China where fish were bred in close proximity to the thriving rice paddies, and by the ancient Aztecs who built floating barges called chinampas in Mexico. Chinampas were largely a network of canals that supported the growth of various crops on these floating islands. Plant growth was fed and sustained by the nutrient-rich waste material that was at the bottom of these canals.

In China, rice paddies were grown together with a variety of fish that were local to the region. At this time, they not only made use of fish, but also practiced caging ducks that were suspended in these ponds, where the excrement was used to feed the thriving rice paddies. The ancient Chinese were the first to practice the art of symbiosis where there was sustainability between ducks, fish and rice that was being grown. It is thought that this particular technique of agricultural farming with fish began as early as the 5th Century A.D. by Chinese settlers who had brought the concept with them when they migrated from the Yunnan region.

Aquaponics is sometimes referred to as aquaculture and is a marriage between aquaculture and hydroponics. The main difference between the two is that you are adding fish to the equation and the waste that the fish produce is what is turned into a beneficial bacterium that forms nutrient-rich food for your plants.

In the pages that follow we are going to take a look at how some of these aquaponic systems have changed and developed over the years, and which systems that are currently being built and utilized are not only cost effective, but also successful.

The main aim for anyone getting involved in aquaponics is to look at sustainability and reduce their carbon footprint, as well as make the best use of the resources we currently have at our disposal.

CHAPTER 1: UNDERSTANDING AQUAPONICS IN THE 21ST CENTURY

"Just one square meter gives you more yield that in one acre of land. That's an ideal system for a developing country. [It] will produce up to 300 cucumbers a year… A system like that can supply a family with fresh vegetables and with minerals and also with protein." ~Dr. Nick Sadiov, aquaponics researcher and leader at the Aquaculture Centre of Excellence in Lethbridge

The secret to successful aquaponics is being able to combine the art of hydroponics and aquaculture. Hydroponics is where you can successfully grow a wide variety of plants, vegetables, herbs and even flowering plants in a soil-less environment, making use of very little water. In hydroponics, much of the work is done by both the water, as well as the circulation of oxygen that reaches the roots of the plants being grown. One of the biggest differences between the two forms of gardening or farming is that with hydroponics, the nutrient system feeding the plants is already pre-mixed. This mixture contains all the nutrients needed in the water. The plants make use of all of the nutrients for them to grow to their maximum capacity. Getting this nutrient mix correct can take loads of practice and time. It can take trial and error resulting in plants suffering from root rot, which is extremely common in hydroponics.

DECIDING WHAT YOU WANT

Your very first step when it comes to setting up your aquaponics system is deciding on what you want. You should have a clear image or picture in your mind as to what the end result should be. If you currently have a lot of the equipment necessary to build an Ebb and Flow or Flood and Drain system, and you know that you can upcycle a lot of what you have right now, it doesn't make sense to go out and spend money on setting up another system where you have to purchase all of the necessary components from scratch. Rather, use what you have but invest in those things that are going to make a genuine difference to the success of your system. This would include investing in a better quality growing medium for your plants and possibly even better quality fish for stocking your setup.

Once you have a clearer idea of the end result you are trying to achieve, you can then begin to put pen to paper and plan the layout of your design. This could include taking physical measurements so that you are confident that the space that you have available will meet the needs of the system that you are designing. If not, it will be time to go back to the drawing board and re-measure or redesign so that your plan is workable.

Due to aquaponics becoming more and more popular, it is becoming easier to purchase existing systems either online or via a number of suppliers. Maybe you are really handy and would enjoy the challenge of physically building your system yourself. Whichever route you plan to take, the single most important factor to consider with aquaponics is patience while waiting for your system to cycle. Impatience will end up costing you a lot of money in both plants and fish.

SYSTEMS CURRENTLY BEING USED

Aquaculture would incorporate rearing an entire range of aquatic animals, which could include fish, prawns, crayfish and even snails, in a tank-based environment. When combined with hydroponics, growing plants, vegetables, herbs and even certain flowering cultivars are added. This environment is usually mutually beneficial and much of the growth that takes place is interdependent on one another.

When it comes to nutrients in aquaponics there is no need for any of these pre-mixed solutions that would need to be purchased and added to the water in a hydroponic system. Instead, water from the aquatic system is channeled through to the hydroponic system. Here the waste-products and excrement from the fish are broken down by bacteria that turn into nitrates. These nitrates are what are necessary for the plants in the hydroponic component of the system to grow. Once each of the plants have taken up whatever nitrates and nutrients they need into their root system, the water is recirculated back into the ponds where the fish live.

One of the most interesting parts of beginning an aquaponic journey is that your system can be as large or as small as you want it to be, it's completely up to you. Aquaponics is becoming increasingly popular and is moving from just being a home-based hobby, where it could be just a smaller system in a basement, in the lounge area or on a kitchen countertop. Some make use of their patio or invest in larger commercial enterprises fitted to greenhouses. These commercial aquaponics systems usually contain a number of ponds that have fish at different stages of their lifecycle, or age. The main reason for this is so that the aquaponic farmer knows which of the fish are ready for breeding, which of the fish are still babies and need more time to grow, and which of the fish are ready for consumption.

Depending on the size of the system, they can range from being fairly simple units, to being extremely complex in nature—although the main purpose is exactly the same. It mimics and copies a natural aquatic ecosystem that has the plant-based or plant-growing component attached to it.

Instead of making use of a pre-mixed nutrient system, the waste from the fish is broken down by bacteria and recirculated to feed the plants. While hydroponics focuses solely on the growth of soilless fruit, vegetables, herbs and even flowers, aquaponics incorporates the use of fish to produce the required nutrients for these plants to grow.

Agriculture is being transformed in the 21st century by the incorporation of these two methods of food production and agriculture for a number of reasons:

Whether you are looking at self-reliance and sustainability within your own home, aquaponics is a means that can quite easily support a family with its plant-based food needs, as well as protein in the form of fish.

Our global climate is currently under threat and this is a method of being able to provide renewable resources for homes and larger, commercial-based sustainability.

One such place is The Aquaponics Innovation Center, located in Montello, Wisconsin, which offers extensive training as a college. They are operating from the perspective of a collaborative, private–public venture that conducts state of the art demonstrations and research. According to their website, in their article entitled, Aquaponics Transforms 21st Century Agriculture (n.d.), there is a massive transformation taking place in the agricultural sector at the moment. Some of the main reasons for these changes over to aquaponics is because it results in both safe food movement and the food production is sustainable. The course that they offer is only one semester long, however those who attend qualify for a professional aquaponics certificate, in partnership with a local industry leader (https://www.uwsp.edu/cols-ap/aquaponics/Pages/default.aspx).

They operate with six replicate aquaponics production units that are capable of nutrient film technique (NFT), media and deep water, or raft aquaponic production. During this training they also cover things that are vital to mastering the art of aquaponics. Some of these include:

- Measurement and manipulation of lighting;
- Entomology (study of insect movements by collecting them, identifying them and monitoring);
- Analysis of water chemistry;
- Analysis of microbiology;
- Purging and quarantine systems;
- Measurement of plant growth and plant physiology; and
- Adaptability of production units.

This gives us a better understanding that aquaponics is being taken seriously as a modern day solution to many agricultural challenges that we face in terms of space availability, climate change, land availability, and our ability to provide healthier food sources that are genuinely organic versus growing crops treated with harmful pesticides and carcinogens that are used on most commercial farms.

WHAT CAN BE GROWN USING YOUR AQUAPONICS SYSTEM

An important consideration when choosing the plants to grow as part of your aquaponic system is whether both the plants and the fish have the same or very similar pH requirements. It is not just the pH that comes into play with successful aquaponic plants and harvesting, but also the water temperature. The closer you are able to match these two factors, the more the system will be successful and thrive. There needs to be close synergy between the two. An example would be that lettuce, herbs, and certain vegetables do well with warmer fresh water and fish such as Tilapia that thrive in these conditions.

You would need to look at heavily stocking your system if you want success with fruiting plants like peppers and tomatoes. Of course, similar to its counterpart, hydroponics, there are some plants that do well under any conditions in an aquaponic system, and those are:

Arugula:

(*Eruca sativa*) is also known to many as garden rocket,

roquette or rucola and is an edible plant that is often added to salads, although it could also be cooked. Originating from the Mediterranean, it is often used in both French and Italian foods. It has a peppery taste and adds bold flavor to whatever dish it is added to. Many people choose to make pesto with it. While this is an extremely popular plant to grow in aquaponics, it is recommended that it is grown indoors. They can easily reach about 15cm in width, making it important to harvest and cut back regularly. From the time that your seedlings start germinating, it takes only about a week to sprout completely. The benefit of working with Arugula is that you can either harvest the baby flowers and use them in salads, or you can wait until they are fully grown and ready to be harvested. If you want to improve your harvesting conditions, cut around the center of the plant, leaving the new growth still in place. It is going to take about 55 to 60 days for the plant to reach full maturity. If the plant begins to taste too peppery, this is an indication that your plant is over-mature. Some of the benefits of arugula are that they are high in vitamin C, potassium and antioxidants. It is even believed that they can ward off cancer.

Basil:

Another name for basil is St. Joseph's Wort and it is an herb that belongs to the mint family. It's thought that basil possibly contains anti-inflammatory benefits while being antibacterial as well. A lesser known fact is that it could possibly assist in fighting off aging. The ideal growing conditions for basil is a pH of between 5.5 to 6.5. They should ideally be spaced about 20cm apart or with around eight to forty plants per m^2. Average germination takes around a week with a full growth cycle of about five to six weeks. You can look at harvesting as soon as the plant is about 15cm tall. They do best in a sunny environment where temperatures are around

68°-75°F. While they prefer sunlight, they grow much better in a slightly sheltered environment. Plants grow to be between 30 and 70cm in height and about 30cm wide. You can successfully grow basil in media beds, using the Nutrient Film Technique or DWC. Basil is an extremely popular herb to grow in aquaponics and is most successful in Italy.

Chives:

Chives belong to the onion family and most aquaponics growers tend to purchase these as seeds, plant them in smaller planters with the right grow medium and within a few days they are already beginning to shoot smaller, brightly colored shoots. Chives do extremely well in organic matter. You can rely on a germination time of around 5 days. After the shoots have begun to appear, they are ready to be transplanted into pots that are suitable for the DWC method of aquaponics. Expanded clay offers great support when it comes to your chives thriving. Full growth takes place between 75 to 90 days, although you should watch your plants closely as this growth cycle could be shortened in an aquaponic environment. Remember that when you harvest chives, you need to leave approximately an inch from where the roots are, to ensure continuous growth.

Kale:

Kale is one of the easiest vegetables to grow when you are first starting out with aquaponics. It is a member of the cabbage family and is extremely healthy for you to eat as well. Kale is high in calcium, and vitamins C and K, as well as beta carotene and is also a great antioxidant. Something worth mentioning about kale is that although it doesn't grow very high, as a leafy vegetable it needs quite a bit of space to grow. You will need to make sure that you have enough space, which may mean only being able to do so in an outdoor system. If you are planning on growing kale, look for one of the varieties that is common to your region because there are many available out there. You stand a much better chance at success if you choose one of these rather than something exotic that doesn't grow very well in your region.

Kale is better suited to growing in the cooler months and usually flourishes early springtime. For kale to survive and thrive it needs to remain moist all the time and the water temperature should be in the region of 55°–70°F. Because it is better suited to cooler temperatures, keeping the air temperature to within the same sort of range as the water temperature shouldn't be a problem.

Kale prefers a pH of between 6.0 – 7.5. Surprisingly it is not a nutrient-demanding plant and can be matched with most fish that are easy to maintain. Koi and tilapia would be ideal. In an aquaponics system, your kale should be ready to harvest in only six weeks (from seedling to fully grown). If you are planting seeds, this process will take a little longer. There are loads of benefits to considering kale with your aquaponics crop but one of the most important of these is that they are easy to maintain and highly nutritious.

Leafy Lettuce:

This is one of the most successful of all leafy green vegetables that can be grown in an aquaponics system because the lettuce plant thrives in water. The most successful water temperature to grow lettuce would be between 70° and 74°F. If you are only starting out with aquaponics as a beginner, lettuce is a great choice of vegetables to begin with. It's also recommended that you start your lettuce off from seedlings, rather than from planting the seeds yourself. If you do decide to plant your own seeds, make sure that these are planted in a germinating tray and once the plants are big enough, carefully transplant them over to your aquaponics system. Lettuce grows best in media bed, DWC and NFT systems. They require an ideal pH of between 6.0 and 7.0. Lettuce begins flowering only once the temperature reaches over 75°F. While lettuce generally prefers full sunlight, they enjoy light shade when the weather is warmer than usual. At full growth, you can expect your lettuce to be about 20 to 30 cm in height, and anywhere between 25 - 35 cm in width. The average growing time for lettuce is around 24 to 32 days, this could be longer depending on the variety you are growing. It normally takes lettuce about 3 to 7 days to germinate. Part of the reasons why lettuce do so well in aquaponics is because of the levels of nutrients in the water produced by the fish.

While we have mainly mentioned leafy lettuce here, there are a variety of lettuce that are especially popular when it comes to being grown in an aquaponic environment. These are iceberg lettuce which are better suited to cooler climates than warmer temperatures; butterhead lettuce that is a popular variety for adding to salads all over the world. Romaine lettuce grows in an upright fashion and the leaves are quite tightly folded over. This variety of lettuce is slow to bolt and tastes sweet. The final type of lettuce is the first that we have mentioned here, leafy lettuce. Because lettuce is always in such high demand, it is great to consider as a commercial crop or commercial venture. Lettuce is a winter crop and does much better in cooler climates. The pH levels need to be closely monitored when it comes to growing lettuce so that the lettuce doesn't display signs of nutrient deficiency.

Seedlings can be transplanted within a few weeks as soon as they have about two to three leaves. If you supplement with phosphorus fertilizers as well as exposing them to direct sunlight for a few days before transplanting usually results in the plants becoming hardier and their survival rate is higher.

If you want crisp lettuce, you need to grow your plants at a rapid rate making sure that the plants receive all of the nutrients required for them to grow, keeping pH and temperatures at the levels necessary for the crop to thrive. You can look at harvesting your lettuce as soon as the heads are big enough to eat. If you are growing lettuce commercially, they should be harvested as soon as the heads reach an average weight of between 250g to 400g. The secret to harvesting lies in harvesting your lettuce as early in the morning as possible and then chilling the heads.

Mint:

Mint can be grown using an aquaponic system but because it grows so quickly and prolifically, it is one of those herbs that should be avoided. It is extremely difficult to control once it starts growing and you run the risk of choking out your system. One of the other major reasons why mint is not a great idea for aquaponics is that it is likely to take over any of your other plants, making it impossible for them to thrive.

Most house plants:

You could successfully plant and grow most house plants in an aquaponic system as long as you stick to the rules regarding matching the pH requirements of the plants to the fish that you are wanting to stock. The air temperature also needs to be factored in so that you can decide whether to grow your plants indoors, in a greenhouse or outdoors. There are a large variety of houseplants that can be successfully grown, especially edible houseplants such as nasturtium.

Sunflowers grow really well, although with these they do need support as the top of the flowers are really heavy. You can also consider the brightly colored tulips, but these would need to be rooted first because the bulbs don't like to be fully submerged in water. Once these have taken root though, they are good to go.

Tulips prefer cooler temperatures initially – 60°F but, once they are growing, their temperature requirements jump to 70°F. An excellent solution to this cool and warm requirement is to keep the bulbs in a refrigerator for approximately two weeks while they are rooting and then place the shooting bulbs into a flood and drain system with fish that can withstand the temperature range of between 60°–75°F.

Other flowering plants that do really well are roses, marigolds, and water hyacinth.

Watercress:

Watercress is another vegetable that you may want to consider growing as a beginner because it multiplies so easily. This could also be challenging though because if not controlled it can cause problems with your grow bed, causing it to become clogged. By only planting a single, small plant, it will multiply at a rapid rate. If you are planning on growing your watercress from seeds the best way would be to add the seeds to the top of your growing media, you would do this in a similar way that you would plant them in conventional soil, but remember that this is a soil-less growing method.

Watercress can be cultivated from cuttings if this is going to be easier for you—all that you would need to do would be to sprinkle the cuttings across the tray instead.

Place each of the trays gently into the water and wait for them to grow. Because they grow so quickly, you may want to keep some of the cuttings or seedlings from the best watercress to be used for propagation at a later stage.

The following plants require a great deal more nutrients and will usually only do well in an aquaponics system that is well established and heavily stocked.

Cucumbers:

Depending on the variety of cucumber you are planning to grow, the average spacing should be between 30cm to 60cm apart or between two to five plants per m^2. They need a pH of between 5.5 to 6.5. It only takes them between three to seven days to germinate, but the germination temperature should be around 20° to 30°C. Total growing time is between 55 to 65 days at a temperature that ranges between 71° to 82°F. Notice how cucumbers have quite a high tolerance for temperature fluctuations. The evening temperatures can go as low as 64°F, but your plants must be protected from frost at all cost. They thrive in a fully sunny environment. When harvesting, your plant height should be about 20cm to 200cm tall and 20cm to 80cm wide.

Cucumbers are best grown using the DWC method or in media beds. A benefit of growing cucumbers is that you can grow them along with other members of the same family, including squash, melons and zucchinis. They are a summer crop. Part of the reason that they are suited to growing in media beds is because they have a longer and larger root structure. Although you could try and grow them in a raft-based system, the roots could potentially block, or clog filters, creating further problems down the line. They need a lot of nutrients and potassium and this should be factored in when planning on stocking your fish. Cucumbers love humidity and so consider growing these if your climate supports these types of conditions. Watch for problems if your temperatures drop below 50°F because your plants are going to stop growing at that time.

You can transplant your seedlings after two weeks and once they have between four to five true leaves. Be aware that these plants grow very quickly, and it is a great habit to get into to cut certain tips when the stem is about two meters long to remove lateral branches. This will also give the plant better ventilation. Other plants can be secured by leaving only two buds that are furthest apart from one another that are coming from the same stem. Cucumbers also need a support structure for them to grow properly as this also gives them necessary aeration. Cucumbers could be susceptible to a number of problems like powdery mildew and grey mold—be on the lookout for any of these diseases and treat with natural methods as we have already discussed.

In ideal conditions one cucumber plant can be harvested between 10 to 15 times. It's also important to make sure that you harvest every few days so that the plants don't become too large and so that you can allow the others along the same plant to grow.

Broccoli:

The ideal time to grow broccoli is in the winter. It's recommended that the media bed method is used. Please note that this is quite a difficult vegetable to grow because it doesn't like warm temperatures at all. When you are growing your broccoli, make sure that your pH is between 6.0 and 7.0. Average temperatures during the day should be between 55° to 64°F, which you can see is a lot cooler than most of the other vegetables we have spoken about here. Although they prefer a cooler climate, they enjoy full sun and can endure some shade. If they are in the shade all the time though, they will grow much slower. When growing broccoli, the average spacing between your plants should be between 40 to 70cm or approximately three to five plants per m^2.

It should take your broccoli about five to six days to germinate at an average temperature of 77°F. You will notice that the plants need a much higher temperature for germination than actual growth. The full growth cycle is anywhere between 60 to 100 days from being transplanted.

You can harvest your crop once the height reaches 30 to 60cm and the width reaches the same: 30cm to 60cm.

I mentioned above that the seedlings take about a week to germinate. Once they have germinated, it's time to transplant them into your media bed. This should be done once there are about four to five true leaves on the plants and they are about 15cm to 20cm tall. Getting the spacing correct when transplanting the seedlings is important, otherwise their growth will be stunted.

When harvesting your broccoli, the buds of the heads need to be both firm and tight. If you notice that the buds are beginning to separate from one another, or they are beginning to flower, make sure that you harvest immediately.

Peas and Beans:

Both peas and beans can be grown in aquaponics. The climbing varieties are recommended because they take up less space than normal beans and peas do. The yield for the climbing varieties is also two to three times greater than normal. The pH for both varieties range between 5.5 to 7.0 and ideal temperatures are between 71° to 79°F during the day and a minimum of between 61° to 64°F at night.

Both plants enjoy full sun and should be grown in either summer or autumn, depending on the cultivars. It is recommended that the media bed aquaponic technique is used to grow these. Consider spacing your plants between ten to thirty centimeters depending on the variety, with bush varieties having between twenty to forty plants per m² and approximately only ten to twelve climbing plants per m². Depending on the variety and cultivar, growing time can take anything between 50 to 110 days to reach full maturity. By this time, the plant would have reached a height of about 60cm, with a width of about 250cm for a climbing plant. The normal bush variety will have a height of about 60cm and a width of about 80cm.

If you are planning on growing beans and peas you can place your seeds directly into the grow media beds about four centimeters deep, making sure that the water level will be high enough during germination. This process usually takes about eight to ten days and the temperature necessary for correct germination is between 70° to 79°F.

Because they are extremely difficult to transplant successfully, any supporting equipment needs to be in place before or at the time of planting your seedlings. Special care should be taken to watch out for spiders and other aphids that are fairly common with beans and peas. Wherever possible avoid planting companion plants or pay close attention to what you plan to plant with them to avoid contamination of these diseases.

When harvesting snap beans, the pods should be crisp when harvesting, with the inside seeds being small or undeveloped. To harvest successfully, remove the pod by holding the stem in one hand and the pod in the other. This will allow for further growth at a later stage.

When harvesting shell beans, the pods should be picked as soon as they change color. The pods should be plump. Try not to leave these on the plant for too long as this affects the quality of the beans.

For dry beans, the opposite is the case. The shells or pods should be left to dry as much as possible. This makes harvesting easier as the pods split open easier when they are dry.

Peppers:

While it is difficult to grow peppers in a conventional gardening system because they require plenty of sunshine and are very particular about the water they use, they are suited to smaller indoor aquaponics systems. The reason for this is because you can control the temperature to exactly meet their specific needs.

A Deep-Water Culture (DWC) method of growing peppers is not suitable—they do much better using a "flood and drain" technique (more about each of these systems in the following chapter).

There are four main genus of peppers which will help you to understand which is going to best suit your needs—whether you are after the Capsicum, Pimenta, Piper, or Red pepper, the important consideration is that they all have exactly the same needs and requirements for growth in aquaponics. Before you begin to grow peppers, the single most important thing to do is to decide which of the above four peppers you are wanting to grow. If you are only starting off with aquaponics, it is highly recommended that you begin with the conventional bell pepper.

Peppers enjoy warm temperatures, which is why many people prefer to grow them in greenhouses. You may want to build a trellis that would aid your peppers to flourish in your aquaponic system.

The water temperature for peppers should be a minimum of 60℉ to 70℉, although this can go even as high as 75℉. Beware of water temperatures exceeding 80℉ as this will cause your peppers to become deformed. As a side note—the hotter the pepper, the warmer the water requirement.

Air temperature is as important as water temperature and

this should be between 70°F – 90°F.

The ideal water pH should be between 5.5 and 6.5 but peppers can thrive in pH as high as 7.0.

Peppers need a lot of sunshine and a warmer climate. If you live in a moderate climate and you plan to grow peppers, you may consider growing them in a greenhouse instead.

I mentioned earlier that you may wish to build a trellis to support your pepper plants. This is because peppers can grow between one and three feet tall and the same width. It's important to note that the leaves of the peppers hang over the to protect them from direct sunlight.

Swiss Chard:

This is a hugely popular aquaponically grown plant. It can also be grown using all aquaponic methods, i.e. NFT, DWC and grow beds. The recommended pH for swiss chard is between 6.0 to 7.5 and prefers temperatures of between 61° to 75°F. Ideal growing conditions are in full sun, although when temperatures exceed 79°F, the plants will need to be moved into partial shading. When planting swiss chard, make sure that you leave spacing about 30cm x 30cm apart, or plat between 15 to 20 plants in a m² area.

It takes about 30 to 35 days for your plants to fully mature and be ready for harvesting. This should normally be grown in late winter or early spring. Something to be aware of when growing swiss chard from seedlings is that they grow more than one plant per seed and so you may need to thin your crop out from time to time. You can easily achieve this by removing older leaves that will also encourage new growth with your plant.

The right height for harvesting is around 30 to 60cm, with a width of around 30 to 40cm.

A major benefit of swiss chard is that you can continuously harvest your plants. As you cut off the plants that are being harvested, this will encourage new growth and new leaves will begin to grow and the cycle continues. The only recommendation when it comes to harvesting is to avoid damaging the central growing point when you are harvesting your crop. Otherwise the next new leaves will battle to grow.

Tomatoes:

One of the main reasons why tomatoes do exceptionally well in aquaponics is that you are able to control how much sun the plants get. Surprisingly, they are a popular choice for newcomers to aquaponics, however, they are more difficult to grow than you would imagine at first. It's important to understand the requirements that tomatoes need to grow successfully before you even begin to consider this particular crop. Tomatoes not only have specific needs in aquaponics, but there is also a special way that they need to be tended to. Because the tomato is actually a berry and not a vegetable, but rather a fruit. Originally from South America, you would then understand why it prefers a warmer climate to other vegetables. A lot of nutrient-rich water is also necessary for your tomatoes to grow successfully. Temperatures should range between 65° to 85°F, but they will stop growing if it is warmer than 95°F. As a matter of interest, if the evening temperatures are higher than 85°F, the tomatoes will not turn red at all.

Although your tomatoes need a constant supply of water, they also need to be drained. Keeping tomato plants submerged constantly will cause the crop to fail.

The water pH needs to be between 5.5 and 6.5 for tomatoes and so the best possible fish to match to these pH levels would be Tilapia, Koi, Crappie, Goldfish, Angelfish and as a last resort, possibly Trout (remember that trout prefer cooler water temperatures).

Tomato plants need sufficient space between them, with enough support for them to be able to grow upwards unencumbered. Your crop could grow anywhere between two feet to six feet in height and so when you are initially setting up your tomato system, make sure that they are placed at least two feet apart from one another.

Watch potassium levels in your system. While they require plenty of nitrogen during their early stages of development, this requirement quickly turns to needing more potassium to make sure that the fruit forms correctly. To keep your tomato plants thriving, you need to trim them once they reach approximately two feet in height. You may also want to remove some of the leaves from the bottom of the plant as this will help the nitrogen flow from the stems to the fruit, allowing them to grow bigger quicker.

On average, you could expect anywhere from 25 to 35 tomatoes per plant, variety dependent of course. They grow quickly and you should be able to see growth over a two-week period, with fully developed flowers around four weeks. You can plan to harvest your tomatoes within eight weeks of planting.

There has been success in growing the following crops under highly monitored and regulated environments:

Bananas, Beets, Carrots, Dwarf citrus trees: lemons, limes, and oranges, Dwarf pomegranate trees, Edible flowers: nasturtiums, violas, and orchids. Also: Microgreens, including Onions, Radishes and Sweet corn.

BENEFITS OF GROWING YOUR OWN FRUIT, VEGETABLES, HERBS AND FISH USING AQUAPONICS

Some of the most important benefits of being able to grow your own fruit, vegetables, herbs and fish are listed below:

- The biggest advantage of making use of aquaponics is that it takes an environmentally friendly stance towards saving the planet. Because it mimics the natural ecosystem, it makes use of very little water and also limited to no power at all (unless you are running heaters or filters in your pond setup. If you are using a normal aquarium with ornamental fish, then you would use whatever amount of water your tank would require. You would only need to top up water from time to time to keep your aquarium levels stable. This would also be an indication of whatever water your plants would use to grow.
- For me it is all about sustainability and becoming self-reliant. A good aquaponic system would easily

be able to support a family of between four to six people continuously once it is up and running and maintained correctly. Larger systems would be suitable for commercial farming and could even feed communities in regions where it is not viable for an entire farming setup to be established.

- The start up costs are fairly low. This would definitely prove a cost saving at the end of the day. Because there are not costly premixed nutrients required in your aquaponic system, your only real costs are your fish food (when required) and the cost of your initial set up. If you are looking at designing a commercial aquaponic system then you can expect your costs to be higher than a home-based system, but you would still save on heavy commercial farming equipment, pesticides, labor and many other cost factors that commercial farmers face daily.
- You may even currently have a fish tank in your home right now that could be converted into an aquaponic system for a reasonable price. It's worth mentioning that a fish tank can only support smaller ornamental fish with limited stocking capacity. The moment you are looking at bigger fish such as Koi or Tilapia, you would need to consider larger tanks and bigger systems.
- Because aquaponics operates as a closed recirculating system, there is little to no water that is lost throughout the growing process. This makes it by far the most economical way to grow food in a cost-effective way.
- Your initial outlay is extremely small because you only need to consider your fish, the food that they eat and water, as well as either seeds or seedlings of the crop that you are planning to grow.
- A huge plus factor is that aquaponics really is completely organic. There are no synthetic, premix addi-

- tives, pesticides and chemicals that need to go into growing the vegetables and fish of your choice.
- While some of your fish could be picky eaters and you will need to buy them their own food, but remember that whatever you are feeding them will eventually feed you and their pellets are going to turn into protein that you would eventually consume. It makes sense then that you feed your fish the very best food available, that matches their specific needs. Naturally this is for the larger edible variety of fish versus ornamentals.
- Due to the nature of this type of farming many of the plant varieties are easy to grow and the growing time is drastically reduced. This means that harvesting takes place a lot earlier. In some instances, it is said that growing times can be shortened up to six times the average growing time required under commercial growing circumstances.
- While this can support individual families with their food requirements, including protein (contained in the fish), when one considers this type of farming on a larger, commercial scale, entire communities can become fully sustainable. It is recommended that you consider the size and scale of the system that best suits your particular needs. Also take into account exactly what crops you are going to eat. There's no point in growing cabbage if it's a vegetable that none of your family ever eats.
- The amount of space required for a full ecosystem is a lot smaller than conventional agriculture and it is suited for indoors, on patios, in greenhouses and areas that have space limitations.
- You are not limited by any one specific crop as you can produce a variety of different vegetables simultaneously, as long as the temperature and pH of the crop and fish match.

- Should you ever reach an overstocking system with your fish, there is also a market for them to be sold to other aquaponics enthusiasts.
- It's an important benefit that you can grow at the source—that means that you can harvest and eat immediately without your crop having to be frozen, stored, or injected with various hormones to keep them fresh to be transported to your local convenience store. The nutrient benefits of this in itself are huge as you are getting all of the goodness that nature intended.
- One final benefit that I can think of to mention here would be that there are limited diseases in aquaponics, opposed to hydroponics where many of the plants are highly susceptible to root rot.

CHAPTER 2: DIFFERENT AQUAPONIC SYSTEMS

"Recirculating aquaponic and hydroponic farms are sustainable options that can have controlled inputs and known outputs, like other existing organic farms. In fact, many recirculating farms not only meet, but can exceed current organic standards. They can be eco-efficient and have versatile designs and reduced use of water, fossil fuels, fertilizers and electricity." ~ Marianne Cufone, Executive Director of the Recirculating Farms Coalition

The three most important decisions that you need to make before you decide which system is going to work best for you is to:

1. Decide which system is going to work best for you?
2. Obtain all of the necessary components required to construct the system, and
3. Put it all together!

Every single aquaponics system needs the following to be effective:

- An aquarium, tank or pond for the fish.
- A grow bed for the plants.
- A means of transporting water both to the plants and

the fish and back again (a recirculating system). Most people find that a pump of some description works best.
- A means of draining the water from the grow bed back to the aquarium, tank or pond where the fish are, siphon type pipes are often used to serve this purpose.

There are three main different types of aquaponics systems: Deep Water Culture (DWC), Nutrient Film Bed (NFT), and Media Bed. While these are certainly not the only aquaponics systems available, they are the three that we are going to focus on because they are the most common.

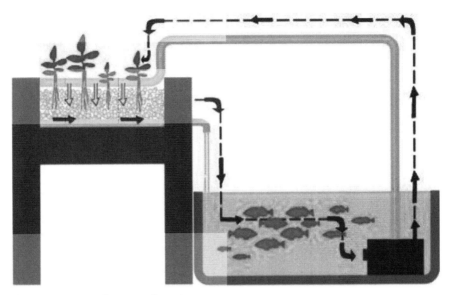

aquaponic system

A Typical Aquaponic System

Before beginning with your design or deciding on what system you are planning on using, it is important that you consider the end use of your system and ask several questions that can help you make the best decision possible. Are you planning on only building your system as a means of supporting your household with some additional organic vegetables all year round? Are you planning on considering a commercial venture with a much larger farm that will grow a large variety of different crops? Are you planning on using your system for educational purposes? Whatever your chief use is going to be, there are a number of other considerations that you need to consider:

These are as follows:

- What is your environment like? Do your seasons fluctuate radically between heat and cold? If this is the case, would it be better for you to consider your system inside versus outside, or in a greenhouse environment where it can be protected by some of the

natural elements?
- How much space do you have available to you? This will also directly impact your decision on how much you will be able to produce and where. There is no point in looking to begin a commercial venture, when you live in a small 2-bedroom tenement building (unless you convince the landlord to allow you to convert and utilize the entire roof area, which could then provide food year round for all the tenants).
- What are you planning on growing—as a sidebar, there really is no point growing fruits or vegetables that you do not eat. This will naturally be a waste. It is the same as stocking the fish that you do not find palatable to the taste. All that will happen is that these will go to waste and that is the complete contradiction to this type of sustainable farming.
- Consider the different technical capacity and capabilities that you have. Some systems are pretty straightforward to put together and you would be able to manage on your own, while others require a slightly more professional approach. Make sure that you understand how your system works, what can go wrong, how to correct it if it does go wrong and how to maintain the system. Remember that when your system is faulty your fish and your crop are at risk. Initial close monitoring of a number of factors are important to the success of whatever system you choose to use.

DEEP WATER CULTURE (DWC):

Deep Water Culture Aquaponics, also known as (DWC):

Closely modeled after the same principles that the ancient Aztecs and Chinese cultures used, this method is really just a modernized version. As the saying goes, "if it ain't broke, don't try and fix it!" This method has been used for hundreds of years successfully, so it has been a natural progression to duplicate this method today with a couple of modern tweaks. This method of aquaponics is really low maintenance and is best suited for fruits, vegetables and herbs that grow rapidly. Examples of these would include leafy greens and lettuce. The setup costs for this system are also reasonable, so you won't break the bank if you decide that this addictive hobby is not for you.

Once you understand how a deep-water culture design works, you will find it easy to adapt and design your own system that will meet the demands of your crops, your fish, your water, your pH and temperatures. Being able to monitor these will literally provide you with all that you need to run a successful aquaponics system.

Understanding that the DWC is very similar to the other systems, in that they still need to be monitored to make sure that both the fish and the plants are healthy and that the main ingredient, bacteria cycling, is necessary before starting your system. In any aquaponic system, the crucial ingredient to the success of the system is that the bacteria colony needs to be established before you "cycle" or let your system "go live". In a DWC system the roots of the plants remain submerged all the time or are mostly submerged all the time. Unlike hydroponics where premix nutrients are added to meet the needs of the plants being cultivated, here, the bacteria, fish, pH, water temperature and air temperature factor into the growing cycle and are the only things that need to be monitored closely for the first month that the system is up and running.

While some people use lightweight pots for their plants, the pots of choice are called net pots and are a popular choice for this method.

DWC is also an extremely popular choice for hydroponics. Although the main difference in using it with aquaponics is that you don't need to include grow media. The simplicity of this system is that the floatation device or beds are literally on top of where the fish are and there should be some form of aeration system included.

The design variations are only limited by how far your imagination can stretch, so grab your pen and paper and start thinking about the following:

- How much space do I have available?
- What crops am I planning on cultivating and how will this impact my system?
- With the crops I would like to cultivate, which fish are closely aligned to the temperatures and pH required to sustain optimal growth?
- What is my budget?

Once you have all the answers to the above questions, the next thing would be to physically measure out your system according to your plan. Remember that your system is a recirculating system and so all plumbing components need to be able to move the water between the plants floating in the net pots and back to the fish. (In the following chapter we will go through the nutrient cycle. This will give you a better idea of how the plants receive nutrients from the waste products of the fish).

If you would like to consider a canal system, the tank housing the fish is separate from where the plants are grown, while water is being pumped between the different areas where the plant beds are floating in the water. While this system is a little more intricate and involved it is also more effective as the water is circulated between the plants better.

Building Your DWC System

If this is the system that you have decided to build, then you are going to need the following:

Aeration:

I mentioned aeration above—it is important that oxygen is added to the water, irrespective of the system you design or choose to make use of. In aquaponics, this is referred to as dissolved oxygen or (DO). This is a vital ingredient to the growth and health of your plants and fish. You can increase the aeration in your system through a number of different methods. Whether you would like to look at diffusers, air stones, air pumps, helping to improve on the DO is something that needs to be monitored closely as it affects both plant and fish.

Biofilter:

Next you will need something called a biofilter. This is where the bacteria go to work to turn the waste produced by the fish into nutrients that are suitable to feed the plants. This process is known as the nitrification process. It is also this process that replaces the chemical premix that would typically be used in a hydroponic system.

Canals:

While we refer to these as canals, what they actually are in a recirculating system is a series of pipes (like large plumbing pipes) or trenches that transport and hold the water pushed through the various tanks by the pumps. Each of these pipes or trenches have holes in them that support the net pots so that they are "floating" in the nutrient enriched water. Depending on how you set up your system, you can add more pipes or trenches to your canals as your planting requirements grow. This could be as a result of your current cultivars growing and needing more space, or it could be that you are planning on adding additional herbs, vegetables, or plants to your system.

Conventional Filter:

A conventional filtration system that is able to filter out anything else that could get into the system. Some prefer screens, reverse osmosis, or even swirl filters to complete this process. The last thing that you want is for the system to become clogged up with leaves or anything that cannot be processed by the biofilter into nutrients to feed the plants.

If you are planning on building a canal system, you will definitely need a pump to help force the water from the fish tanks through the filters and to each of the canals where the plants are floating on the "rafts". Remember that the secret to aquaponics is to keep the water recirculating and moving at all times for the plants to be aerated with the nutrients to help them grow. When choosing your pump, take the size of your tanks into consideration.

Grow Beds – Floating:

These are usually manufactured from a lightweight substance that is able to float easily, that can also support your net pots. In most instances these allow for only the roots to be exposed to the water. The net pots provide the plants the necessary support that they need to grow.

Tank:

A tank for your fish. This can be as large or as small as you require but remember that it needs to meet the needs of the breed or type of fish that you plan to stock. Your fish need to be comfortable and have sufficient space to grow. Some people prefer to have separate tanks that will accommodate their hatchling or fingerling fish (those that are still really small). This is a great idea because it prevents them from becoming food for larger fish, especially if the more mature fish are carnivorous. This tank will be home to them until they become large enough to be moved over. Your tanks will also become the collection point for the waste product that your fish produce.

Gordon L. Atwell

Important Tips for DWC Aquaponics

Some important things to take into consideration when it comes to DWC aquaponics are to ensure that there is enough dissolved oxygen in the water. This is achieved with air stones, or pumps. You will need to monitor this regularly to ensure that your plants and fish are healthy and thriving. Without dissolved oxygen, neither your fish nor your plants can survive.

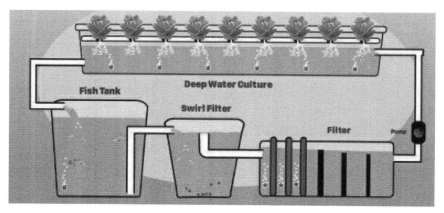

Deep Water Culture System

Remember to monitor your water temperature and pH levels constantly. These need to be in range to match the fish that you have stocked, as well as the plants that you are growing. Also make sure that your nitrification process is happening correctly. (We will discuss this in greater detail in the next chapter).

Check all of your filters, pumps and piping on a regular basis to make sure that there are no blockages so that your water flow is not restricted in any way.

If you are planning on adding any plants to the fish tank, make sure that these are easy to maintain and aren't likely to cause disease for your fish.

Because this system is relatively easy to setup, with costs that can be controlled on the basis of your design, it is ideal for someone who is first starting out with Aquaponics.

FLOOD AND DRAIN OR EBB AND FLOW SYSTEM

This system is by far the most popular system for beginners because it is easy to build and results in fairly good yields for someone who is just starting out.

This system works as follows:

- The plants or grow beds are situated above the aquarium, allowing drainage to take place naturally via the force of gravitation.
- Typically, plants would be planted in a grow medium such as clay pebbles. These will support the roots of the plant and will substitute soil.
- Water from the aquarium or fish tank is pumped into the grow beds by means of a submersible pump.
- The amount of water being pumped into the grow bed is usually monitored with a timer that is turned on and off. This allows for initial flooding and then draining back into the fish tank.
- An automatic timer is placed to control the flood and drain cycle. This makes use of a bell siphon, which means that it operates without electricity.
- The average timing for flooding would be around fifteen minutes per cycle, with a drain cycle of forty-five minutes.

ORGANIC GARDENING

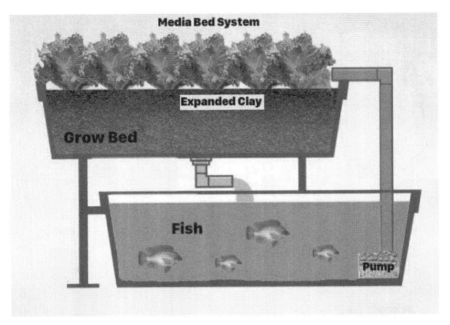

Flood and Drain or Ebb and Flow Technique

NUTRIENT FILM TECHNIQUE (NFT):

While this system is very similar to the DWC method, the difference between the two is that the roots of the plants are watered by a steady flow of water in much smaller volumes. This is why they call it the 'film' technique. The nutrient filled water virtually only moistens the plants root system, but it is constant.

Again, each of the plants sit in net pots in each of the channels or closed recirculating systems while the roots are fed as the water containing all of the nutrients passes by the bottom of the plants, also known as the root zone.

Just like the DWC method, there is constant flow between the different components. The water from the fish tank, pond, or aquarium is pumped into the NFT channel, where the roots are lightly covered, and this water then returns to the fish tank. With each of these systems a separate biofilter is needed.

NFT is one of the best choices when it comes to larger commercial farming. If you are planning on starting out with aquaponics for the first time—the Ebb and Flow system is better suited.

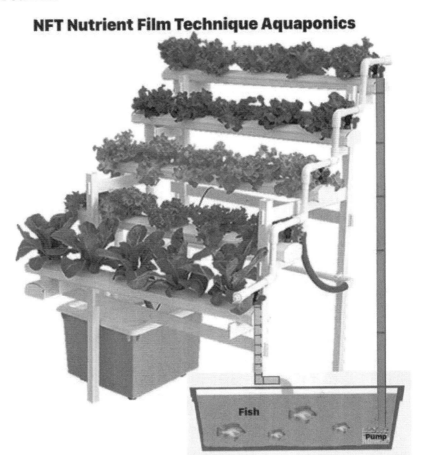

Nutrient Film Technique or NFT

CHAPTER 3: UNDERSTANDING THE NUTRIENT CYCLE

"[Plants] grow extremely rapidly because they have all the nutrients and water they need. It's much better than field production because in the soil, you have insects and not enough water or nutrients." ~ Dr. James Rakocy, "Father of Aquaponics," and former professor at the University of the Virgin Islands

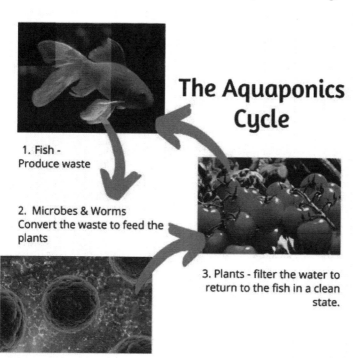

The Aquaponics Cycle

1. Fish - Produce waste

2. Microbes & Worms Convert the waste to feed the plants

3. Plants - filter the water to return to the fish in a clean state.

The Nutrient Cycle

UNDERSTANDING THE IMPORTANCE OF THE NUTRIENT CYCLE:

Most aquaponics enthusiasts are impatient and want their system up and running as soon as possible. Before you can, or should get your system going, it should be cycled correctly. When fish create waste as a byproduct, ammonia and nitrates are created which can be poisonous to the fish and pH levels in the water can also increase. You can cycle your aquaponics system with your fish or without your fish. I'm going to share both methods with you.

When we refer to "cycling" it's not riding a bicycle—it's ensuring that your beneficial bacteria system that you need for your aquarium, pond or tank are up and running correctly and are effectively changing the harmful nitrates to beneficial nitrites. The good news is that you can do it with your fish or without fish. The ideal is to do it fishless because it could potentially save you a lot of money in fish if you happen to get it wrong!

UNDERSTANDING THE ROLE THAT NITROGEN PLAYS IN AQUAPONICS

Nitrogen is crucial for all living organisms. It's what keeps us alive, but at the same time keeps all other living organisms alive as well. The drawback of nitrogen is that in many different ecosystems there is limited supply of nitrogen present. There are different forms of nitrogen available. These include atmospheric nitrogen (N_2), ammonia (NH_3), nitrate (NO_3^-) and nitrite (NO_2^-). Animals excrete nitrogenous waste in the form of ammonia, while plants require nitrogen in the form of nitrates to survive. Because plants absorb nitrogen in the form of nitrates and convert this to atmospheric nitrogen (N_2), in the ecological system continues to be recycled.

CYCLING YOUR SYSTEM IN THREE EASY STEPS:

Add water to your aquarium tank, or pond and turn on your pump, allowing it to run for two days. This will dissolve any chlorine from tap water that may be present. Whatever you do, don't add any fish or plants at this stage.

Once this process is complete it's time to add a couple of smaller, cheap fish that you are possibly prepared to lose, think of something like a couple of goldfish. The purpose of adding these fish to the tank at this point is for them to produce waste which will contain ammonia.

Wait at least two weeks before adding some seedlings to your grow beds. For the next ten to fifteen days it's important that you don't feed your fish, as this will only create problems for your system. Don't worry too much, fish can survive for as long as three weeks without food. At this stage the ammonia levels will be high because the beneficial bacteria required to turn this into nitrites haven't become sufficiently established to begin the nitrogen cycle as yet. Remember the two nitrifying bacteria — nitrosomonas (NO_2), and nitrospira, which converts the nitrite into nitrate. It is this nitrate which is required by the plants as nutrients. This type of nitrate is beneficial to both plants and fish and is the final step in the nitrogen cycle.

So how do you tell if your system is ready?

You will be able to confirm that your system is now ready as soon as you find nitrates in the water; your water will test with both nitrites and ammonia levels lower than 0.5ppm, and regular feeding will not increase nitrite or ammonia levels.

The ideal should be zero or less than 1mg/liter of ammonia and nitrites in your water within 40 to 50 days. At this stage the nitrate level should be higher than 100ppm.

You can now slowly begin to add more fish to your system, although only a few at a time with a couple of days in between. The main reason for this is that even though your biofilter is ready and functioning, it needs to populate and grow at the same rate to support your fish. This would happen quickly in a fully cycled system, but you need to remember that this is still taking place and you don't want to run the risk of losing your fish at this time.

You can begin to add plants at the same time as you begin to cycle your tank, aquarium or pond. Plants are helpful in absorbing nitrogen from ammonia nitrates and nitrites throughout the cycling process. Your plants will definitely be happiest once the biofilter is fully established and nitrates are available from the beneficial bacteria and the cycle is 100% complete.

As soon as you have added your plants, they will begin to take root in your new system. You may initially notice some of them turning yellow or dropping a couple of leaves here and there. This is completely normal. You will not begin to see normal growth in the next couple of weeks. Part of the reason for adding plants at the beginning of the cycling process is that it allows them to catch up with the rooting process and makes sure that they are ready to start absorbing the nutrient-rich fish waste from the system as soon as it becomes available.

MONITORING YOUR CYCLING PROCESS

The full cycling process normally takes anywhere upwards of four to six weeks to complete. Knowing this will give you a much better understanding of where in the cycle you are as you move forward. You will know that you need to have monitored your pH, nitrite, nitrate and ammonia levels to make sure that each of these are within range. If not, you know what to do to correct it. While this entire process is fascinating to watch, unfortunately the only way that you get to see it properly is via a test kit. As soon as everything is within the ranges as mentioned above, you can begin to slowly add more fish to your system and the monitoring process that you have had to rigidly follow takes a bit more of a back seat. You then get to sit back and do the fun stuff like watching your fish, feeding them and tending to your plants.

Remember to consider each of the following while you are monitoring your cycling process.

Temperature:

Both types of microorganisms or bacteria mentioned are living and are altered by temperature. The ideal temperature range is between 77° to 86°F for them to grow. Should the temperatures be out of these parameters, the levels of dissolved oxygen will be affected, and the bacteria will be unable to process the waste as needed.

pH:

The pH plays a vital role in the nitrification process. pH levels outside of 7.0 will begin negatively influencing bacterial performance. This will become completely restricted and virtually non-existent at 6.0. Ideal ranges for Nitrosomonas are between 7.3 to 7.5 and for Nitrosomonas is between 7.0 and 8.0.

Nitrification:

During the nitrification process, ammonia is transformed into nitrates which can be used by plants. These nitrates are what makes up the nutrient-rich water that is pumped from the aquarium, tank or pond to water your plants through whatever method you have chosen.

Nitrification includes two steps involving nitrifying or beneficial bacteria:

1. Ammonia is changed into nitrites (NO_2-) by bacteria called nitrosomonas.
2. Nitrites are changed into nitrates (NO_3-) by bacteria called nitrobacter.

The product that results from this transformation, nitrates, can then be absorbed as nutrients by your plants.

Chloramines and Chlorines:

It's vital to make sure that all chlorine is neutralized completely before adding any form of bacteria to your tank, aquarium or pond. Any chloramines or chlorine that remain is highly toxic to the fish, as well as the nitrifying bacteria (beneficial bacteria).

Light Sensitivity:

Nitrifying bacteria are especially sensitive to both ultraviolet and blue light. This light only causes problems during the cycling process and so you should make sure that all lights are turned off for the duration of this period. Once your system has cycled through, it is quite safe for you to turn these lights back on.

Dissolved Oxygen (DO) Levels:

We have discussed how dissolved oxygen levels can adversely affect both plants and fish, but this comes into play much earlier during the nitrification process, as soon as dissolved levels of oxygen concentrations reach below 2.0 mg/liter. Hitting this level will not affect the nitrosomonas as much as it will affect beneficial bacteria. Nitrosomonas will increase levels of poisonous nitrates in the water. You can reach maximum nitrification rates at dissolved oxygen concentrations above 80% capacity.

Salinity:

Also referred to as the salt content, this needs to fluctuate between 0-6 ppt with a specific gravity between 1-1.0038 which is best suited to the growth of the freshwater nitrifying bacteria. Adjustments to differing salt levels or content could take between 1-3 days before they start to grow at a rapid rate.

Micronutrients:

All nitrifying bacteria require micronutrients. The most important of these is phosphorous as this is necessary for Adenosine Triphosphate to be produced. Cells obtain their energy from ATP conversion. Cells would normally be able to get phosphorous in the form of PO_4. Nitrites cannot be oxidized by nitrobacter into nitrates without phosphates.

Absorption:

During the absorption stage, nitrogen is absorbed into the living organisms. Plants take in nitrogen in the form of nitrates through their root hairs. This nitrogen is processed by the plants further and used as both amino and nucleic acids.

Ammonia:

As living organisms produce waste, decay or die off, nitrogen is converted to ammonia and is given off by the organism. This process is called ammonification.

Denitrification:

Occurs as nitrogen is once again recycled back to the atmosphere in the form of nitrogen. This happens when nitrates, and nitrites are converted back to the N2 gas via anaerobic bacteria. This completes the nitrogen cycle.

Avoid the following:

Beware of using any other aquarium products like algae preservatives, water conditioners or other products that you would normally use for pet fish. None of these products are going to be beneficial to the mini aquaponic ecosystem that you are trying to establish.

Remember to reduce feeding as much as possible to ensure that less destructive ammonia enters the system. Ammonia substantially reduces the production of nitrites.

Leave the pH levels alone. They will automatically take care of themselves over time and should lower accordingly. You may potentially have to add certain things to maintain your pH at 7.0.

IMPORTANT POINTS TO REMEMBER

Invest in a really good quality water test kit and educate yourself as much as you can about water. You can do this online, by asking those in the know or even reading books such as this one. Testing the quality of your water on a regular basis is one of the few activities that will be ongoing and something that you should learn to master. I would recommend that you look for a proper testing kit rather than trying to rely on the testing strips, as these are not always accurate and can often be difficult to read.

The only time that you should add any salt to your water at all should be during your cycling time. This should also only occur if you are cycling with fish. Remember that I mentioned that salt does not evaporate, so it is extremely important to add this in moderation and keep accurate notes of how much salt you are adding at a time.

Before you add your expensive fish that you plan to populate your system with, go out there and buy some cheapies that you are prepared to sacrifice if the system is not yet ready. This decision and small exercise could end up saving you loads of money in the long run.

Something that we have not discussed up till this point, but will be hugely beneficial in giving your system a kickstart—consider adding a couple of red worms that you would normally find in composting to your plant bed once your system has cycled and you begin adding your fish.

CHAPTER 4: IDENTIFYING THE BEST FISH FOR AQUAPONICS

"Only by adopting a mentality that focuses on maximizing conservation and ethical food production techniques, can we establish a future of production that works. We have to intensify production. But it needs intensifying the right way, not just relying on the finite resources, because in the long run it won't work. It's a false economy, we'll run out." ~ Antonia Paladino, Founder of Bioaqa, biggest integrated aquaponic trout farm in Europe

Finding the very best fish for your aquaponics system is dependent on a number of factors. You need to consider the climate that you live in, what species of fish are actually either indigenous or common to the area, and whether you are going to settle for fish that are just decorative or whether you plan on eating them as a means of obtaining your source of protein. This is one of the benefits of moving towards aquaponics rather than hydroponics. There are many other differences and benefits between the two and we will list them further in this book for you to make an educated decision as to what will work best for you.

Before you should even be considering which fish are going to work best for you, think about your needs and whether you are going to buy your fish from a hatchery, a local aquarium or online. Buying fish online is now in fairly high demand and so you will probably find someone in your area who delivers directly to your door. A small sidebar here, if you are planning on ordering your fish online, please make sure that you are there to receive them, or someone else has access to receive them. Please remember that they are live produce and will need to get into their respective tanks as a matter of urgency.

There is no right or wrong answer when it comes to purchasing your fish—some people prefer to go to the supplier, hatchery or aquarium and select the fish that they want themselves, while others are content to accept whatever they order online.

Some of the most successful fish for aquaponics include Angelfish, Bluegill or Sea Bream, Crappie, Goldfish, Guppies, Koi, Mollies, Sunfish, Swordfish, Tetras, Tilapia, and Pacu. Some of these are purely ornamental, while others can be reared for eating. The following fish are also widely used in aquaponics:

Barramundi, Carp, Catfish, Largemouth Bass, and Golden, Silver and Yellow Perch.

The main consideration is how well the species of fish will do within your own specific climate. This dictates pH and water temperatures, which we will discuss a bit later—but it doesn't help bringing in a tropical fish to a climate that is not conducive to its survival. Remember that the aim is for the fish to be able to both survive and thrive.

To give you a better understanding of this, let's look at each of these fish and see what sort of conditions they need to thrive in.

ANGELFISH

If you were considering using these beautifully colored fish in your tank for aquaponics, this would definitely be an option for the ornamental variety of fish. They can be very pretty to look at and can have a calming effect over you while your plants are being nourished, however they are not suitable for consumption at all. Most angelfish only grow to around four to five centimeters in length, making them a small fish by comparison to a Tilapia or Largemouth Bass. Another concern when it comes to choosing Angelfish for aquaponics is that they are extremely inbred as a species and can become prone to carry diseases around with them—this would not really make them ideal, unless you were running a pretty small unit somewhere in your home and the protein component was not an issue for you.

Source: Emperor Angelfish - Pixabay

BLUEGILL OR SEA BREAM

The Bluegill, also referred to as bream or sometimes even perch (which is incorrect), is a freshwater fish that can be found in North America. It's happy to live in either shallow or deep-water conditions, which makes it great for aquaponics. If you are planning on stocking these, it may be worthwhile to add some tree stumps or other types of structures in your ponds as they enjoy hiding in this type of environment.

They would be great to stock for protein if you were situated in North America as they can grow to a reasonable size, ranging anywhere between 12 inches (30cm) long and approximately 4½ pounds (2.0 kg) in weight.

They are omnivorous and will pretty much eat anything, which is also important when it comes to aquaponics. With Bluegill, you could even feed them scraps and they would be quite happy.

When it comes to reproduction, Bluegills spawn between May and August each year, and water temperatures should then be between 67° – 80°F. The males will create spawning beds in shallow water and are extremely protective of these nests. During mating, one female will choose only one male who she can spawn with, but when this is done, the male will chase her back out of the nest and then protect the young. Smaller females can produce around 1,000 eggs at a time, while larger females can produce over 100,000 eggs. The male will closely guard the eggs until they hatch, and the larvae are able to

Gordon L. Atwell

swim away.

The lifespan of a Bluegill is approximately four years when they reach full maturity, but others have been known to live up to eleven years.

Source: Bluegill or Sea Bream – Pixabay

CRAPPIES

Source: Wikimedia Commons

There are a number of species that fall into the Crappies family. Some of these are actually Bluegills as discussed above, while others are Largemouth Bass. Crappies actually form part of the Sunfish family and are the biggest of the entire Panfish species. There are only two different types of crappies, white and black!

The White Crappie looks slightly different to the Black Crappie and although it grows to around the same size (6.7" to 20.9"), they weigh the same as the Black Crappie. While their coloring is much lighter and blotches that they have on their body often appear more like stripes, they also have only five or six dorsal fins, compared to the Black Crappie who have seven or eight. Counting the dorsal fins is actually the easiest way to tell these two apart, because while in the water, they can often appear to be exactly the same color.

BLACK CRAPPIE

The length of Black crappies can vary between 5" and 19". The average weight is around ½ pound to a pound, although if they really get big, they could weigh in at 3 or 4 pounds. A black crappie is distinctive by its evenly spaced blotches that are located on the sides. The white crappie is usually silvery green, while the black crappie is more olive colored.

Because crappies are extremely hardy fish, they are a great choice for starting out with aquaponics. Ideal temperatures for crappies are between 70°-75°F, although they can still survive at temperatures as low as 55°F. Allowing temperatures to fall down to 55°F should be avoided as much as possible though because by this stage, the fish become lethargic and the amount of waste produced is a lot less than when water temperatures are optimal.

Crappies can even thrive in temperatures of up to 80°F. Remember that it's not just the water temperature that affects the survival of the fish that you decide to stock, much of the success rate also depends on the pH of the water, which should ideally be between 7, and 7.5.

ORGANIC GARDENING

Source: Black Crappie - PNGKey

GOLDFISH

Source: goldfish-672126_960_720.goldfish-aquarium-Pixabay.jpg

Goldfish make for amazing aquaponic fish, although remember that if you are going to choose to use Goldfish, these are usually just ornamental in nature and can obviously still produce hours of fun and enjoyment in being able to watch them while you unwind after a hard day's work. Some further reasons for choosing to use Goldfish to support your aquaponic system is that they are extremely hardy. They can survive in diverse water temperatures and so this doesn't become a case of having to double check water temperature or consider which side of the continent you are living on. Another huge benefit of using Goldfish for your system is that they produce a lot of waste, which is exactly what your plants are going to need to thrive on.

Goldfish come in two main varieties—fancy and slim-bodied.

The variety of Goldfish that you choose for your aquaponic system would depend on where you plan to build or house your system. If you are planning on having your system outside or in a cooler environment, it is recommended that you look for the Slim-bodied Goldfish because they are hardier and less likely to survive the elements. Some of these would include Bristol Shubunkins, Comets, Commons, Shubunkins, Wakins, and Watoni. Even outside in cooler climates these don't require a heating unit, as long as the water is not likely to freeze over. If it does get cold enough that the water is going to freeze then you would need to shut your system down in winter. You would need to bring whatever plants are in the tank inside as well because it will be highly unlikely that these would be able to survive the icy climate.

Source: goldfish-3687937_960_720-Goldfish-Pixabay.jpg

If your system is indoors, then Fancy Goldfish are the answer if you are after ornamental fish. They are ideal for placement where there is little to no temperature fluctuation. A great idea when it comes to using fancy goldfish are the addition of goldfish-safe snails. These speed up the process for breaking down waste, while being natural algae eaters at the same time.

If you are planning on using either of these varieties of Goldfish, the quality of the food that you are planning on giving them is extremely important. Remember that it is really going to be the waste from this food that is going to feed your plants and you want to ensure the highest quality waste will be produced. Some problems that could arise if you feed them cheaper and lower quality food could lead to things like cloudy water and swim bladder problems, which not only affect the tank, but also the fish. It makes perfect sense that if you are growing plants to be harvested and consumed by yourself that the quality of what is going into the fish will affect the quality of the waste by-product.

GUPPIES

While guppies would probably be the last fish that you would consider to be suited to aquaponics, they are in fact very suitable. There are a couple of reasons why they work really well for aquaponics—firstly they are really entertaining to watch because they dart backwards and forwards really quickly, and the second reason is that they are another resilient fish. There are several factors that you need to get right before you can proceed with guppies. You must understand their different tolerances before you include them in your aquaponic tank. Once you understand this, you can create the best conditions in your tank for success. While they are extremely hardy and resilient, they can take work to maintain and look after some other species and you need to do your research before taking the plunge.

Gordon L. Atwell

Source: aquarium-4446625_960_720Pixabay.jpg

I bet that you never knew that there are more than 40 different species of guppy out there, some of them being the Common Guppy or the Rainbow Fish. These are available worldwide and are usually a popular choice for aquariums and aquaponics systems; Endler Guppies are related to the common guppy but are green, red and silver in color. They love a tranquil environment and warm water. One of the most important questions that are asked when it comes to guppies is whether they can be combined with other fish. Not always in an aquaponics setup because you need to make sure that temperature and pH are suited to the needs of the fish that you are rearing, which is seldom the case when it comes to any two varieties. With Guppies however, they could be combined with non-aggressive fish like Catfish or Tetra. The main reason for not including them in other systems would be for the fear of inbreeding, which won't happen with these two varieties.

KOI

Source: koi-1298672_960_720Koi-Orienntal-Fish-Pixabay.jpg

Next to Tilapia, Koi are the second most popular fish that aquaponics enthusiasts' stock as their fish of choice. The main reason for this is because they are highly suited to aquaponics tanks and setups whether indoors or outdoors. Koi live fairly long and breed in the system. This is because as a species, Koi are used to being kept in ponds or tanks as ornamental fish all their lives. Not that you would ever guess, but Koi are related to both the Goldfish and Carp species. Being highly resistant to diseases and most parasites, they are ideal to be kept in close surroundings with other fish. Because they are used to being in ponds, using Koi are best suited to an outdoor aquaponic environment. You can even design your setup so that your Koi pond becomes the main feature in your garden. Because of their unique patterns and designs, watching Koi can prove to be both therapeutic and relaxing. Another major benefit to stocking Koi is that they are easy to sell should you find yourself in a situation where you have too much stock.

The downside of using koi for your aquaponics fish species is that depending on where you are located in the world, you may require permits to stock them. The best way to resolve this would be to check with either your local forests and fisheries department or the suppliers of the Koi. They should be able to provide you with this information.

Some key considerations when you have your Koi pond outdoors is that they could be prone to predators. The best way to prevent this from happening and protecting your Koi would be to consider net covering, fencing around the pond and possibly even covers should you be aware that you have birds such as Fish Eagles in the area that could possibly endanger your fish.

MOLLIES

Source: fishy-3214876_960_720 Pixabay.jpg

Mollies are another ornamental fish that can be used for your aquaponic system. As you can see by the image, they are pretty and would be great to look at in an aquarium-based system. It is not recommended for you to use them for any larger outdoor system where a lot of waste is needed, purely because they aren't able to produce the amount of by-product required to feed your plants sufficiently.

If you are only considering a smaller indoor system then they would be ideal and are recommended along with Goldfish and other ornamental fish.

TILAPIA

Source: tilapia-799876_960_720-Tilapia-fish-pond-Pixabay.jpg

Ask any aquaponics expert which the most popular fish is to use for their system, and they will more than likely answer 'Tilapia'. There are also many reasons why they are so widely used and popular. Some of the main reasons they work so well is because they are resilient and hardy, they can be an ideal fish to begin aquaponics with on a small scale until you are confident to move on to bigger things. Another major plus is that they are actually quite friendly and will be friendly towards whoever feeds them. They also get on quite well with Catfish.

Tilapia are quite pleasant to the taste and grow big enough for a decent meal. They thrive in warmer water than other fish, opting for approximately 80°-86°F. They can survive fluctuating temperatures that range between 60°-95°F comfortably.

You will be able to farm Tilapia in cages, ponds or tanks without any problems. A Tilapia breeds on average every 4-6 weeks, making them a constant source of protein. While they themselves are omnivores and only require between 22-33% protein as food, a Tilapia will grow to be approximately 600g in six to eight months.

One of the only drawbacks when it comes with farming Tilapia is that if they are in a cooler climate, you may require a heating system in your tank to keep the water temperatures within the above ranges.

If you live in an area where you need to get a permit for Tilapia, consider the Nile Tilapia rather than the Mozambique Tilapia. Most commercial aquaculture or aquaponics farmers have opted for the Nile Tilapia as their fish of choice. The main reason for this is that it has been genetically modified to yield and produce more over a shorter time frame. Evidence suggests that the Egyptians used to keep them in ponds along the Nile some 3,000 years ago, however, the records of them being used in local aquaponics only date back to around the 1980s.

CHANNEL CATFISH

These are highly recommended for larger systems. Most people use these in areas where Tilapia is illegal. They are extremely well-suited to much cooler climates. If you live in an area where your winter is colder and you are running your system outdoors, these should be your fish of choice. Because they are accustomed to being in cooler water, you don't need to invest in water heaters to keep water temperatures constant, as you would do with Tilapia.

Source: catfish-4377964_960_720Pixabay.jpg

There are a couple of pointers when it comes to rearing Channel Catfish. Firstly, they like to live at the bottom of the tank. It is important to know this so that you don't overstock your tank or try and raise them as this will cause them to get hurt.

It's not ideal to keep them in deeper or smaller tanks. A recommendation when working with Channel Catfish would be to raise them with other fish species that mainly use the top of the tank. These would include fish such as Tilapia, Bluegill and Perch. Because they only live at the bottom of the tank, a much larger tank is recommended, i.e. in excess of 250+ gallon.

The ideal temperature for a Channel Catfish to survive and thrive is between 75°-80°F, although they can tolerate temperatures between 40°-90°F, making them also fairly flexible in nature.

Channel Catfish grow pretty quickly and can reach maximum sizes of between 40 – 50 pounds. Although they only need 32 – 38% protein. Their feed conversion ratio is around 2:1 (2 pounds of feed to 1-pound size fish).

Catfish can be eaten and are rich in Vitamin D. Before eating them though you need to skin them when preparing them for cooking.

LARGEMOUTH BASS

Source: photo-1551464664-222eeb2d2034largemouth-bass-unsplash-Luis-Vidal.jpg

These fish are usually popular to North America and are known more as gamefish rather than a fish to stock for aquaponics. Largemouth Bass are part of the freshwater fish family, making them ideal for aquaponics. They have a very wide temperature tolerance range, which means that they can be safely bred and reared through both winter and summer months quite safely.

Their temperature tolerance ranges between 50°-86°F, although their optimum temperature is around 68°-97°F.

The Largemouth Bass is carnivorous and needs more than 40% high protein diet. You can eat Largemouth Bass. It has white flesh and is rich in omega-3 fatty acids. The bonus of eating this fish is that it is boneless (for those like me that can't stand picking bones out of fish).

Due to its size, the Largemouth Bass does require a much larger tank – the smallest that you will get away with will be around 1200 gallons.

RAINBOW TROUT

Source: trout-277056_960_720Rainbow-Trout-Pixabay.jpg

The Rainbow Trout belongs to the Salmon family and because of this, they are not only edible, but have a really pleasant taste. Trout thrive in colder water with average temperatures ranging between 57°–60°F and minimum temperatures for survival being 50°–64°F. Trout are also carnivorous and need up to

50% high protein diet.

You can expect rapid growth amongst your Trout, they are some of the fastest growing fish of all those used for aquaponics, adding between 800 to 1000 grams every 14 to 16 months. Rainbow Trout are better suited to colder climates because they don't survive in warm waters.

Trout need clean water to thrive, unlike Tilapia. They can be quite high maintenance because you need to ensure that their water is well oxygenated at all times and that the dissolved oxygen level never drops below 5.5ppm. Trout also like to jump, so a covering of some description on your tank is going to be a necessity. While you may have your heart set on rearing Rainbow Trout for their specific taste and flavor, the climate that they survive in leaves you only a limited variety of plants that you could grow.

Because they are carnivorous, they need to be fed commercial fish pellets, and smaller fish, flies, snails and even bloodworms. There is also a genuine danger of them attacking and eating smaller Trout as part of their feeding routine, which would need to be closely monitored—our recommendation on trout rearing for aquaponics would be to keep them only if the climate dictates and you have sufficient experience to work with them. They take a lot of time and effort to rear successfully.

The last two fish that we are going to discuss that could potentially work best for your aquaponic system will be the Jade Perch, and the Carp.

JADE PERCH

Here is another resilient and hardy fish that grows rapidly. It stems from Australia and so is used to much warmer environments. Some interesting facts about the Perch is that they are really placid and get on well with other species, making them an ideal option for aquaponic enthusiasts where the climate is right. Additional bonuses are that they can be harvested within about a year and they are delicious to the taste. Another fish that is high in healthy omega 3-fish oils.

The ideal temperatures for Perch would be between 70°–80°F. It's worth mentioning that if temperatures drop below 65°F, the Perch will stop eating, could become inert and die. As omnivores, they eat almost anything, but still need a medium protein diet. Another downside of Perch is that they won't breed while in captivity unless they are injected with a specific hormone to allow this to take place.

Being fairly peaceful, they get on well with other fish in an aquaponic system.

Even though they are resilient, they still need a fair amount of dissolved oxygen to survive. These can easily be pumped into the tank using traditional stones and an aerator. The best pH for Perch is between 6.8 and 7.8.

ORGANIC GARDENING

Source: perch_3585165_960_720Perch-fish-Perca-Pixabay.jpeg

CARP

This would be your "go to" fish if you were planning on setting up an aquaponics system in the UK and they are ideal for larger scale aquaponic farming. Part of the reason for this is that they have a high tolerance level for both hot and cold temperatures and can therefore survive the UK winter as well as summer conditions quite comfortably. Carp do favor warmer temperatures and therefore a greenhouse would be ideal for them because they grow better in warmer waters. There are a large variety of different Carp available and while they all belong to the same species, the most important three to remember would be the Common Carp, the Mirror Carp and Koi Carp.

Similar to both Tilapia and Catfish they can survive and thrive in water temperatures between 32°–90°F, although the ideal water temperature range for maximum growth is 75°–82°F.

Carp are omnivores and can survive with only medium levels of protein in their diet. They only need about 35–45% protein. Feeding Carp pellets is a good idea, with the regime of fewer pellets but more often because they do not have a stomach to process the food. On average they would eat approximately 2% of their body weight per day.

Regular Carp - Source: animal-2029698_960_720carp Pixabay.png

Koi Carp - Source: carp-217229_960_720Carp-Koi-Pixabay.jpg

CHAPTER 5: COMMON MISTAKES IN AQUAPONICS AND HOW TO AVOID THEM

"My green thumb came as a result of mistakes I made learning to see things from the plants point of view." ~ J. Fred. Ale, posted on Instagram by Harperponics

There are a large number of very common mistakes that most people make when it comes to aquaponics. Below is a list of those that are most common, and we are going to discuss them in greater detail so that you know exactly how to avoid them at all costs.

ENSURE THAT YOUR WATER QUALITY IS CORRECT

Avoid adding poor quality or tap water into your system at all costs unless the water has been tested and reported as being suitable. Because water is the key component ingredient to any aquaponic system, this is the very first thing that you need to get right. This is what is going to make sure that your plants receive all the nutrients that they receive to survive and thrive. And, it is also home to your fish. In a nutshell, if your fish are happy, your plants should thrive.

There are five key areas that you need to monitor for your water to be suitable and effective. These five things are:

- Your dissolved oxygen level (DO) as we have discussed above. The correct DO is actually 5mg/liter of water.
- The pH of your water should normally be around 6.0–7.0 (having said this, remember that your pH is directly linked to the requirements of your fish, so take this into consideration now as well). Does your pH match up to the pH of the fish that you are stocking?
- Your water temperature should ideally be between 64o-86oF, although, like the above comments on pH, water temperature is also directly linked to the type of fish you stock and you need to adjust your water

temperatures accordingly. If your fish needs warmer temperatures, consider some form of a heating unit that can be added to your system that will raise the temperature sufficiently. Be careful not to overheat the fish tank, pond or pool either.
- Total nitrates — this is the ammonia, nitrites and nitrates.
- The final thing you need to consider is your water alkalinity.
- Chlorine, pH and parasites or pathogens also need to be checked before you even begin to use your aquaponics system. With the chlorine and fluoride content being different all over the world, it is vital to test this before simply adding your fish. This can easily be tested with a chlorine test kit. Remember that too much chlorine can be deadly for fish. Most test kits make for easy testing and you can easily diffuse water by allowing it to sit with an aeration unit running for approximately 48 to 72 hours.

ENSURE THAT YOUR FISH TO WATER RATIO IS CORRECT

Many new aquaponics enthusiasts want to grow as many fish as quickly as possible and this leads to a number of problems. The first is an obvious one, overcrowding your tank, pool or pond. Imagine how you feel in an overcrowded train, not great! This is how your fish feel when they are squashed in a small space. The results of overcrowding can result in losing fish because they simply cannot survive the high levels of nitrate that will be in the tank, but it can also stunt their growth, which is exactly the opposite of what you are trying to achieve.

Let's look at what too much nitrate does to a fish, and how you can avoid it or treat it if it does occur?

While ammonia poisoning is common among fish, believe it or not, nitrate poisoning is even more common. Your entire system is likely to go into nitrate poisoning mode as soon as your nitrate level reaches or exceeds 6ppm. This level typically occurs the moment there is more pollution in the tank than what can be handled and broken down by the beneficial bacteria.

New tanks are way more susceptible to this phenomenon, especially when they have not yet been completely colonized by the beneficial bacteria yet. The most critical point is just before the tank is beginning to cycle. This is another reason why you need to be patient in setting up your system and make sure that you aren't too impatient to get your system up and running. There are two different strains of nitrifying bacteria. The one that breeds, and feeds bacteria is known as nitrosomonas and these both eat the ammonia and produce nitrites. The chemical term composition is $NH_3 \rightarrow NO_2$, while the other is known as nitrospira and this converts nitrites to nitrates ($NO_2 \rightarrow NO_3$). This has slower reproduction rates and takes much more time to establish itself. Nitrate is what is needed for the plants to grow and does not have a harmful effect on the fish.

Nitrite poisoning can also occur in established systems due to overstocking of fish and overfeeding. The most common causes of this happening are poor filter maintenance and new tank syndrome. If you wash your grow beds, this could also result in the beneficial bacteria being washed away, causing the same symptoms. While this won't have any effect on your plants, it is deadly to your fish and could cause their death.

Remember that aerobic bacteria cannot colonize in the lower layers of the media that is dense with fish waste and muck. If oxygen levels are too low a rather nasty strain of anaerobic bacteria begins to form and thrive. If you think of the beneficial bacteria as the engine that is running your aquaponics system, think of this particular strain of bacteria as hitting the engine into reverse at high speed! It immediately begins to once again convert the beneficial nitrates back into nitrites.

You will be able to recognize that this is starting to happen by watching the color of your fish. The moment that they start turning pink or red on the fins and tail, this is an indication that your fish is under stress due to nitrite poisoning.

Fish survive through moving their gills rapidly, as well as consuming oxygen from the surface. You will notice that healthy fish will begin to move more rapidly around the tank when they are in a state of shock. Fish suffering from nitrite poisoning will appear sluggish with little activity. Here are a couple of other signs that you could look out for:

- Their gills begin to move more rapidly.
- Their gills begin to turn tan or brown in color.
- They seem to be gasping for more air on the surface of the water.
- They are way more passive or limp and often remain near the water outlets.

Nitrite poisoning prevents the blood cells from carrying vital oxygen into the fish's bloodstream, often turning the bloodstream of the fish brown in color. Because of this, the fish will become weaker and weaker, often suffocating because it simply cannot get enough oxygen from the water.

If the fish is exposed to nitrite poisoning for any length of time, its immune system becomes compromised and this allows secondary diseases to suddenly appear. Often, these are a result of bacterial infections. You will also notice that there will be a string of fish deaths in your tank simultaneously, or directly one after another.

Make sure that your nitrite level should always be zero or really close to zero. Even levels that are 0.25mg/liter can cause some stress to species that are more sensitive. Your nitrite levels should never exceed 0.1mg/liter.

HOW TO LOWER THE NITRITE LEVELS IN FRESH WATER

- **Add salt to your water**—by adding about half an ounce of salt per gallon of water, methemoglobin build up will be prevented. This prevents or reduces the influence of nitrite to remove oxygen from the bloodstream of your fish. While this technique has been researched and recommended that the most effective dosage is 1lb of salt to 150gal of water, you should keep an accurate record of how much salt you are adding and when, because salt does not evaporate.
- **Add bacteria**—whenever you change either the media, filter or the tank itself, it's a good idea to add some beneficial bacteria to your tank. This is easy enough to do by simply taking some of the gravel or medium from your existing tank that is running optimally. This will help to establish a new colony of beneficial bacteria fairly quickly. If you are going this route however, it's important to make sure that the gravel or grow media that you use is clean and pathogen free.
- **Don't use treatments or medications**—while it may be tempting to simply treat with chemicals, remember that many of these chemicals actually kill off the beneficial bacteria as well. This will leave your fish

open to other infections and diseases such as fungus. The most important thing to do should be to make sure that your water quality is as good as possible.

- **Change the water**—changing out between 25% to 50% of the water with water that has been dechlorinated and repeating this pattern every day until the ammonia and nitrate levels are at zero is the quickest way to resolve this issue.
- **Stop feeding**—stop feeding your fish and avoid adding any new fish to your tank until the ammonia and nitrate levels return to normal.
- **Increase aeration**—this is easy enough to achieve by adding an additional aerator to the tank, aquarium or pond. Not only will the additional bubbles keep your fish alive, but it will assist your beneficial bacteria to continue to grow.
- **Clean the tank**—remove all uneaten food from the tank and make sure that the bottom of the aquarium or tank is completely free from any uneaten food that is decomposing.

While these are ways to solve your nitrite poisoning problem, prevention is always better than cure. As suggested at the beginning of this section, there are ways to avoid nitrate poisoning. These include avoiding overstocking, choosing fish that are not susceptible to disease, avoiding overfeeding (it's better to feed your fish in smaller doses over the course of the day, rather than a massive feed once a day).

You should also make sure that your grow beds are acting as a biofilter and are effectively removing or stripping the impurities from the water that is recirculating. If your water ever looks cloudy or foamy then you know that you have a problem and you should be looking at solving it as recommended above.

The water pump that you are currently using should also be

Gordon L. Atwell

able to circulate the entire volume of water in the fish tank approximately four to five times per hour. If it is not doing this then you may require a more powerful pump.

CHOOSING THE RIGHT GROWING MEDIA

This is probably one of the most common mistakes made in aquaponics today. People make poor decisions on the growth medium that they are going to use. Most people look for what is readily available and accessible to them, without doing the necessary research and finding out exactly what the best grow media are.

Before we go into the list of what is available it should be mentioned up front that certain grow media that are suitable for hydroponics are NOT suitable for aquaponics. Remember that you need a grow medium that is going to support the needs of your plants, allows you the greatest yields possible and it also takes the least amount of work to maintain. Your grow medium will also need to suit the aquaponic system that you have chosen, whether you are working with DWC or NFT or any other system, make sure that the medium is working for you and not against you. The rule of thumb when choosing your grow medium is that it needs to be the easiest to maintain. For example, when using the raft-based technique, all that is required are net pots that sit within the rafts themselves.

There are no right or wrong grow media, other than utilizing anything that contains soil or small particles that can be washed through the system. The most important thing to consider should be that they meet the needs of the system that you are using to grow your plants in. They also need to support the plants that you are growing with the main objective of keeping the roots moist, without suffocating the roots, causing oxygen deficiency, resulting in root rot. While this disease is less common in aquaponics, it can still occur. Before embarking on your project, it's worth gathering some information on what is available, and what could potentially best meet your needs.

Here are a couple of options, along with their cost indications, pH factors and lifespan:

- Coco Fiber & Chips are low to medium priced with a neutral pH but have a short lifespan.
- Floral Foam has a low price with a neutral pH and is reusable.
- Hydroton or Leca Clay is expensive with a neutral pH and is reusable.
- Net pots are low priced and are reusable.
- Oasis Cubes is mediumly priced with a neutral pH and is reusable.
- Pine bark is low priced with a neutral pH and a short lifespan.
- Pine shavings have a low cost with a neutral pH and a very short lifespan.
- Polyurethane foam insulation is low priced with a neutral pH but has a short lifespan.
- Rice Hulls are low priced with a neutral pH and a short lifespan.
- River rock is low priced with a neutral pH and is reusable.
- Rockwool has a medium cost with a basic pH and is renewable.
- Sand is low priced with a neutral pH and is reusable but is NOT recommended for aquaponics.
- Starter plugs for seedlings are low priced and are re-

usable.
- Vermiculite has a medium cost with a basic pH and is reusable.
- Water absorbing polymers are low priced with a neutral pH and are reusable.

For aquaponic systems, apart from the starter plugs for growing your seedlings, it is recommended that you consider:

Growstone Substrate which is manufactured from recycled glass and is extremely lightweight. Similar to growing rocks, they are porous and provide excellent aeration to the root zone while retaining moisture at the same time. They can hold water up to three to four inches above the grow media, while still allowing for great drainage. The benefits of making use of this grow media is that it is sustainable, lightweight, holds both air and water (more so than Hydroton) and the air to water ratio is a major plus factor. On the downside they can be quite difficult to clean (although being made from glass, even if they break, they won't cut you).

Hydroton Leca Clay, aka Grow Rock is also known as expanded clay. LECA stands for Lightweight Expanded Clay Aggregate. These roundish shaped balls are manufactured from clay that is expanded. They are extremely porous. Even though they are pretty lightweight, they are still heavy enough to provide support to your plants. Because they are pH neutral, they won't release any nutrients into the water. Due to their spherical shape they don't get waterlogged and can retain oxygen.

Cleaning and sterilizing these on a large scale can take quite a bit of time and they are reasonably expensive, but when you consider the benefits of them being reusable, it makes their price worth it. In aquaponics, using these in both the Ebb and Flow system and the drip system are highly beneficial to the plants and fish. The benefits are that they have no additional solvents added to the clay; they are pH neutral and are reusable. Because they are coarse, aerated and expansive clay, this acts as a great support to plants as they are trying to grow. Working with them is extremely easy, especially when it comes to planting crops. They are not compact at all. The disadvantages are that they drain and dry pretty quickly and you would need to make sure that your roots are not going to dry out quickly. They are also initially quite expensive, but when you factor in the benefits, the cost is worth it.

USING HARMFUL ADDITIVES TO LOWER THE PH

The balance and relationship between temperature and pH and fish requirements is a vital component in the success of your aquaponics system. This area seems to catch a lot of aquaponics enthusiasts. Most individuals are too impatient in waiting for their system to be ready to cycle and try and reduce the pH using various chemicals that are available. Some try adding acid to the system. While adding these chemicals may have the desired effect immediately, ultimately, they will destroy your plants and fish. Do not add any chemicals to your system other than what is recommended.

Remember that the nitrification (beneficial bacteria) will reduce the pH of your system gradually over time. This slower, gradual decrease is better for the health of your fish as well.

If you are really that impatient, consider adding a little vinegar to the water. This is another slow fix. Keep each of the dosages small and remain patient, all good things come to those who wait!

GROWING THE WRONG PLANTS

Be aware when it comes to trying to grow plants that aren't native to your area. Even if you manage to find seedlings at your local nursery, if the crop, cultivar or plants are not native to your environment, temperature and climate you could battle to get them growing. Remember to also grow each plant in its correct season.

It seems as though this point is repeated throughout this book, but this speaks to its importance, make sure that your fish and plants are compatible. Your fish should be suited to the crop that you are planning on growing. Remember that the water temperature, pH and air temperature all need to be taken into consideration when choosing your crops. Once you get the match correct, you will have healthy, thriving and bumper crops all year round.

There are three main components that are like the three-legs of a stool in aquaponics. When you get all three right there is perfect harmony and balance. When one of them is out, the entire system falls apart. The three legs are: Bacteria, Fish, and Plants. On top of the seat of these three legs falls water temperature and pH. The reason why these two factors affect the three legs is that they affect each of the three legs in different ways. For most fish there is a temperature range that they can function effectively in and each of these have a high and low range. Temperatures also affect the DO (dissolved oxygen) levels as well as the toxicity of ammonia in the tank. A rise in water temperature will decrease dissolved oxygen levels but will increase ammonia levels.

TEMPERATURE CHANGES IN GROWTH CYCLES

Most plants can survive in temperatures that range between 64° to 84°F. While others prefer much cooler temperatures. We have considered temperatures with each of the cultivars discussed in Chapter 1, and the temperature requirements of each of the best fish to choose from in Chapter 4. By matching each of these to your specific climate, your seasonal requirements and crops that are usually grown at that time of the year, you should be off to a success within no time at all.

Remember that temperatures will also be affected if you are making use of a greenhouse or growing your plants indoors.

When water temperatures become too high you could experience some of the following symptoms which result from heat stress:

- Calcium absorption could be negatively influenced.
- Lettuce plants will become elongated and seed rather than growing like conventional lettuce.
- Lowered levels of dissolved oxygen in your water.
- Plant roots will possibly turn black and die.
- Wilting leaves on your plants.
- Your plants could start to drop flowers or stop the fruiting process altogether.

Remember that water temperature is influenced by both air

and humidity levels as well.

Lower water temperatures mainly have only one disadvantage when it comes to growing: Growth is stunted or you could notice that it takes a lot longer for your plants to wake up in the day.

Because nitrates are the beneficial bacteria and the nutrients that plants need, it's important to understand how this nitrogen cycle works. Because all the nutrients that the plants are going to need are transported or distributed to the plants through the water, we need to make sure that there is enough nitrogen in the water that the plants can be sufficiently nourished and fed. In aquaponics, this works via ammonification, assimilation and nitrification in the following ways:

When the fish excrete their waste into the water, this takes on the form of ammonia and is known as ammonification.

- The first Nitrosomonas bacteria is found in the grow medium and converts this ammonia to nitrates. A specific example of growing media for your aquaponic system could be grow rocks or gravel in your plant bed.
- Next comes the second bacteria, called Nitrobacter, which is also found in the grow medium. This converts the nitrites to nitrates.
- The final step is when the plants absorb the nutrient-rich beneficial bacteria that is in the form of nitrates.

The results of this cycling exercise are that:

- All nitrogen compounds that would normally be toxic to fish are removed from the water.
- Plants receive nutrient-rich, beneficial bacteria that will help them grow.

The cycle continues as the fish are fed on a regular basis, water is replenished as it evaporates or is taken up by the plants.

Gordon L. Atwell

Plants are harvested in their season and the cycle continues.

INCORPORATE A PEST CONTROL STRATEGY

It's not too often that your system will be affected with pests of any description. It's still a good idea to have a pest control strategy in place should you ever need it. One of the most important things is to check your system on a regular basis to make sure that you don't have any pests, bugs or unwelcome visitors. Remember that using pesticides and other chemicals is a huge NO, NO when it comes to running an aquaponics system, so you need to come up with a workable alternative.

One of the best solutions is to react as quickly as you possibly can to resolve any problems that you come across, especially when it comes to pests on your plants. The ideal solution in getting rid of them is to feed them to your fish. All those little bugs, slugs, caterpillars, and other beetles will be a tasty treat for your fish to enjoy and they are rich in protein as well.

Consider using natural predators to reduce any bugs—you may want to consider adding some beneficial bugs, beetles and spiders to your plants that will naturally ward off harmful bugs. The ladybug is an excellent example of this, they feed on aphids.

ORGANIC WATER

There are a number of organic water sprays available that could be used to control larger insect infestations without harming your plants. Remember to make sure that they are not harmful to the beneficial bacteria, your fish, your pH levels in your pond, aquarium or tank. This organic water will run off into your system so this should almost be a last resort scenario.

FEEDING YOUR FISH

Make sure that your fish are being fed sufficiently and at regular intervals. Some of the biggest mistakes with aquaponics are either overfeeding or under-feeding. Fish can survive without food for up to three weeks, however you will notice changes in your system. Remember that the whole reason for having the fish there in the first place is to provide your plants with the nutrient-rich water solution. If the fish are not producing waste, this cannot happen. Over-feeding is just as big a concern as this could lead to the unconsumed food lying at the bottom of the aquarium, tank or pond and clogging up filters. These filters need to be checked on a regular basis to make sure that any unwanted waste or food that hasn't been consumed is removed quickly enough.

NOT WAITING FOR YOUR SYSTEM TO CYCLE COMPLETELY

This is another very common problem when it comes to aquaponic, impatience! Remember to take the time that is necessary to set your system up properly as we have discussed in Chapter 3. You can cycle your system with and without fish but each of the required steps need to be followed to the letter for your system to become ready. This is the part of aquaponics that is most time-consuming. It could also be the most expensive due to the cost of losing precious fish that are placed into the system before it is ready. Rather wait it out for the beneficial bacteria to form correctly and populate within your system sufficiently. You will only ever do this once (unless you plan to set up a second or third system). A little patience will go a long way in producing a fully functioning aquaponics system.

LACK OF OXYGEN CIRCULATION

Sufficient aeration is necessary in your aquarium, pond or tank. The water that is there needs to be circulated sufficiently and often enough so that there is enough dissolved oxygen in the water for your fish. The best way to do this is to make sure that the pump or aeration device that you have included to your system is the very best available and meets the needs of your setup. If you are running a small aquarium with ornamental fish and growing your plants on your kitchen counter, it makes logical sense that you only need a small enough aquarium pump that matches its size. If on the other hand you are running a larger pond or pool setup, the pumps that you require will need to be much bigger with the capacity to circulate the water throughout the closed circuit where your plants are. I have already mentioned that the pumps required must be able to circulate the water throughout the system at a rate of between four and five times per hour. If your current pump is not able to do this then you are likely to run the risk of losing both plants and fish due to oxygen deficiency. As a side note, if you are living in a region where electricity supply is not consistent, please make sure that you have back-up pumps that can run off of batteries or that you have automated generators that can kick in should the power be interrupted for whatever reason.

CHOOSING YOUR FISH

There are many factors that come into play under this heading. We have covered each of the different fish extensively in a previous chapter, but this is another common mistake that is often made when people consider setting up their aquaponic system. There are so many different things that you need to take into consideration when it comes to the fish that you are going to stock. This ranges from the size of the aquarium, tank, pond or pool that you plan on using. Are you wanting to make use of ornamental fish or do you plan on rearing the fish as a means of protein (to eat) as well? While each of these are important considerations, you also need to think about whether the fish that you are wanting to stock are suited to your specific climate. Are they seasonal or would you be able to stock them throughout the year? This would be the first prize naturally! Another common mistake is stocking multiple varieties of fish that don't get along with one another. Fish can be carnivorous, omnivorous or herbivorous. Know which fish you are stocking so that you don't end up stocking carnivorous fish that are going to literally make a meal of the other fish!

The ideal when it comes to looking at what fish to stock is to consider what is native to your region. Whichever fish are likely to survive the seasonal climate of your region with the water temperature changes through summer and winter. These become far easier to maintain and you will save on buying expensive heating systems to increase the water temperature to make sure that your fish survive cooler months or climates. One of the last points to mention when it comes to choosing your fish—make sure that you are stocking fish that you will eat (if you are stocking for protein purposes). Not all fish are palatable, and there's no point in breeding and rearing fish that are going to go to waste. All that will happen in this instance is that your ponds will become overstocked and lead to disease or loss of fish due to overcrowding.

KEEPING RATIOS RIGHT:

It's extremely important to keep the correct ratio between fish and plants correct. Overstocking fish as discussed above will cause death and open the door for disease because they will produce way too much waste. This will have a knock-on effect on your plants by providing them with a nutrient-rich solution that is too nutrient-rich. Just as you would experience in conventional gardening, if you over fertilize a plant it could die. Exactly the same scenario could take place with aquaponics. It's important to try and get the balance between your plants and fish correct. This is going to take some practice. Some ways of being able to do this is by harvesting fish, while harvesting vegetables. This is after all exactly what aquaponics is all about. If you find that you are unable to keep these stocking levels down, then consider selling some of your fish off. This is one of the reasons for starting off small so you can get used to rotating and harvesting effectively and to meet your specific needs. Some other ways to ensure that you can keep this system going effectively is to rotate with seedlings and fingerlings, this should give you the time that you need to allow both to grow without having an overstocking problem. There really isn't a right or a wrong way to do this, initially it will be trial and error until you can figure out how many fish you are likely to harvest while harvesting your plants.

The final common mistake that I am going to cover is one that has already briefly been mentioned but is a critical error that will cost you in fish, will possibly cost you quite a lot of money to replace fish that die.

OVERFEEDING

It's extremely important to avoid overfeeding your fish. Rather feed them in smaller amounts at various intervals throughout the day. Within approximately 30 minutes of feeding your fish, remove any uneaten food from the aquarium, tank or pond. This will prevent it from beginning to decompose. Once this remaining food begins decaying it uses up all the dissolved oxygen available to the fish and can cause disease. Closely monitor how much food has not been eaten and you have removed from the system as additional waste—you should then try and change the following day's feed appropriately.

CHAPTER 6: ADVANCED TECHNIQUES – HOW TO LEVEL UP YOUR SYSTEM

"Achieve the greatest volume and highest quality of produce possible, while reducing operating costs, and maximizing your profitability by growing smart." ~ Tom Blout, Expert at US Hydroponic Association

THINKING OF GOING COMMERCIAL?

So you have successfully set up and got the hang of a smaller system that is able to sustain your family with regular seasonal crops and fish. Where do you go from here? the natural progression is being able to share this with others. Due to the current crisis when it comes to sustainable agriculture, insufficient land availability, high costs of conventional farming, high costs of labor, seeds, climate change, drought and an entire host of other challenges that threaten agriculture as we know it, aquaponics can genuinely provide an answer. Let's take a brief look at each of these challenges.

Firstly, climate change has brought about irregular seasonal changes all over the world. The change in weather patterns is apparent and is felt globally. Areas that were used to seasonal rainfall are now experiencing crippling drought conditions that are literally bringing the conventional crop farmer to their knees. They are unsure as to whether or not to plant their crops because rain is not guaranteed and even a few weeks out can make all the difference for any cultivar. Aquaponics addresses this issue because there is very little water used other than in the aquarium or pond where the fish are kept. The plants are grown in a recirculating closed system, preventing water loss and therefore the only water that is used throughout the entire process is either via evaporation, or plant uptake. You don't even need to drain and replace water like you would in a hydroponics environment.

ORGANIC GARDENING

This system can be designed to fit into any space, making it convenient in meeting your specific requirements. If you live in a small apartment building, you may only have the space available on a countertop for a small aquarium with ornamental fish, with the grow beds above. Alternatively, you may live on a larger property where you have access to a greenhouse, and you are looking at upscaling your operation to become a commercial one. The message of this chapter is that whatever space you have available, aquaponics can utilize to full capacity in the most cost-effective way possible.

You will have noticed that in one of the previous diagrams of a system that the troughs are stacked or separated above one another. This saves space, while allowing you maximum yield for your plants. You can adopt similar systems in a greenhouse environment, interconnecting the closed-circuit pipes or adding raft systems that cover the space that you have at your disposal.

Aquaponics is sustainable because with a little training, anyone is able to do it. The most challenging part of setting up an aquaponics system is the cycling process. Once you have managed to get this right and under your belt, there is very little work that needs to be done. Most of this work involves monitoring your pH, water and air temperature, your fish and your plants. Pretty simple stuff when you compare it to the complexities involved in conventional agriculture and the amount of labor involved. It's no wonder that many countries are beginning to teach communities how to design, build and manage their own aquaponic systems as a means of sustainable food supply.

Communities that don't have access to regular water or power can look at adopting this method of supplying themselves with organically grown fruits, vegetables, herbs and protein in the form of fish. A reasonably small area would be able to produce enough produce to feed a community.

Conventional farming costs are extremely high when you think about all the equipment that you need to invest in to plough the land, plant seeds, irrigate the land sufficiently and then to harvest the crop once it has grown. It's not just the equipment cost that you need to take into consideration but also the cost of fuel, and labor (even seasonal labor when necessary). All of these costs add up—compared with a smaller aquaponics system, this can be run at a fraction of the cost and once it is up and running, the operating costs are reduced.

The cost of seeds, pesticides and other chemicals required in conventional farming is exorbitantly high. In aquaponics, there are no pesticides and chemicals used whatsoever. The only costs that you would be faced with would be your seeds, seedlings and your fish, once you have designed and set up your system.

For environments that face extreme weather conditions such as drought, deserts or land that has eroded and is non-arable, aquaponics can be a cost-effective solution. There have even been instances of large aquaponics facilities being set up in the middle of the desert, that are able to support the surrounding environment.

Additional benefits to upscaling to commercial aquaponics would be that food could be grown close to the source of consumption. This would save time, energy and money on refrigeration, transportation and chemicals that are currently being used on the foods that we are currently purchasing from your local grocer.

By growing close to the source of consumption, you are genuinely producing vegetables, fruit, herbs and protein that is truly organic. There have been absolutely no chemicals or additives included as part of the entire growth cycle.

INTERESTING FACTS ABOUT AQUAPONICS:

An interesting fact about aquaponics is that it can be run totally off the grid. Because running your system is so energy efficient it can very easily be run off of alternate energy sources, reducing your carbon footprint even further. Think about installing your own solar panels, windmills or wind turbines or even a form of hydroelectric power and you are good to go. This is great news for those areas that don't have access to regular electricity, or if you just want to be that eco-friendly enthusiast.

Water efficiency is a major bonus for aquaponics, even a large-based, commercial aquaponics system uses only 10% of the water that would be used for conventional farming. There is no wastage of water as the system circulates water throughout and with limited evaporation, the only water that is lost is what is absorbed by each of the plants. The system never needs to be flushed out like with a hydroponic system. Instead, there is only limited topping up of water required to the aquarium, pond, or tank where the fish are kept. If you are operating in a greenhouse this is further reduced, and there are even pool covers that can be added to reduce the evaporation even further. There may be a slight loss when removing any excess solid waste, but it's not really worth mentioning because it's a tiny amount of water.

Year-round growing is another major benefit to aquaponics. This is especially beneficial to those out of the way places, those regions where climates aren't always suitable for growing crops throughout the year. Think about desert climates as well as those that have shorter seasonal growing periods for certain cultivars. Imagine being able to grow tomatoes all year round, having delicious Trout available throughout the year. In many of these regions finding this fresh produce was almost impossible and if so, it was extremely expensive. Think of the costs involved in getting these herbs, vegetables, fruits and fish to these out of the way places. Through the solution of aquaponics many, if not all of these problems can be overcome and fresh, healthy, organic food produce can be grown, delivered and consumed very close to the source.

UNDERSTANDING FISH DISEASES:

There are three different types of stress that your fish could be subjected to and we are going to look at each of these here. They are:

1. Biological Stress
2. Chemical Stress, and
3. Physical Stress.

Each of the above can be recognized and dealt with as follows:

Biological stress—when your fish is facing biological stress there are various parasites, viral diseases, bacteria or fungi in the area that are affecting them. These unwanted organisms are normally always around, but only become a problem as soon as the conditions for them to thrive are just right. You will know that there's a problem with your fish if they begin to behave in the same way as if they were under physical stress. This includes eating less or not eating at all. They visibly move from the state where they were thriving, and you can begin to see that there is a distinctive change happening. They could also begin bumping into the walls of the aquarium, trying to escape the light because they are feeling more sensitive towards it. Many of these symptoms will have a genuine threat for your fish.

You can sort out biological stress by adding salt to the water to help them fight off some of these unwanted diseases, however it is important to get the ratios right because too much salt can be harmful to your plants. It's recommended that instead of adding sodium chloride to take care of the problem, look for just chlorine (but in really low doses). It's actually the chlorine that has a positive effect on the fish and warding off this unwanted bacteria. There are also some more plant-friendly solutions out there like magnesium chloride or potassium chloride. These will not only benefit your fish but will keep your plants safe at the same time.

Chemical stress—is usually as a result of your water quality. If there's a problem with either ammonia or nitrites in your water, your fish are going to become stressed. If your pH levels are low this can also place your fish under undue pressure. Remember that your nitrate levels can go up to 500-700ppm quite safely without disrupting any of your fish. Remember to remove any unconsumed food from the tank or pond within 30minutes of feeding (every feed). If there is a problem with your filter and it is not working sufficiently well in removing unwanted waste from the tank or pond, chemical stress is likely. All this unwanted waste in the tank reduces the amount of dissolved oxygen (DO) in the water and your fish will soon start being oxygen deprived.

Physical Stress—is probably the most common type of stress that your fish could ever go through because there are so many external and internal factors that could apply towards the creation of physical stress. Some of these include water temperature. Fish do not have the means to self-regulate their internal body temperature because they are cold-blooded animals. We need to know the temperature range that our fish is going to thrive in and maintain the water temperature within those ranges to prevent them from going into shock. Symptoms of temperature problems are very similar to those of when they are suffering from biological stress – they either stop eating completely, or the amount of food they consume will be reduced. We need to watch for optimal thriving temperatures with our fish because they can also become more susceptible to diseases that are always present.

There are a number of other things that physically stress fish out, these are things like sudden change in light (when we turn lights on and off the fish become confused—we are telling them that it is now daytime). If they are confused, they will start swimming into the sides of the tank. Loud noises and tapping against the tank are also a problem for your fish. Because they hear throughout their bodies via vibrations, something as simple as tapping against the tank can sound like screaming for them, and this will set them into a state of stress.

Finally, most fish prefer to live in calm waters. Examples of these would be Perch and Tilapia. Other fish prefer to have a form of a current available in their tank – think of any typical river fish such as Trout.

We need to think about all of these things and monitor for any undue stress that we may be causing our fish.

CHAPTER 7: MAXIMIZING YOUR SYSTEM

"You can convert 1.2kg of fish food into one kilo of fish. The lost 0.2kg dissolved into nitrogenous waste. For every kilo of fish you rear, you grow about 10kg of plants and vegetables. All of a sudden, you're producing a lot from very little." We are potentially taking a system that's evolved over millions of years and we are just copying it. While it can be seen as complex, it is incredibly simple."
~ Charlie Price, from the social enterprise Aquaponics UK

Getting an aquaponics system up and running doesn't need to be an expensive exercise. In this chapter we are going to look at a couple of different options that you could consider as a way to get your feet wet and test the waters of aquaponics for yourself without losing out on a lot of money.

The first system we are going to consider is one that is going to be upcycled from an existing fish tank that many people already have in their homes. Side bar—when I refer to a fish tank, I am referring to a proper aquarium and not just a gold-fish bowl!

The pond component in this particular exercise is an existing aquarium that houses five Goldfish. There is a corner pump that pumps the water upwards to the "plant bed" which is another repurposed window-sill rectangular flower pot. The pot has been filled with Hydroton Grow Stones. This becomes what is known as our grow bed. The grow bed input pipe fits snuggly into a regular aquarium filter floss. This floss makes sure that the water flow is reduced to a gentle flow rather than flooding.

EBB AND FLOW:

This system has been designed on an **Ebb and Flow or Flood and Drain** system and has a timer. The timer allows the water to flood the grow bed for a total time of fifteen minutes, then switches off and lets the water drain back into the fish tank. The flooding only takes place once an hour. For this particular system, it was also equipped with artificial lighting to assist with enhancing plant growth. This aquarium is therefore best suited for areas that don't have much natural light. Building this system is extremely easy with a relatively low cost because most of the items necessary were already available and were modified or repurposed. The most expensive part of setting this system up would be for the hydroton grow stones. Remember we mentioned that these could be pricier at first, but, because they are reusable the costs are worth it.

DWC OR RAFT SYSTEM:

There are many advantages to deciding to build a **DWC** system versus an NFT system when it comes to aquaponics. Some of these benefits are that they have an even light distribution across all of their plants, you can look at the correct temperature distribution because of the large amount of water in the system. Other benefits include being able to care for each of your plants individually because you can get to them and last but not least, they are extremely inexpensive to build. Let's unpack it and look at some of these benefits more closely:

Even distribution of light—because all of the plants in a deepwater culture system are on the same horizontal plane, they each have access to the same amount of light which is required for growth. When compared with a vertical system, plants are potentially cut off from direct sunlight by some of their neighboring plants. This can be seen by the lower plants especially and the growth of these plants are likely to be affected by reduced sunlight because as we all know, plants require sunlight for growth.

Less expensive—for a normal, conventional greenhouse you would look at spending anything upwards of US$50,000 to build and install a drip tower system rather than installing a DWC system instead.

Oxygen—raft or DWC systems ensure that the roots of the plants are always submerged in water. This would mean that you would need to make sure that the type of plants that you are planning on growing are suited to this type of aquaponics. Because roots are always under water, additional aeration methods should be used to increase the amount of oxygen available to both plants and fish. This can be done reasonably easily with stronger air pumps or air mats that are added to the bottom of the tank. When setting up your system in the first place, it is always a good idea to make sure that the air pump you are making use of is suitable for the amount of oxygen needed for your fish and plants.

Spacing of Plants—working with this method means that you can evenly space your plants to meet their specific needs. For those cultivars that need more space around them, pots can be skipped or moved around accordingly. It becomes easier to thin out those that need to be thinned out and move those that are only beginning to grow closer together. This versatility isn't always possible when you are using other systems.

Thermal Mass—A DWC system has approximately three times more water available to your plants than a drip tower system because of the volume of water that the troughs. A drip tower system works with only about 18,000 liters of water, whereas a DWC unit that takes up exactly the same amount of space will hold around 66,000 liters of water. The benefits of this additional water are that it supports water temperature fluctuations especially in cooler and warmer temperatures. Due to the amount of water, your plants and fish are protected from major fluctuations. Most of this protection happens around the plants where it is needed most.

CONCLUSION

As we reach the end of this book, by means of quick revision, let's go over some of the things that we have covered and that you should remember when venturing out into this fantastic hobby of aquaponics.

Firstly, decide exactly what it is that you want and make sure that you have the right amount of space available to meet your needs. There is an old adage in the carpentry game that says measure twice and cut once—this could easily be applied to aquaponics as well. Make sure that your system is suited to the plants that you are planning on growing as well. There are some systems that are only suited to some of the plant varieties or cultivars and more of this information can be found under each of the plant headings in Chapter 1.

Remember that there are many benefits to growing your own herbs, vegetables, plants and fish apart from saving water and energy. You are also producing crops that are 100% organic with no chemical additives whatsoever, while reducing the time between harvesting and consumption. This is a wonderful benefit for those growers who live in remote locations and can set up their aquaponics farms or gardens and supply to the local communities where it is difficult to reach or transport. Often there are steroids and chemicals used to keep produce fresh for longer while it is being transported across vast areas to out of the way places. Aquaponics provides a solution to this dilemma. Further in this chapter, we take a closer look at how many different plants, vegetables and herbs can be grown in aquaponics and what is required for them to be grown successfully. If you are wanting to match your pH to your fish, this is where you need to study up to make sure that you are getting it right!

In Chapter 2 we discussed the various different systems with diagrams of what they look like to give you a much better indication of what system is going to work best for you. This chapter also gives you a clear picture of where everything needs to be situated for your system to work properly.

Chapter 3 covers the nutrient cycle and understanding the important role that these nutrients play in building up your system. It also explains why it is so vitally important to practice patience and allow your system the time to cycle properly before just rushing out, buying your fish and your plants and throwing everything together. While it may look like it's a hobby that could be quick and easy, practicing patience is the key to setting up your system correctly. It's getting the ammonia, nitrites and nitrates correct and making sure that the beneficial bacteria is formed properly and that your fish are going to survive and thrive, along with your plants. On average, it could take up to three months for your system to cycle correctly before you even add your fish. Remember to take it slowly and add only one or two fish at a time that you are prepared to sacrifice, so that you don't waste any of your expensive fish on a system that is not yet ready. Your cycling process is going to take the most time and the most attention in this entire aquaponics journey. This will literally set the tone for your success or failure. If you can take the time to get the very basics right and build up your beneficial bacteria colony so that it is working and functioning correctly, the rest is smooth sailing from there.

While you are cycling your system, pay special attention to your pH levels that they are aligned with both your crops that you are planning on growing, as well as the fish that you are planning on stocking. It is really that simple. If both your fish and the plants fall within the same pH requirements, then you are all set to harvest a bumper crop at the end of the process. When there are variations in pH levels, or you are mixing cultivars that have different pH tolerances or requirements, this is asking for headaches because changing pH levels in aquaponics is way more involved than in hydroponics.

Remember that you are running an entirely chemical free system here!

Go through the list of fish that I have given you some solid information on and make sure that the fish that you are planning on stocking are local to your region, that they are going to survive the water temperatures and if you are planning on co-stocking with companion fish, that they are fish that get along with one another and have good temperaments rather than those that could potentially eat one another, or cause one another harm. Remember that overstocking is something that could cause your fish undue stress and you could lose fish and money that way.

Chapter 5 covers an entire host of common mistakes to be avoided from water through to dissolved oxygen levels, to pest control and feeding your fish correctly, even avoiding overfeeding and how to adjust feed levels if you find that there's a lot of food left over once you have fed your fish. Remember that it is extremely important to clean out and remove any uneaten food thirty minutes after your fish have initially been fed. This will prevent uneaten food from building up and decomposing into ammonia which would be extremely harmful for your fish. At the same time, check that your filters are clean and clear at all times and working effectively. The only way to know that this is happening is by keeping a regular check on your system to ensure that it is still functioning at an optimal level.

Oxygen in the tank needs to also be sufficient for both plants and fish. This is achieved by making sure that the air pump is strong enough to support the system. If not, it is worth investing in one that will do the job. Oxygen deficiency is another major obstacle that will cost you plants and fish. The entire objective of this book is to help you avoid some of the common mistakes that are made by those venturing into aquaponics for the first time.

If you are considering moving into a commercial route with aquaponics, then Chapter 6 will be beneficial for you and provide you with much of the information that you could possibly need to decide whether this is indeed an option for you or not. This chapter also covers a variety of fish diseases, what they look like, how to recognize if your fish are under stress and how to deal with these diseases effectively. The aim of this chapter is to assist you in being able to recognize when your fish are under stress as soon as possible, look for potential reasons why this could be so and then come up with a workable solution to reduce the situation, or minimize the stress that the fish find themselves in as a matter of urgency. It's also being able to recognize basic diseases that your fish could be susceptible to.

Our final chapter focuses on how to maximize your systems to work to your best advantage.

Having all this information at your fingertips right now, it's time to get out there and go and dream up the very best aquaponics system that you can that is going to meet your specific needs. Don't just build something for the sake of building—take the time to make sure that your system is going to be exactly how you want it to be. Remember that there will always be opportunities for you to upskill and upgrade your system as soon as you feel confident enough to do so.

Thank you for sharing this journey into the fascinating art of aquaponics with me—I wish you may hours of relaxation watching your fish and tending to your crops and may you always have a bountiful harvest of whatever plants you choose!

REFERENCES

A brief history of aquaponics. (n.d.). Retrieved from https://www.stuppy.com/aquaponics/aquaponiclearn/history/

Aquaculture North America highlights UWSP. (n.d.). Retrieved from https://www.uwsp.edu/cols-ap/aquaponics/Pages/default.aspx.

Aquaponics: Chives. (n.d.). Retrieved from https://www.aquaponicsblogspot.com/2014/10/aquaponics-chives.html?M=1

Aquasi. (2019). Carp aquaponics – A sustainable production system. Retrieved from https://www.aquapona.co.uk/carp.aquaponics/

Backyard koi pond for aquaponics. (n.d.). Retrieved from https://www.aquaponicsexposed.com/backyard-koi-pond-for-aquaponics/

Bernstein, S. (2011) Aquaponic gardening: A step-by-step guide to raising vegetables and fish together. Canada: New Society Publishing.

Bradley, K. (2014). Aquaponics: a brief history. Retrieved from https://www.milkwood.net/2014/01/20/aquaponic-a-brief-history/

Brooke, N. (n.d.) Crappie aquaponics system. Retrieved from https://www.howtoaquaponic.com/fish/crappie-aquaponics/

Brooke, N. (n.d.). Guppy aquaponics: Everything you need to know. Retrieved from https://www.howtoaquaponic.com/

fish/guppy-aquaponics/

Brooke, N. (n.d.). How to grow tomatoes in aquaponics. Retrieved from https://www.howtoaquaponics.com/plants/tomatoes-aquaponics/

Brooke, N. (n.d.). How to grow watercress in aquaponics. Retrieved from https://www.howtoaquaponics.com/plants/watercress-aquaponics/

Brooke, N. (n.d.). The best plants for aquaponics systems. Retrieved from https://www.howtoaquaponics.com/plants/best-plants-for-aquaponics/

Clawson, M. (n.d.). Goldfish aquaponics: ultimate guide. Retrieved from https://puregoldfish.com/aquaponics/

Deep water culture in aquaponics. (n.d.). Retrieved from https://www.aquaponicsexposed.com/deep-water-culture-in-aquaponics/

DIY aquaponics system plans. (n.d.). Retrieved from https://www.uponics.com/aquaponics-plans/

Editorial Staff, (2019). 20+ common mistakes people make in aquaponics (& how to fix them). Retrieved from https://www.leaffin.com/mistakes-aquaponics-guideline/

Editorial Staff, (2019). How to avoid & treat nitrite poisoning in your fish tank? Retrieved from https://www.leaffin.com/avoid-treat-nitrate-poisoning-aquaponics/

Editorial Staff, (2019). How to cycle your new aquaponics system? Retrieved from https://www.leaffin.com/cycle-new-aquaponics-system/

Editorial Staff, (2019). Top 17 best growing media for hydroponics and aquaponics. Retrieved from https://www.leaffin.com/growing-media-aquaponics-hydroponics/

Editorial Staff, (2019). What are the best fish species to use in aquaponics? Retrieved from https://www.leaffin.com/

aquaponic-fish/

Editorial Staff, (2019). What is the optimum range of temperature for aquaponics? Retrieved from https://www.leaffin.com/optimum-temperature-aquaponics/

Genello L. (2015). Why Tilapia? Species selection at the aquaponics project. Retrieved from http://liveablefutureblog.com/2015/01/tiapia-species-selection-aquaponics

Goering, C. (2019). Types of aquaponics designs. Retrieved from https://www.ecolifeconservation.org/updates/types-aquaponics-systems-design

James, N. (2018) Know your Tilapia strains. Retrieved from https://www.farmersweekly.co.za/animals/aquaculture/know-tilapia-strains/

James, N. (2018). The best fish species for aquaponics. Retrieved from https://www.farmersweekly.co.za/animals/aquaculture/best-fish-species/aquaponics/

Ki-moon,B. (n.d.). Quote on climate change. Retrieved from https://www.brainyquote.com/topics/sustainability-quotes/

Kirsten, B. (2014). Aquaponics: a brief history. Retrieved from https://www.milkwood.net/2014/01/20/aquaponics-a-brief-history/

Malzberg, R., Weissman, R., Fleiss, A (2018). Aquaponics: How advanced technology allows Dr. Simon Goddek to grow vegetables in the desert. Retrieved from https://www.google.com/amp/s/www.rebellionresearh.com/blog/aquaponics-how-advanced-technology-allows-dr-simon-goddek-to-grow.amp

Masterclass. (2019). What is arugula? Plus easy arugula pesto recipe. Retrieved from https://www.masterclass.com/articles/what-is-arugula-plus-easy-arugula-pesto-recipe

Nordqvist, J., Gill, K. M.D. (2018). Why everyone should eat basil. Retrieved from https://www.medicalnewstoday.com/articles/266425.php

Quotes from hydroponics and aquaponics experts. (n.d.). Retrieved from https://www.uponics.com/quotes-from-the-experts

Recommended plants and fish in aquaponics. (n.d.). Retrieved from https://www.aquaponics.com/recommended-plants-and-fish-in-aquaponics/

Sawyer, T. (2019). Aquaponic fish facts. Retrieved from https://www.theaquaponicsource.com/aquaponic-fish-facts/

Southern, A., King, W. (2017). The aquaponic farmer: a complete guide to building and operating a commercial aquaponic system. Canada: New Society Publishing.

Storey, A. (2016). How to grow mint in hydroponics – all you need to know. Retrieved from https://www.university.upstartfarmers.com/blog/how-to-grow-mint

Stout, M. (2013). The complete idiot's guide to aquaponic gardening. USA: Alpha a member of Penguin Group (USA) Inc.

University of Wisconsin Stevens Point. (n.d.). Aquaponics transforms 21st century agriculture. Retrieved from http://supportuwsp.org/aquaponics-transforms-21st-century-agriculture/

Why aquaponics? (n.d.). Retrieved from https://www.stuppy.com/aquaponiclearn/why-aquaponics/

MICROGREENS

*An Essential Guide to
Grow Nutrient-Dense
Organic Microgreens for
Your Health or Profit*

GORDON L. ATWELL

INTRODUCTION

Do you want to get healthy, strong, and vital, with only a handful of plants daily? Perhaps you're familiar with microgreens, and you want to grow them. If you're unfamiliar with these popular plants but want to find out more, this book will give you the right answers! If you know a good deal about microgreens and want to learn to grow them like a pro, this book will even show you how to turn your kitchen hobby into a six-figure business! This book aims to provide you with all essential information needed for understanding microgreens, their origin and history, benefits, and best use. Once you're finished with this book, you'll be equipped with thorough knowledge to use and cultivate these gentle herbs to your greatest benefit.

This book will present you with explanations, tips, and strategies for growing and consuming microgreens, whether for personal use or commercially. This book will help you if you're looking to improve your diet or only looking to find out more about the newly-discovered superfood. If you want to grow your own garden, this book will give you thorough instructions for cultivation of microgreens, from choosing the variety and seeds, to planting, harvesting, and storing. If you're looking to start a business with microgreens, this book will give you the exact advice on what you need to do to commercialize the small plant production.

Moreover, you will find out how microgreens can improve your health, all based on study of scientific research. In this book, we reviewed only reliable, science-based information and facts, to give you only the best instructions and strategies.

This book resulted from a detailed review of best practices, recommendations, and research projects dedicated to studying microgreens. As a result of their growing popularity, researchers worldwide are trying to figure out whether the hype surrounding the plants is justified, or they're simply a trend that will pass with the "next big thing."

First, you'll learn what exactly microgreens are. To be able to make your own judgment about microgreens, you'll first learn their definition, after which you'll find out about their history, development, and rise in popularity. The first chapter of this book will tell you whether the hype around microgreens revolves around fiction, or if the cultivation of the varieties has been around for a long time, and they're just now receiving due attention. With this knowledge, you'll be better able to understand the culture and history behind microgreens and know how to distinguish genuine, accurate information from false advertising that aims to dig into your wallet. Once you start to understand the history behind microgreens, you'll proceed to learn about their nutritional benefits.

Once you start to learn about the health benefits of using microgreens, which you'll find in the second chapter of this book, it will become clearer why microgreens are esteemed as they are. You'll learn what science discovered about the nutritional value of these herbs, and what the greatest health benefits are from using them. Here, you'll learn how you can improve your health using targeted microgreens, and why they're so powerful when it comes to supporting not only a healthy diet but also recovery from many illnesses. With this knowledge, you'll be better able to understand how to use these plants to improve your well-being and target specific health areas that need extra support.

Once you've learned how exactly you can benefit from microgreens, you'll learn how to choose the best plants and top-quality seeds. As you'll learn, seeds have enormous value for

ORGANIC GARDENING

a future crop. Any farmer will tell you that the quality of the crop depends on the quality of the seed. In the third chapter of this book, you'll learn not only why seeds matter in cultivation of microgreens but also how to find and choose top-quality seeds. Once you learn that, I'll show you how to take good care of your seeds to preserve their shelf life and protect them from decay. With this knowledge, you'll be able to cultivate microgreens with certainty and confidence that you're giving them the best chance to grow.

After this, you'll learn how to plant and cultivate microgreens step-by-step. In this book, you will find the exact instructions needed for easy-breezy microgreen cultivation. You'll find out what exact tools and supplies are needed, and you'll also learn how to plant, maintain, harvest, and store the crops properly. With this in mind, you will be completely equipped to start growing microgreens right now!

In the fourth chapter of this book, you will learn what exact tools and supplies you need to grow healthy microgreens. In this book, you will also learn more about how to get the right containers, watering systems, fertilizers, and lighting to grow healthy and nutritious microplants. After this, you will learn about the very process of growing microgreens.

In this chapter, you will also learn the right steps for growing microgreens, from obtaining seeds to planting them in the trays and the process of harvesting. This will help you get ready to do your own creative work while choosing the species that you will love and enjoy. Finally, you will learn how to provide your plants with the best conditions to thrive in terms of lighting, supplementation, temperature, hygiene, and more. With this knowledge, you will prevent withering and contamination of your plants and produce an optimum number of healthy crops from the seeds you purchase.

In the fifth chapter of this book, you will learn how to properly eat and use microgreens. To experience the true health benefits from microgreens, you have to know how to store and use them properly. First things first, we will tell you how to make microgreens a steady part of your daily diet. We will show you how to incorporate them into common meals to enrich their flavor and nutritional value. You will also learn how to cook microgreens properly to preserve their nutrients and intensify the taste that they will release into your meals.

Last but not least, you will find out how to turn your microgreen hobby into a business. If you stay persistent in following the guidelines from this book, you will easily be able to grow your own healthy crops. Once you're certain of your knowledge, you will be able to grow greater amounts and profit from your work. The final chapter of this book will guide you through establishing and maintaining a microgreen business. First, we will explain how and why microgreens are profitable and what you can do to enhance the profits from starting your own business. We will first explain what the advantages are of growing microgreens for sale and how you can start doing it using the tools and supplies you already have in your home.

Next, we will give you exact calculations of possible profits and startup costs for a microgreen business. With this knowledge, you will be able to determine whether you'll be satisfied with small production and keeping your cultivation as a hobby, or you want to aim for bigger goals and conquer the market. Next, we will show you how to properly sell microgreens. As with any other business, selling microgreens will require adjusting to the rules of the market. We will show you how to evaluate your competition and learn from them to improve the quality of your own crops. Next, we'll show you how to maintain a good relationship with your customers so that your brand becomes visible and grows in popularity and profitability. With this knowledge, you will be fully equipped to not only grow and eat microgreens for optimal health benefits but to also grow your own income. Thank you for taking the time to read this book! We hope you will enjoy it and find it invaluable.

CHAPTER 1: WHAT ARE MICROGREENS, AND WHY GROW THEM?

Welcome to the first chapter of your manual for growing and using microgreens! If you've picked up this book, you are probably at least a little bit aware of what microgreens are and how to use them. But, do you know everything you need to cultivate them on your own? Probably not. Plant cultivation requires attention and knowledge of individual species, growth calendar, planting, and proper conditions needed for successful growth of rich-tasting, nutrient-boosting plants. Perhaps you are only interested in finding out how to successfully plant pots of micro basil, onion, or celery? Or, you want to transform your diet, and you're looking for ways to add more nutrition to your daily meals? It could be that you see a business opportunity in growing microgreens and want to find out how to produce and sell them on a large scale. Whatever your motivation is, this book will provide the answers.

First things first, you'll need to learn the very basics to be able to understand microgreens. In this chapter, you'll first find out what microgreens are and what distinguishes them from the regular vegetables and spices you find on grocery store shelves. With that understanding, it will become clearer what makes these small plants so special and why they are worth the effort. You'll also learn about some complications that come with large-scale produce and a couple of vulnerabilities that make these plants attention worthy.

More than that, you will learn the history behind microgreens. In this chapter, you will also learn where microgreens came from and how they came to be as popular as they are today. With this knowledge, you'll better understand how to interpret the information about their value and be able to distinguish real benefits from targeted advertising. Here, you will learn why, despite being so simple to grow, these plants become very expensive to obtain unless you grow them on your own. With this knowledge, you'll be able to better understand the benefits they can offer but also a couple of drawbacks to industrial production. Without further ado, we'll begin our manual with some basic information about microgreens.

WHAT ARE MICROGREENS?

Microgreens are small, young greens that are grown and used to enrich the flavor of numerous dishes. These plants are grown until they reach the first hue leaf stage and are then harvested and sold (Kyriacou et al., 2016). They belong to a species of plants that are typically harvested and consumed either in baby stages or as sprouts. Microgreens are a third category of herbs and contain seed leaves, or cotyledons, along with stems. Most often, they're used for salads, smoothies, and as additions to numerous other dishes to enrich the flavor and boost the nutritional value of an otherwise regular dish. While there's no legal definition for either microgreens or baby greens, you'll typically recognize them as being up to two inches tall depending on the species. Much like sprouts (e.g., pumpkin and almond), where you'll consume either the shoot, root, or seeds, microgreens share the same vulnerability to microbe contamination. In addition, they're fragile and sensitive but valuable for their vibrant color, strong flavors, and distinct textures.

Compared with microgreens, sprouts are only partially germinated. This means that they only contain the seed, root, and the stem, while a microgreen doesn't contain the root. Compared to sprouts, microgreens are more intense in flavor, with wider selections of colors, textures, and shapes. Simply put, microgreens are a slightly more grown version of a sprout. To grow microgreens, you'll use materials called substrates that resemble soil, and you'll need to provide them with enough sunlight to increase their nutritional value and support healthy growth. Sun and water are the two most important elements that help the plants process the nutrients absorbed from soil to not only grow but also synthesize the substances we find to be so precious and beneficial to the diet. In addition, to grow microgreens, you will use less seed density, meaning that only a couple of seeds will be enough for growth.

Microgreens usually grow anywhere from two to six weeks, with expanded leaves signifying that the time to harvest has come. If you're purchasing microgreens, you'll often find them sold in pots while not yet fully developed. This is to avoid oversaturation of the plant, giving you the opportunity to cut it later as you need. However, keep in mind that you should only purchase microgreens for quick use, as they lose color and flavor with maturation.

While microgreens are less labor intensive than sprouts, they come with somewhat bigger risks from pathogens and safety concerns. This increases the probability of safety risks due to factors like the lack of knowledge of good practices, overly dense seeds, insufficient light and air, and ignoring recommended safety procedures. There is also a probability of accidentally growing toxic plants, as some of the species—like nightshade plants that include potatoes, tomatoes, and eggplants—can become toxic.

There's a lot of variety when it comes to the taste of microgreens. While a common assumption is that they lack flavor, the truth is that they can be very spicy and sweet to the palate. They're commonly considered to be a "superfood" due to the high amount of nutrients they contain in small amounts. They are also popular due to simplicity and ease of growth, the reasons which make them desirable for personal cultivating. You'll find species like arugula, cabbage, kale, beet, kohlrabi, amaranth, swiss chard, radish, and mustard equally as home grown plants and as a seasoning in expensive dishes in prominent restaurants that feature extravagant cuisines.

Currently, nearly 100 species are known to be grown as microgreens, including common plants like celery, buckwheat, sweet pea, spinach, lemongrass, fennel, broccoli, onions, chives, and basil, and also plants like carrots, arugula, and cress.

While growing microgreens in the comfort of your home isn't at all demanding and difficult, marketing is quite a different story. If you want to sell greens, you have to be aware of all the intricacies of not only mass production but also complex production strategies that produce the maximum amount of quality produce to sell. Since harvesting times depend on the species, their growth calendar doesn't care much for demands of the market. While minding successful production, you'd also have to be considerate of the revenue flow that will supply the funds to settle financial duties and taxes.

With this in mind, the best advice is to focus production on the crops with similar harvesting times so that you can harvest and sell them all at once. In addition, you have the choice of planting different seeds and mixing them up after harvest.

As you can see, there are numerous options and considerations to think about when contemplating growing microgreens. However, their nutritional value and the opportunity to enrich your life and diet with the replenishing substances they're known to possess make them worthy of studying and growing. In the next section, you'll find out more about the history of microgreen cultivation.

HISTORY OF CULTIVATION

Nowadays, microgreens are known for their nutritional value and satiating flavors that can turn a plain dish into a delicacy. But, what's the history behind microgreens? While microgreens turned popular in mainstream culture only a couple of decades ago, rising from home-grown specimens to the secret ingredient of upscale culinary establishments, their quality and variety of uses range further back in history.

While the use of sprouts and baby plants ranges back to ancient societies, the cultivation of microgreens is fairly new. Their popularity first arose with the insight into the potential of adding flavor to otherwise plain dishes, while subsequent studies proved their nutritional benefits. The production of microgreens across the US began in the 1990s, spreading from San Francisco and other parts of California. As with most innovations, the cultivation began in small yards, only to spread and become an industry to supply food chains and restaurants.

Here, the most popular crops included basil, arugula, kale, beets, cilantro, and a popular Rainbow Mix. They're now being grown across not only the US but also the rest of the world. Aside from natural plants grown in homes and gardens, microgreens are found in numerous other forms, like cellulose pulp, which has been present in Europe since 2002. However, sales of living microgreens are just becoming popular, as more and more people are aware of their benefits and ease of cultivation. However, living microgreens are rarely found in stores because of higher costs and smaller yields that impact production and packaging. In addition, large-scale production and shipping tend to negatively impact the quality of produce, due to the difficulty of keeping the plants hydrated and nourished enough to preserve the flavor and nutrients. With added costs that come from industrial production and packaging, commercial use of fresh microgreens on a large scale remains a challenge. However, they can come at a somewhat luxurious price when grown organically in greenhouses.

The use of fresh microgreens is challenging for restaurant owners as well, since they quickly decay after being harvested and refrigerated. For this reason, systems and strategies for large-scale commercial growth are still being developed. Meanwhile, home cultivation remains a primary source of healthy flavor for individuals interested in these plants.

But, what makes these small plants so popular? What are the reasons for increased interest in their cultivation and possible health benefits? In the next section, you'll find out more about what lies behind the popularity of microgreens and what makes them a so-called "superfood."

WHY MICROGREENS BECAME POPULAR

Nowadays, the nutritional benefits of microgreens are well known, and their cultivation makes an attractive hobby for those looking to refresh their kitchens with fresh-smelling herbs grown by their own hands. Aside from that, the small plants are getting attention and are heavily featured in culinary shows, popular cookbooks, nutritionists' recommendations, and diet plans for those looking to lose weight and get rid of fat and cholesterol. Simply put, they're all present, from farmers' markets, to TV. This had led to an increased interest in their growth and cultivation, driving people to further learn about the art of microgreen growing. However, there are more factors contributing to their popularity than simply mainstream trending.

A rich taste is one of the biggest reasons why microgreens became popular in the first place. Naturally, the flavor of young plants is stronger than that of the adult's, and their quick growth only contributed to the hype. Aside from that, the richness in flavor comes in the compact form of a little stem that offers vibrant tastes that range from sweetness to spiciness and are disproportionate to their size.

Nutritional value is a benefit beyond question when it comes to growing microgreens. In fact, plants that are harvested in the microgreen stage tend to contain 40% more nutrients than adult plants. However, this comes at a price. Arguably, greater quantities need to be planted and harvested with small plants to achieve the same amounts and volume that one would have with adult plants. This small obstacle can be easily surpassed with their quick growth. Within only a couple of weeks, the tiny plants are ready for use and are also suitable to grow on small spaces, like kitchen countertops. They don't require typical gardening equipment and skills, such as taking care of the soil, hydration, and fertilizing. Instead, simply planting them into a substrate of your choice and watering regularly will suffice to enjoy lush, healthy produce.

Aesthetic appeal is among the reasons why many homeowners love microgreens. They spread adorable fragrance and can serve as decoration in kitchens and dining rooms. Many look at them as an art, carefully planning to build stations and choose decorative pots for their small plants, to add not only scent and flavor but also a touch of freshness into the ambience of their living space.

Whether you find microgreens appealing as decor, or you simply want to add more flavor to your food without continuously having to buy spices, microgreens will provide more than a treat for the eye and the palate. Compared to fully-grown vegetables, they are richer in many vitamins, like C, E, and A. They can be a quick and easy way to improve your diet, with larger concentrations of vitamins and minerals in small doses. On the other hand, they are a low-calorie food that allow you to enjoy taste without fearing gaining weight. In fact, they average only 29 calories per 100 grams. However, one thing to consider is that you'll have to purchase or grow greater amounts of microgreens to reap the health benefits. With an average of 75 grams being recommended for daily use, just sprinkling the greens over your salad isn't enough to make a noticeable dietary impact. In this case, it remains up to you to decide whether the investment is worthwhile.

In this chapter, you learned what microgreens are and what

makes them so popular. You learned that there's nothing specific about these small plants except the fact that they are harvested at the microstage of growth, where they contain the highest percentage of nutrients and the most intense flavor. However, you also learned that the consistent use of these plants can become a bit of a luxury, considering the amounts that need to be consumed for health benefits.

You also learned that, despite mainstream hype created around so-called superfoods, there are many challenges to their production and harvesting. First things first, microgreens include many species, of which each has their own time of the year to grow and be harvested. From the beginning, this shows that cultivating microgreens will require thoughtful planning. With this in mind, proceed reading this book while staying aware that the best choice is to choose the species of interest and plan their production in accordance with that. In this chapter, you also learned that the majority of the hype surrounding microgreens comes from nutritional benefits one can enjoy with a little bit of time and effort.

But, what are these benefits? Are microgreens truly as healthy as one might assume, or does the attention surrounding them come from advertising and exaggerated claims? We will review these aspects in the following chapter, where you'll learn more about the potential health benefits of microgreens. In the next chapter, you'll learn what makes microgreens so healthy, about their nutritional value, and what health benefits you can expect from regular use. With this knowledge, you'll be able to make an educated decision about the exact species you want to grow and the amounts you want to produce.

CHAPTER 2: NUTRITIONAL AND HEALTH BENEFITS OF MICROGREENS

In the previous chapter, you learned what microgreens are and what makes them so popular. You learned that their intense flavor and convenience of growth has made them highly desirable both for personal and commercial cultivation during the past couple of decades. However, the nutritional value of these gentle plants remains one of the biggest reasons why people are so eager to grow and use them. The nutritional value of microgreens has been intensely studied recently, with research examining many different varieties and individual species to measure their nutritional value and conditions for optimal growth. I will now present you with scientifically proven information about the health and nutritional benefits of microgreens.

After all, you are probably interested in microgreens due to their nutritional potency. Nowadays, both agriculture and medical experts are looking into the potential of microgreens to contribute to a sustainable, simple, and easy, yet optimally healthy diet. For this reason, numerous industries, from agriculture to medicine, and even economists, have been studying the potentials of microgreens and their implications for modern eating habits, human health, and the food industry.

The research I came across mainly revolved around the potential and optimal use of these low-maintenance plants for personal and commercial purposes, and measuring their quality when produced on small farms, served at restaurants, and sold on store shelves.

In this chapter, we will explain the proven health benefits of using microgreens. We will first look into studies that examined the nutritional compounds found in different microgreens and compare them to regular fruits and vegetables. With this knowledge, you will know exactly why microgreens are worth the effort. You will find out more about their potential to enrich your diet with nutrients that are otherwise hard to preserve in regular vegetables that can't be eaten raw. As they don't require cooking, nutrients are preserved that would otherwise decay while baking or boiling, which would otherwise be required in order to prepare regular vegetables. The information given in this chapter will show you the exact nutrients you can directly ingest from only small amounts of microgreens.

Further, we'll present you with the nutritional richness of the most popular microgreen species, aiming to present you with those that have proven to contain the most abundant number of nutrients, yet remain the most practical to grow and cultivate at home. With this knowledge, you will be equipped to obtain the right supplies and purchase the right seeds of these plants and start growing them right now. As you will learn, growing these nutritional bombs is super easy, even when done on your kitchen counter. With the information and instructions given in this chapter, you will be able to start growing your own favorite microgreens right now.

In addition, you will find out how exactly your health benefits from a daily dose of microgreens. From simply boosting your immune system to avoiding seasonal flu, to getting more fiber to improve your digestion and speed up weight loss, and even improving your blood pressure and cardiovascular health, you will learn which exact plants you can use to to alleviate issues that might be bothering you. Whether you decide to cultivate at home or purchase microgreens from your local farmer's market or grocery store, you will know the exact species to choose for your own health and nutritional needs.

WHY ARE MICROGREENS SO HEALTHY?

When it comes to the nutritional value of microgreens, researchers measured a couple of nutrients that are thought to be vital for human health. Here are some of the most potent micro- and macronutrients found to be abundant in microgreens (Xiao et al., 2012; Choe & Wan, 2018).

Vitamin K

One of the nutrients known to benefit blood coagulation is phylloquinone or vitamin K1. This nutrient is most often found in leafy greens, like spinach, broccoli, kale, and other dark-green vegetables. The biggest concentration of this nutrient is found in garnet amaranth, green basil, pea tendrils, and red cabbage. On the other hand, greens like popcorn, golden pea tendrils, magenta spinach, and red orach microgreens showed less than 0% of this compound.

Color seems to be a valid indicator of content, meaning that you can rely on your judgment to assume that the darker greens and bright reds are richer in this nutrient than light-oranges and yellows. You don't have to be a scientist nor put each microplant under the microscope to conclude its dominant nutrient. If you're working to boost your blood circulation, this nutrient will give you exactly what you need.

The maturity of the plant also plays a vital role, meaning that grown varieties contain less of this nutrient than microgreens.

Vitamin C

Vitamin C, or ascorbic acid, is an important antioxidant. However, to preserve vitamin C in microgreens, you'll have to protect them from stress and provide optimal, stable, and continuous conditions for healthy growth. The varieties known to have the greatest amounts of vitamin C include garnet amaranth and red cabbage, with opal basil and china rose radish being runner-ups. In fact, the amount of vitamin C that was found in these plants was nearly double the amount found in mature species.

While this doesn't mean adult vegetables are useless, it shows how you can navigate food supplementation, like seasoning, juices, and smoothies, to boost the number of nutrients lacking in your regular diet. If you find yourself lacking vitamin C yet hate eating cabbage, you can disguise it into a tasty smoothie by adding a small amount of the microgreen substitute.

Carotenoids

Microgreens can become a potent source of carotenoids, like beta-carotene, also known as provitamin A. This essential nutrient has antioxidative properties, protecting cellular membranes of your body from passing through free radicals. The words "antioxidant" and "free radicals' are often used when discussing cellular regeneration and cancer prevention, with antioxidants helping the body release toxic chemicals instead of absorbing them. The microgreens found to be richest in this nutrient include red sorrel as the most substantial source, with cilantro, pepper cress, and red cabbage following closely. You'll find the least amount of beta-carotene in popcorn shoots and golden pea.

Compared to adult plants, the leading carotene microgreens contain anywhere from 10 to 260 times the nutrient levels. This only goes to show the abundance of the nutrient compared to adult plants and how much antioxidant benefits you can gain with only small dosages.

When it comes to the health of your eyesight, lutein and zeaxanthin are carotenoids that accumulate in the macula of your eyes, supporting healthy, sharp vision. In fact, they're believed to reduce the possibility of developing cataracts and prevent the degeneration of ocular tissues.

To boost your eyesight, you can grow cilantro, garnet amaranth, red cabbage, and red sorrel. Studies have shown that these microgreens contained significantly higher amounts of the eye-nurturing compound compared to adult specimens. The secret lies in the leaves of these plants, which seem to be most saturated with lutein.

Another carotenoid called violaxatine, which is an orange carotenoid, was found to be most concentrated in cilantro microgreens, with lush amounts of it present in other microgreens as well. Again, the amounts were highly abundant compared to grown plants.

Potent Micronutrients

When it comes to researching the nutritional value of microgreens, it's been proven that micro elements and macro elements like potassium, calcium, iron, copper, sodium, manganese, phosphorus, magnesium, and zinc are all very high in all brassica microgreens. While this varies based on varieties and species, the vitamin K, manganese, potassium, calcium, and phosphorus levels show the highest concentrations in wasabi microgreens, with the lowest value being in daikon radish microgreens. The concentration of phosphorus and calcium was the highest in savoy cabbage and lowest in wheatgrass. Magnesium showed the highest values in microgreen cauliflower and lowest in red mustard. The concentration of sodium showed to be the greatest in watercress and lowest in ruby radish.

The levels of the important macro elements of phosphorus, calcium, potassium, and iron were also high in microgreens, showing that purple kohlrabi and red cabbage had the greatest concentrations of these nutrients, alongside zinc and copper. The majority of other microgreens were also very potent in these ingredients, which are considered to be of vital importance for maintaining a strong immune system.

On the other hand, grass microgreens had great amounts of manganese, while the least nutritious microgreens showed to be mustard, Chinese cabbage, red kale, and ruby radish. Typical commercial selling conditions didn't prove to affect the microgreens negatively, as the tested samples didn't contain any heavy metals.

If you are looking for true superfoods, research suggests that you should cultivate pea shoots, followed by kohlrabi, which also contains high amounts of valuable nutrients. Red mustard seems to remain the least nutritive. However, it still had an abundant number of vitamins. One of the reasons why microgreens are so potent in nutrients is that, at this stage of growth, the plants accumulate numerous vitamins and minerals. In fact, plants pile up vitamin K, phosphorus, and zinc, so that they can support their further growth functions. On the other hand, iron and calcium will be accumulated during more mature phases of growth when the micro green is ready to harvest.

Tocopherol

This is a substance that qualifies under vitamin E. Vitamin E also includes the substance known as tocotrienol. These substances are soluble in fat. What research showed was that the most important types of substances in this category, like alpha-tocopherol and y-tocopherol, were abundant in microgreens. They are most concentrated in green daikon radish, which was highly rich in both types of the substances. If you are aiming to boost your nutrition with vitamin E, you should aim to plant opal radish. The lowest rated microgreens when it came to the saturation of this nutrient were golden pea tendrils. However, even this small plant contains more vitamin C than mature spinach leaves. Red cabbage microgreens are found to contain a large amount of vitamin E as well.

To sum up, microgreens contain enormous amounts of important nutrients that often range from 10 times to 200 times compared to adult green leaves and vegetables. Considerably higher amounts of keratinocytes and vitamins, compared to adults of the same plants, were found in their microversions. You'll find the greatest amounts of vitamins K and E in green daikon radish, cauliflower, amaranth, garnet, and red cabbage.

On the other hand, the lowest-rated microgreens, when it comes to concentrations of essential nutrients, include golden pea tendrils and popcorn shoots. However, these microgreens still contain large amounts of nutrients compared to fully grown vegetables. This concentration severely reduces with insufficient light. It's been proven that, for example, gold pea tendrils lose a lot of vitamins and keratinocytes if they don't have enough light. If you're thinking about boosting your diet with microgreens, you need to be aware that their environment and conditions seriously impact the amount of nutrients that they will be able to synthesize. Always keep in mind that the nutrients don't come from the plant itself but instead from the conditions that were provided.

When it came to commercially grown microgreens, the results were slightly different. Whether microgreens are grown for commercial purposes or for personal use made a lot of difference with the amount of vitamins they contained and desirable dietary intake. When cultivating microgreens for personal use, consider the fact that many conditions affect their nutrient density.

NUTRITIONAL BENEFITS OF MICROGREENS

It is beyond question that you can use microgreens to enrich your diet with healthy nutrients. As they are undoubtedly more saturated with nutrients compared to full-grown plants, they have proven to be highly beneficial for average users. Flavor seems to be one of the biggest factors contributing to the general acceptance of microgreens. However, this greatly depends on quality of maintenance, which is best done with modified atmosphere packaging and keeping the plants at moderately low temperatures. If the plants found in stores get exposed to direct light, their nutrient concentration will decay significantly and quickly. Forms of transportation and light exposure also contribute to faster decay of vitamins and other nutrients found in microgreens. There are other additional risks when it comes to commercial microgreen growing and shopping for the plants in grocery stores.

Some research revealed low-to-moderate contamination from *E. coli*. However, this risk is still smaller compared to sprouts.

One of the reasons why microgreens are more nutrient dense than mature plants can be explained by gene expression and biosynthesis during growth. It seems that microgreens process enzymes differently while the seeds are growing, which can have a great impact on their nutritional value.

When selling and purchasing ready-to-eat microgreens, it is important to note that postharvest storage and wash treatment need to be done in optimal conditions for good quality and prolonged shelf life. While there's little-to-no fresh microgreens appearing in stores, it is important to note that the way you wash and dry the plants, as well as how you package and sanitize them, can increase the risks of losing nutrients and contaminating the plants with different pathogens. However, the majority of microgreens can be found as live plants, sold in grocery stores, and served in restaurants completely safely and without any consequences.

However, a great misconception about microgreens is that they will last longer because they're living plants. Note: a plant being sold alive, in its pot, doesn't guarantee long shelf life! Considering the fact that they need constant and moderate exposure to light to maintain their photosynthesis or else they wither; they can also lose a lot of their potency during transportation. This can negatively impact their nutritional quality and flavor. When it comes to the risks of developing germs, microgreens usually carry low risk of contamination by *E. coli* and other pathogens.

When looking into the nutritional value of microgreens, it is clear that they are far more abundant in all sorts of replenishing nutrients. You also have to understand that this doesn't diminish the importance of adult vegetables. When thinking about the right species to grow, you should think about your own nutritional needs and preferences when it comes to taste. Microgreens are very sensitive to environmental influences, so it's important to think about what kind of conditions you can provide and whether the particular species aligns with your ability to take care of it properly. There are many important microgreens that demand complete emulation of their natural conditions. For this reason, think about whether you can provide these conditions.

Nutritional Value of Individual Microgreens

Now, let's look into some individual properties of different microgreens. Types known to be among the most beneficial include:

- **Amaranth** is most suitable to grow either hydroponically or in soil. While it takes only about 12 days before you can harvest it, it will have a vibrant red or rose color. It tastes sweet and very fresh. It is also highly rich in beta-carotene, iron, calcium, and vitamins C and K.
- The next most popular microgreen is **Arugula**. This small plant doesn't need presoaking before planting, and you can choose any medium to grow it in. It develops quite fast, being able to reach the harvest stage after only eight days. It will be colored deep green and have a strong, peppery flavor that will resemble cabbage. Its stems are fresh and crisp, and the plant is rich in phosphorus, iron, calcium, and vitamin C. It is also a good plant to fight free radicals, as it contains many carotenoids and minerals such as calcium, manganese, and iron, which are all essential for a healthy diet.
- **Barley** usually grows after nine days, when you can harvest it and enjoy its sweet taste.
- **Basil** is another popular microgreen that grows in 12 days. However, it is ideal to harvest it after 10 days, as this is the time when it will have the most intense flavor and the highest amount of nutrients.
- **Beets** are highly rich in protein, zinc, iron, magnesium, calcium, potassium, and vitamins C, K, E, and B. This highly nutritive microgreen will take between 11 and 21 days to mature, and you should grow it in soil. It tastes somewhat earthy, but sweet, and can be compared to wheatgrass.

- **Broccoli** will mature after only 12 days and provide you a steady supply of phosphorus, calcium, and numerous vitamins. Since it grows fast and requires minimum maintenance, you can grow it both hydroponically and in soil. It is one of the healthiest microgreens to cultivate.
- **Brussels sprouts** are rich in fiber, folic acid, and vitamins C, K, and B. They taste similar to cabbage and broccoli, only slightly more bitter. You can grow them on any medium of your choosing. You will recognize that it is mature for harvest after its stems become purple or pink. Most likely, this will happen after 14 days. However, it is important to know that Brussels sprouts don't respond to warmth very well.
- **Buckwheat** is yet another super food that contains plenty of fiber, vitamins K, B, and C, as well as folic acid. It is another microgreen that is painless to grow, with a high germination rate. However, you will need to soak the seeds in cold water a day before planting.
- **Microgreen cabbage** is rich in beta-carotenes, iron, and vitamins A and C. It has a soft, fresh texture with a typical brassica flavor that resembles broccoli. Its leaves can be colored different shades of green, or even red and violet. You will find it in numerous variations. However, all of them are very easy to cultivate. The green varieties contain a substantial amount of beta-carotene, while the red ones are rich in vitamin C. In addition, these plants are highly decorative, and you can use them to refresh the ambience of your home.
- **Cauliflower** is rich in iron, beta-carotenes, and essential vitamins like C and E. It shares a crispy texture and light taste similar to broccoli. Its stems, when maturing, become a purple or pink shade, with deep-green tops. It will take only up to 14 days before you can enjoy this nutrient-dense microgreen
- **Chia** is another food that is known to be a genu-

ine nutritional bomb when it comes to iron. It contains abundant amounts of this nutrient, and it will take only up to 10 days to harvest. Chia microgreens are also rich in proteins, amino acids, and omega oils. They have a soft, tangy flavor, and also a pleasant smell.

HEALTH EFFECTS

Health benefits of microgreens are one of the major reasons why they became so popular and well-accepted among those who care about their health and well-being. But, what are the true benefits from consuming microgreens?

Improved Digestion

Studies have found that microgreens offer great benefits when it comes to nutrient richness. In fact, they are abundant in fiber, which replenishes your digestive system, as well as vitamins and minerals essential to create, preserve, and regenerate cells and tissues inside the body. Overall, these nutrients contribute to strengthening your immune system and preventing diseases. In addition, microgreens help you manage weight due to the high amount of fiber that improves digestion and high amount of nutrients that can make every diet nutritional regardless of the calorie count. If you are dieting and trying to lose weight with microgreens, you will ingest a lot of nutritional value without growing your fat cells and creating the fat supplies that will frustrate you when stepping on the scale.

Cellular Regeneration

Perhaps, one of the most beneficial health benefits of microgreens is the antioxidant property. Microgreens are abundant in antioxidants, aside from vitamins and minerals. While antioxidants help you eliminate the unstable molecules from your body, which is found to prevent cancer, vitamins found in these small plants support the essential physiological processes that boost your immune system, improve your mental abilities, and also affect beauty.

The antioxidant properties help you remove free radicals from your body. These substances result from the body's natural processes and numerous negative environmental influences. Free radicals start to form in your body when you live in a polluted environment, eat foods that are saturated with unhealthy sugars and fats, consume a lot of alcohol, as well as when you smoke and drink a lot of caffeine. Free radicals are also linked to a stressful lifestyle, which results in increased amounts of cortisol secretion. While your body has a certain ability to remove these harmful substances, they can still accumulate when the body is overwhelmed with negative influences. Consuming nutrient-dense foods that contain antioxidants can help you get rid of these harmful chemicals.

While the exact antioxidant types depend on each plant, they are generally known to possess multiple types of these beneficial compounds, regardless of species.

For example, the microgreens that come from the brassica family, which includes broccoli, are rich in vitamin E, which is a phenolic antioxidant. On the other hand, keratinoid antioxidants are found in lettuce, chicory, and other asteraceae microgreens. Still, exact details of how microgreens can prevent illnesses remains covered with a veil of secrecy, which scientists are working hard to uncover. Here are a couple more important scientific findings about the health benefits of microgreens.

Kidney Disease

If you have kidney disease, the microgreens that contain high levels of potassium, such as leafy microgreens, lettuce, and chicory, can be very beneficial. In addition, microgreens are a great solution for people who follow a vegan or vegetarian diet, as well as adding more fiber to their daily nutrient intake.

There's some evidence that these foods, since they don't require soil and can be grown in simulated environments, are even suitable for astronauts.

Sustainability is one of the major benefits of the cultivation of microgreens. As they don't require the same amount of labor as classic gardening, they can be a low-cost way to introduce healthy and beneficial foods into your daily life. They are also appropriate for growing in confined spaces while maintaining the variety and bulk amounts of plants. They provide a consistent source of natural nutrients, as they require only a couple of weeks to grow enough to be consumed. In fact, by simply rotating a couple of selected species, you can have a new, fresh batch in your kitchen every single week.

Cardiovascular Health

Microgreens have been found to potentially benefit those who cope with high blood pressure, cardiovascular disease, obesity, and diabetes. They can also help the healing of those who are recovering from stroke.

Sadly, these diseases, alongside cancer, are flourishing in developed countries due to poor work-life balance and insufficient time to rest and devote to health.

While a general recommendation is to consume a minimum of 400 grams of vegetables and fruits daily, as they are a rich source of micronutrients, antioxidants, and vitamins, insufficient exposure to the sun and a diet that consists of fat, processed sugars, and carbohydrates remain most prevalent among citizens in developed countries.

However, it is important to consider that improper handling of microgreens can cause a decline in flavor and nutritional value of crops, mainly affecting potatoes, and other tubers, as well as leafy greens and other horticultural crops. It is also important to consider that seasonal plants that are grown locally are much more saturated with nutrients than those that are imported.

When thinking about the nutritional value of microgreens by species, types of microgreens like legumes, and others that include soybean sprouts, and traditional ones like radish, mustard, and amaranth, contain substantially larger amounts of micronutrients compared to grown vegetables across the different stages of growth, from sprouts to microgreens, and then a fully grown plant.

One of the biggest benefits from microgreens comes from a high saturation of the so-called phytonutrients, which contribute to intense taste and flavor, while helping those with a deficiency of micronutrients. This means that if you are deficient in vitamins like C, A, E, and K, or substances like keratin, beta-carotene, and potassium, you can avoid supplementation and instead use microgreens to compensate for the lacking nutrients, while reaping great benefits in flavor and taste.

Another benefit of these foods is that they can be consumed raw. You don't have to cook or prepare microgreens in any way, which would otherwise reduce their nutritional value. Grown fruits and vegetables contain high amounts of nutrients. On most occasions, they need to be either processed or cooked, which further depletes them of beneficial substances. You are free from having to cook microgreens, which means that you get to consume the highest amount of their potentially regenerative nutrients.

But, what are the advantages of home-grown microgreens?

Growing your microgreens on a windowsill or terrace by simply storing them in containers, with the possibility of growing numerous crop seeds, will give you fresh produce in 7 to 15 days. In addition, you won't have to use any fertilizers or pesticides to protect them from negative influences and possible infections, which means that you get to consume foods that are completely organic and free from toxic chemicals. Compared to store-bought vegetables, which are most often treated with pesticides and require processing before you eat them, microgreens aren't depleted of nutrients, and they won't introduce any additional toxins into your body.

You can grow microgreens by first washing the seeds and soaking them in water for up to six hours. They need to be kept at room temperature. After this, you only need to place them in a suitable container, which can be either a plastic tray, a plastic container, or a plate. You can also pack them into a glass jar or any other container of your choosing. After that, you can simply cover them with a paper towel or a regular cloth, to preserve their moisture and optimal temperature. After this, you only need to rinse and sprinkle the seeds with water daily to support the sprouting process. You need to provide the seeds with drainage as well, which will keep bacteria or fungi from growing. For misting, it is best to use distilled or spring water.

It is important to remember that microgreens need nutrients for healthy growth. For this, you should use a soil substitute, or regular soil, whether organic or inorganic. You can also use hydroponic nutrient film towels, which will help you easily pull out of the plant when it's time for harvesting. Another convenience of growing microgreens is that they need fewer seeds than growing sprouts.

In this chapter, you learned about the amazing nutrient saturation found in microgreens. You learned that they contain from a couple to ten times more nutrients than their grown versions, with some micros exceeding the adult varieties by over 200 times when it comes to nutritional value. This served to prove the potency of these plants and their significance for a healthy diet. Moreover, you learned how and why microgreens become so potent. As you learned, they pile up, preserve, and contain nutrients to secure the next stage of growth. At the stage of a microgreen, a plant gathers all the nutrients needed to become a fully grown plant. This explains why it's essential to harvest at this exact stage, before the plant starts processing the nutrients and proceeds growing.

Moreover, you learned how exactly your health benefits from these amazing plants. If you're looking to simply boost your immune system, the abundance of vitamins, minerals, and other complex nutrients like beta-carotenes, tocopherols, and others, will make you germ proof, and will also contribute to sharp vision, a strong, vigorous heart, and sufficient iron in your blood. In addition, if you're looking for support in recovery from illnesses like kidney disease or cancer, the antioxidants found in microgreens, in staggering amounts, will support your body in getting rid of free radicals, which are the substances that intervene with proper cell regeneration.

The cell-regenerating property of antioxidants is a topic on its own. You see, for your body to remain healthy and rejuvenated, the cells need the ability to process and get rid of their old, decaying parts. If their capacity to do this depletes, old and decaying cells remain in your system. This is as bad as it sounds, as compromised cellular regeneration is associated with illnesses we'd rather not name, from allergies, weakened immune systems, and respiratory infections, to severe ones like autoimmune disease, cancer, lupus, and others. Consume abundant antioxidants from microgreens, and you will support your body in metabolizing the dead, decaying, and flawed cells of your body, to fuel and support regeneration and the growth of new, healthy cells and tissues.

However, whether you're looking to grow at home or turn your hobby into a business, your journey begins with finding the best seeds. In the next chapter, we will present you with the right strategies for finding the best seeds to grow microgreens.

A quality microgreen requires more than care and environment. The quality of seeds comes first, as the seed carries the plant's genetic potential to produce, process, and synthesize nutrients. Furthermore, the treatment and handling of seeds prior to planting also determines the health of the future plant. For this reason, the next chapter will give you the necessary instructions to first choose the varieties you want to grow, and then obtain the best quality seeds.

CHAPTER 3: HOW TO CHOOSE THE BEST SEEDS

In the previous chapter, you learned more about the nutritional benefits of microgreens. You learned that their reputation for being superfoods is firmly backed up by science and that their value goes beyond eye-pleasing and palate-delighting traits. Microgreens are genuinely abundant in the majority of nutrients needed for proper body functioning, a robust immune system, and vigorous cellular replenishment. You learned that the regular use of microgreens can, indeed, help your body wash away toxins and contaminants, battle bacteria and viruses, and more importantly, support your own natural regeneration process (Choe, Yu, & Wang, 2018).

Now that you've decided to start cultivating these potent herbs, the first step is to choose the best quality seeds. The quality of your plant won't only depend on your care. The very basis of nutrient-dense microgreens is a potent seed, that has the right genetic makeup for vigorous growth and has been cared for to preserve the potential it carries.

The importance of quality seeds for microgreens is enormous. First things first, the seed quality mainly determines the germination rate. Simply put, this rate determines how many seeds will sprout and turn into growing plants. A high germination rate means that the seeds are healthy, well-nourished, and genetically suitable to produce healthy plants. The seeds with a high germination rate mainly come from reputable, quality suppliers who pay attention to the way they collect, nurture, store, package, and transport seeds. While genetics is a major contributor to the quality of the seed, it's treatment can either preserve or deplete the seed of its capacity to grow.

On the other hand, suppliers who don't pay enough attention to the quality genetic selection of their crops and the treatment of their seeds tend to market seed packages with a low germination rate. A low germination rate essentially means that only a portion of planted seeds will sprout, and the quality of the plants that grow out of them is also questionable.

On the other hand, good germination capacity is also important to prevent contamination from mold, fungi, and bacteria. This particularly goes for micros like the tender amaranth, peas, and sunflower. These are only some of the plants that will wither with the barest appearance of pathogens, which will quickly infect and diminish the entire plate of growing crops. This can ruin your efforts and demotivate you from future cultivation, which is something I'd like to help you avoid.

In addition, quality seeds are GMO-free and organic, and I'll help you discover the right ways to obtain seeds that possess these two important traits. However, before you head off to purchase seeds, it would be wise to first decide on the crops to cultivate. We've created a short list of beginner-friendly microgreens, which you'll find in the following section.

DECIDE ON DESIRED CROPS

Before deciding to start growing microgreens, it is important to first decide on the varieties you want to cultivate. For starters, it's important to note that you can choose any type of vegetable or herb you like and cultivate it as a microgreen. In fact, you can pick up the seeds of any vegetable you enjoy, plant it properly, and then pluck it once it reaches the microgreen stage. While this is a simple philosophy, deciding on the plants you want needs some contemplation.

The first thing you want to consider is the taste. Which tastes do you prefer? Would you like to use your plants to simply add aroma to your cuisine, or do you want to eat greater amounts of them, in which case you'll focus on veggies you already enjoy? Microgreens vary in taste and can give a mild, spicy, sweet, bitter, or sour effect, depending on the species. The choice of flavors depends on what you usually prefer in your diet, minding the fact that some of the delicate greens vary not only in the type but also the intensity of the flavor.

With this in mind, here's a short overview of microgreens by family. This short list will help you narrow your choices and map out the possible winners for your future DIY kitchen garden. As you browse this list, keep in mind that the tastes are similar to those of adult plants and choose a couple to focus on for starters. You can group microgreens in different families that all encompass different types of varieties. While there are some differences in tastes and textures, usually the

crops from the same family are similar. Here are a couple of most common microgreen crops, grouped by family:
- The **amaranthaceae** family includes quinoa, swiss chard, beets, spinach, and amaranth.
- Popular veggies like onions, chives, garlic, and leeks are a part of the **amaryllidaceae** family.
- Fennel, dill, celery, and carrots belong to the **apiaceae** family.
- The **asteraceae** family includes radicchio, lettuce, endive, and chicory.
- The **brassica** family includes watercress, radish, cauliflower, cabbage, broccoli, and arugula.
- Squashes, melons, and cucumbers are part of the **cucurbita** family.
- Oregano, sage, rosemary, basil, and mint—the herb flavors you enjoy when seasoning meals—belong to the **lamiaceae** family.
- If you want to grow grasses and cereals, which include wheatgrass, gold rice, corn, and barley, look for them under the **poaceae** family.

I didn't compile this list to simply sound smart by using Latin names. Knowing the common traits of each family will help you read packages and get further informed on cultivation techniques and supplements in other sources, which mainly apply to individual families rather than specific species.

Now that you have some insight into the microgreens you're most likely to love, I'll help you make a choice by giving some more technical information about individual plants belonging to these families. Following are some recommendations for the microgreens that are the most beneficial yet very simple to cultivate:

Kohlrabi is rarely used in an average kitchen; you may also know it under the name of cabbage turnip. As it's the same species as cabbage, you will use its roots rather than leaves.

The microgreen version of this plant will take up to 12 days to grow. You will know that they are ready to harvest when their stems grow taller, and the green leaves have thrived. This plant will give your meals a pop of color and a mild turnip-cabbage-y flavor. They are also great for salads and sandwiches.

Clover microgreens grow simple and fast, and they only take up to 12 days. They have a sweet and mild flavor that is most intense when picked young. Additionally, they are abundant in calcium, zinc, iron, and magnesium.

Collards grow hydroponically and are slightly smaller and slower in growth compared to chives. It will take up to 12 days for them to grow, and they will feature a dark green color. They have the same taste intensity as the grown vegetables.

Kale is one of the healthiest plants known and is also considered to be a superfood. If you don't enjoy the taste and texture of the fully grown plant, the microgreen form of this vegetable will taste similar to lettuce, albeit milder and more tolerable.

Alfalfa is another of the hydroponic microgreens that won't require soil. To plant them, all you need to do is soak an ounce of seeds on a paper towel and cover them for between three and five days. After 8 to 12 days, you will notice dark green leaves that will be crunchy and have a mild flavor. They are great to diversify the taste of sandwiches and salads.

Wheatgrass is one of the simplest microgreens to grow. It looks similar to regular grass; however, it is abundant in many vitamins and minerals. Sadly, the general consensus is that the taste of this herb isn't great. If you don't enjoy the taste of this healthy microgreen, you can add it to a smoothie or improve the flavor by adding sugar or honey.

Sorrel will taste sour/tart. It has a lemony flavor and takes 20 days to harvest. Red vein sorrel is the most popular variety of this plant and will look similar to spinach.

Basil. Growing micro basil is also very simple and convenient, and you will get to enjoy an intense flavor that will add a touch of the exotic and Mediterranean to your kitchen. You shouldn't presoak the seeds, but instead directly plant them into the soil and slightly mist until they are damp. It grows quite quickly, but it will require higher temperatures to grow healthy, which is why you should preferably plant it during the spring or summer months. You can choose between multiple types, like cinnamon basil or lemon basil. Each of these species taste different but very intense.

Mustard is a flavorsome microgreen that has a spicy taste and will enhance the taste of many dishes and salads. It grows very fast and will be ready to harvest in about 10 days. The young plants are quite resilient, and they won't lose any of their flavor or properties even if you leave them growing slightly longer.

Buckwheat also grows very fast, and you only need to soak the seeds in cold water and leave them up to 24 hours. After that, before planting, choose either a large cup or a broad tray. You will most likely be able to harvest it within 12 days, after its yellow leaves start turning green. However, this plant will need a lot of light, meaning that you'll either keep it on your windowsill or add supplemental light for bulk cultivation.

Amaranth will grow and spread out after 12 days, when you will be able to harvest it. You can keep it safely in the refrigerator, and it will maintain its flavor for a long time. It should be intensely red and have slender leaves. These microplants are most often used for garnishes.

Sunflower is yet another superfood that will take only up to 4 days to produce green leaves that will make a great addition to any salad or sandwich.

Peas will require sufficient water, as they absorb substantial amounts. After transferring soaked seeds (preferably after 24 hours of hydration) into a ball or a tray, mist them multiple times a day until you notice sprouting. After that, you can transfer them into soil, using around 12 oz of seeds per tray. After you've planted the sprouts, keep them out of light between three and five days, but proceed with misting. The soil needs to be just dampened; otherwise, the plants might get soggy. The peas will take around 12 days before you can harvest them and enjoy their sweet and crunchy taste.

Microgreen **carrots** taste similar to regular carrots, only sweeter, finer, and softer. However, it will take them around four weeks before harvesting. They will be worth the effort, considering they will be highly saturated with beta-carotene and vitamins C, E, and D.

Arugula has a spicy, peppery flavor that will give some flair to your sandwiches and salads. You can harvest in only seven days, as it only takes a couple of days to germinate.

Cress is great for those who are just starting out and can be grown either in soil or on a paper towel. However, you need to take good care of it and handle it gently, as it can easily bruise.

Now, you are free to decide which microgreens you want to plant! We recommend choosing between three and five if you're a beginner, preferably those with similar harvesting times and germination requirements. This will allow planting multiple species using similar techniques and tools, as well as simultaneous harvesting. However, if you're eager to learn, you can always combine the species to diversify tastes and flavors, while learning different techniques.

PURCHASE THE BEST SEEDS

Now that you've decided which microgreens you want to grow, it is also important to choose top-quality seeds. At the beginning of this chapter, we already highlighted the importance of high-quality seeds. Now, we'll present you with a couple of tips for finding the best seeds for your microgreens.

Organic

It is very important that your seeds are untreated and organic. Purchasing seeds that are purposefully cultivated for sprouts and microgreens most likely means they were not treated with any chemicals like fungicides and pesticides. On the other hand, if you're using gardening seeds, it is likely that they were treated with insecticides and fungicides. If your seed is treated with chemicals, the toxic chemicals will also remain in the plant, compromising its growth and nutritional value.

Make sure to get only untreated seeds, whether you are ordering them online or purchasing from farmers' markets. Organically grown seeds are a bit harder to find but worth the trouble. It is also important to distinguish untreated from organic seeds. While purchasing organic seeds means that they are not treated, buying specifically untreated seeds doesn't guarantee that they are organic. This means that the only guarantee of an organic seed is the certification you'll find on the packaging. This is the only way to secure top-quality seed. If you're unsure of whether a seed is organic, untreated, and GMO-free, ask the provider directly.

Find a Trusted Supplier

Purchasing seeds from the cheapest online store is not going to be the wisest decision. Not only will you be unaware of the exact species and the quality of seeds that you will receive, there's also no guarantee that your seeds will be healthy and quality enough to grow. Make sure to research wisely, and pay attention to harvesting dates, as well as the provider's claims on seed longevity. Make sure to pay attention to the germination rates as well, as they suggest how many plants will sprout and grow.

Go for a Limited Variety

For starters, you don't want to stretch your efforts to an overly broad number of varieties. Instead, get to know each of the species that spark your interest, and find out what is best suitable for you. Beginners are usually successful with cultivating the popular brassica family, which can be demanding but worth the effort. This family includes turnip, broccoli, and cabbage. Another easy choice is mustard, which is flavorsome and quick and easy to grow. You'll also find lettuce, cress, sesame, bok choy, and Chinese cabbage to be beginner friendly.

Purchase From Bulk Sellers

As your confidence in your ability to grow microgreens strengthens, you can move on to buying seeds by ounces and pounds. Once you start cultivating larger amounts, it's recommended that you buy from bulk sellers, as they usually offer the best prices.

Take Good Care of the Seeds

The quality and result of the seeds you purchase don't only depend on the supplier. They also depend on how much you care for the seeds. Taking good care of the seeds requires refrigerating them and protecting them from high temperatures, moisture, and air. They also require cold temperatures and low humidity to be stored long term. Temperature fluctuations can promote germination and cause your seeds to sprout before time. On the other hand, refrigeration will keep them fresh for a very long time.

Also, keep in mind that the paper envelopes that serve to deliver the seeds won't be enough protection in the long run. You should remove them from their packaging and transfer them into watertight, but not completely airtight, plastic bags or clamp bags. Alternatively, you can also keep the seeds in glass jars. Keep in mind that, while the seeds are in a dormant state, they are still living organisms that require care with due knowledge and responsibility. If you take care of them well, they will sprout with high germination rates, and grow as beautiful, potent, flavorsome plants as intended.

In this chapter, you learned how to pick, choose, and select the best species and seeds for your future collection. First, you learned the abundance of greens to choose from. With the liberty to grow as many types as you like, we suggested that you choose those you're most likely to enjoy and use, all while focusing to present you with the crops that are easiest to plant and grow. With this in mind, you've probably narrowed down your list to your top five.

After that, we suggested the right ways to obtain quality seeds. It is important to approach microgreen seed selection with great attention, as not only the quality of supply but also the way you care for the seeds determine their germination and the success of your batch. Care for the seeds is a shared responsibility between the supplier and you, meaning that you need to protect the seeds from temperature fluctuations and excess moisture while keeping them away from sunlight. For this, it's recommended to keep the seeds refrigerated, preferably in glass jars. Now that you know which greens you want to grow and how to find the best seeds, it's time for you to learn the exact technique of growing, harvesting, and storing microgreens. We will cover this topic in the next chapter, giving you the exact steps to take for growing lush batches of greens.

CHAPTER 4: HOW TO GROW MICROGREENS

In the previous chapter, you learned how to choose the crops that will fit your needs best. You can make your choice depending on taste, preference, ease of growth, and health needs. Whichever choice you made, now's the time to finally learn how to grow microgreens. After all, this is the most important part of the process. While simple and easy, proper growing technique will make the process effortless if you follow these simple guidelines and adjust your approach to individual properties of the varieties you chose. For that reason, this chapter will show which exact crops require particular environments and circumstances to thrive.

The proper choice of the crops and seeds should yield maximum germination, ensuring that the greatest number of seeds planted develops into sprouts. For this, a careful choice of seed will provide a healthy genetic base, while your efforts to care for the growing plant will support it in transforming soil, water, and light into valuable nutrients.

In this chapter, you'll learn the exact steps needed to grow microgreens. It's essential to follow these steps religiously, as they create the proper conditions for the plant to grow. First, you will find out what tools and supplies are needed for cultivation of microgreens. You'll find the list to be quite simple, mainly containing items you likely already have at home. However, steps need to be taken to prepare these tools to minimize the chances of contamination and trauma to the plants

(Di Gioia et al., 2015).

Next, you'll find out how to properly germinate and plant the seeds. Individual varieties require different treatment for best germination. Most often, the seeds are hydrated with filtered water. However, some crops, as you'll learn, don't require soaking prior to germination, and these are usually the simplest to grow.

Finally, you'll learn about other important considerations relevant to growing a healthy batch. In this chapter, you'll learn about optimal temperature, lighting, storage, and harvesting processes recommended for highest yield. You'll also learn about possibilities to further enhance the potency of your plants with proper drainage, hydration, and fertilization. Bear in mind that general recommendations state that microgreens don't require additional supplementation. However, I encountered some evidence that shows that proper supplementation can, indeed, benefit the nutritional potency of particular microgreens. You may, if you want to, follow fertilization and supplementation advice, keeping in mind it's not a must for growing healthy crops. Now, it's time to start gathering tools and supplies for planting your first batches!

TOOLS AND SUPPLIES

One of the reasons why microgreens are so compelling to grow is the short amount of time that passes from sprouting to being harvested. They aren't a big investment, considering the benefits of having a fresh supply throughout the entire year. Before you start growing your own microgreens, it is important to prepare and get all the supplies you will need. First things first, you will choose the exact variety you want to cultivate. There are dozens of plants that you can grow as microgreens, but you should start with the one that is easiest to cultivate. We suggest starting off with the simplest microgreens, for example, sprouts, arugula, broccoli, cabbage, bok choy, cauliflower, chia, and Chinese mustard. You can also go for kale, as it is a plant that is relatively easy to cultivate. For starters, you want to select the best media to grow your microgreens in.

First things first, purchase only the amount of seed you will need for the first planting. As you already know, seeds can grow stale and get contaminated under the influence of bacteria and mold. To prevent this, purchase only the smallest amounts for starters, and move to bulk seed purchasing once you gain more experience. Now, it's time to list the basic supplies your greens will need to grow and thrive.

Containers

After you've decided on the varieties to grow and purchased quality seeds, the next thing to think about is where you will store your microgreens. You can use anything from a specially built shed to a windowsill or even your kitchen counter. However, you need a clean container; this can be in the form of a regular plastic container or a disposable pie plate. You can also go for salad bowls, fruit boxes, regular plates, or even plastic plates for hydroponically grown microgreens. Since these DIY microgreen containers aren't made for these purposes specifically, you'll also have to think about drainage and pierce or drill holes across the bottom of the dishes so that the soil can release any excess water.

While you can use Tupperware, glasses, glass jars, etc., for more serious cultivation, you'll need microgreen trays. These containers are best to grow healthy microgreens, as they're made for these specific purposes. Whether or not you'll need to drill drainage holes depends on the substrate. If you're using hydroponically grown seeds, you won't need holes, particularly if you're using growth mats. However, soil media will require holes, since the excess water needs to be drained from the tray.

First things first, check all of the instructions, and follow the advice you find attached to products you purchase. Rely on the manufacturer's knowledge of best use, and stick to their suggestions for how to best use the products. Whether it's a container, lighting, soil, or any other piece of equipment, following instructions will ensure that the product performs at its best. Later, when you're more experienced, you can add your own touch of creativity according to the knowledge of what works best.

Water

The quality of hydration greatly determines the health, flavor intensity, and nutrient density of your crops. You'll preferably use either rainwater or a water filter, since regular tap isn't a good choice due to high pH value. When it comes to watering, you want to pay attention to the pH values of water and pre-soak the seeds that require doing so. Soaking will most likely be necessary for plants like buckwheat, beets, sunflower, popcorn shoots, and others. Tap water is usually too high in pH value for microgreens to process. You should get a pH test kit that ranges from pH two to pH eight. Ideally, you will provide water that has a pH value of six for watering your plants.

Growth Media

We already discussed choosing between hydroponic growth pads, soil-less, and soil media. This choice mainly depends on the type of microgreen, with some room to adjust the mix to your own preference.

There are multiple types of growth media to choose from, ranging from soil based to soil-less and hydroponic:

The soil-based mediums will require a planting mix that will drain well. The mix shouldn't contain any stones or clumps. Instead, it should be light and compact. Preferably, you will add nutrients through hydration, keeping in mind not to go overboard. The soil can start developing microbes if it is too wet. You can use soil to grow many greens, including basil. But, keep in mind that soil isn't the best choice for all of them.

The media that don't include soil are made from different mixes like perlite, vermiculite, and coco coir. You can also use organic clay pebbles or hydroponic lava. One of the bigger advantages of this medium is that you can adjust and level it to give a clean surface. This will be important when you start to harvest, as the plants are harvested close to the soil. It will also provide a clean surface that won't spread a lot of dirt.

Using hydroponic methods is very simple and easy for beginners. Hydroponic medium consists of a growth pad, which you will use to retain water and allow the seed to absorb it. This method will also enable germination, allowing the seed to sprout while staying continuously hydrated. If you do this properly, you will have crops that are easy to harvest without having to pull them out.

Keep in mind that the choice of the medium doesn't only depend on your taste. It also depends on the type of the plant. With microgreens, you won't need fertilizer. However, if you still desire to use it, we recommend getting specialized fertilizers that are tailored to fit the individual needs of particular varieties you're cultivating.

Illumination

Besides your growth medium, lighting deserves some attention. We already discussed the illumination needed for microgreens to grow healthy. However, if the place you're storing them in supplies sufficient light, you don't have to think about adding supplemental illumination. However, if you estimate that your plants might need a boost of photons, or you grow them on racks, you can start looking into the alternatives for LED illumination, depending on your needs and budget. After you've planted your microgreens, you will wait an estimated amount of time for them to grow, after which you can move on to harvesting.

In this section, you learned about all supplies needed for successful microgreen cultivation. Once you start the process yourself, keep in mind that the advice given varies by individual species and varieties. Upon choosing a couple of plants to start with, choose those tools and methods that are the best fit for the variety in question. In the next section, you'll learn the exact steps needed to successfully grow microgreens.

THE PROCESS OF GROWING MICROGREENS

Now that you've gathered all of the supplies, the time has finally come to plant your seeds. The following section will give you precise steps and advice to successfully plant the chosen seeds and care for them until they flourish into microplants.

How to Plant Microgreens

Here's a step-by-step guide for planting microgreens.

Prepare the Container

After receiving and presoaking the seeds (if applicable), you will prepare your container. The first step is to carefully read the instructions that came with the seed package. Check all of the instructions, and follow any advice and recommendations given. Read through the instructions carefully and check to see what advice the manufacturer gives regarding hydration and watering, drainage, placement, and other necessary actions to take good care of the growing plant.

When it comes to preparing your trays, you'll have to drill small holes into the bottom, so that plants can dispose of excess water. Of course, you won't have to do this if the trays or storage boxes you purchased already contain drainage holes. Ideally, your trays and storage boxes will measure roughly 10" x20", which is a standard measurement that applies to instructions on planting and dosing the seeds. Choosing trays of standard size will ensure effortless work going forward, as you won't have to do further calculations to adjust hydration, lighting, and temperature.

Add Soil/Growing Medium

The soil should be loose and scattered so that the seeds can have enough air. First, you will cover the bottom of your container with the substrate, or soil, that you intend to plant. It should be a thin layer of only an inch or two of soil, which should be moist but not soaked. You should level and flatten the soil but not press it completely so that it becomes hard.

Plant the Seeds

Next, it's time to insert the seeds. You should scatter them evenly across the soil, and then press gently using a piece of cardboard or your hands. The goal is for the seeds to be sufficiently covered with soil but not so overly pressed as to deprive them of oxygen. The next step is to cover the seeds with another thin layer of soil, keeping in mind that this layer should be loose, again, for the purposes of allowing your future plants to breed.

Light or Blackout?

The next step is to set-up the light. How you manage the light and illuminate your microgreens greatly affects their growth and nutrient richness. The first few days after planting the seeds is the so-called stacking period, which will last throughout four to five days after seeding. The germinating process will require humidity and a lot of hydration. However, during this time, you want to keep the seeds away from light. You can do this by using a blackout dome, which is essentially a tray that you can flip over the seeds. You will have to mist the seeds and the lid at least twice a day to keep a moderate amount of humidity. However, not all seeds require blackouts, so take this step only if required.

After four or five days, your plants will be ready to be exposed to light, and with some crops, you can strengthen their roots by flipping over the blackout dome and allowing it to sit on top of the emerging crop for at least a day. Whether you will use supplemental lighting depends on the natural light of the room. If there's enough light in the room where you keep your microgreens, you won't need supplemental light. Different species will also vary in their illumination requirements. Study each individual species before making this decision. If the crop that is emerging looks pale and soggy, it means that it needs more light. If you are growing using stack racks, you will need supplemental light because racks themselves will create shade.

Mist and Water

You will then mist and dampen the soil and cover the container using plastic wrap or the lid that might come with the container. Your container should remain covered until you notice sprouts. While waiting to see the sprouts, you should mist the container, up to twice a day. However, neither the container nor the soil should be too wet.

When you notice that the seeds have started sprouting, you can then remove the cover and proceed with daily misting as recommended. After this, you will wait a couple of days, preferably for four days, for your microgreens to thrive in direct sunlight. If you are growing them in winter, they may need some supplemental lighting. If the plants become pale, it means that they are not getting enough illumination, in which case you can use supplemental lighting.

How to Harvest Microgreens

There's nothing overly complex or difficult about harvesting. You need a sharp tool to cut as close to the bottom of the plant as possible. Some of the plants can be easily pulled out, after which you should trim off the base and roots. After this, you'll spread them around to check if any of them still have seeds, keeping in mind to remove remaining impurities, like soil.

You can wash the greens if you plan on eating them right away but not if you plan on storing them. Before serving the plants, make sure to remove as much water as possible using a salad spinner. Some plants can spend some time on paper towels to dry, while others whither within minutes and need to be consumed right away.

Keep in mind that each variety demands different postharvest treatment. They are fragile to various degrees, and you want to make sure not to handle them too harshly or else they might wither and turn to mush.

However, a lack of due attention might cause your efforts to fail. Misting, watering, and paying attention to harvesting times is all necessary for quality produce.

For starters, you can choose between different herbs, leafy vegetables, and salad greens. You can grow a wide range of microgreens, including edible flowers. However, beginners do best with cultivating one type of seed and then moving on to a broader range of varieties, as they get to know the process. Usually, this is either buckwheat, sunflower, mustard, cabbage, or cauliflower. These are among the simplest microgreens to grow as they require very little work and can be grown in a single container. However, you can also grow them in different containers. You can take up a different approach with choosing your seeds by determining your dietary needs. Some microgreens are best suited for salads and sandwiches, for example, and you can start by determining which flavors and nutrients you want and make your decision like that.

You can also think about the color. Microgreens can come in a variety of shades, from deep green to intense purple and red. Also, keep in mind to think about your climate and the conditions you have for supplemental lighting and heating. Preferably, you'll choose those microgreens that don't require many environmental adjustments and can be grown in the garden. They will be pretty simple to plant and cultivate. However, those species that are fragile and require LED lighting and protection from weather conditions may easily succumb to environmental influences if you don't have enough time or resources to devote to their care and maintenance. Usually, microgreens are very simple to cultivate. However, many people don't have enough time in their day to devote to their care. If your day is busy and you can't spend too much time tending to your greens, it is best to choose those crops that require minimum maintenance.

The next thing to think about is where you will store your microgreens. Depending on the size of your batch, you'll store them either in your own refrigerator or a specialized appliance. Typically, small produce requires a small space, while larger-scale produce will require additional space and appliances.

IMPORTANT CONSIDERATIONS (SAFETY, HYGIENE, FERTILIZING, ETC.)

Quality of Lighting

For supplementing lighting, you can use four- or eight-inch LED bars for each shelf or microgreen tray. LED lights will give enough illumination to meet the needs of the microgreens and come in a variety of prices, sizes, and shapes. To begin with, you can use shop lights. If you already have them at home, you can attach LED bulbs combined with incandescent light, while being thoughtful of lighting requirements for the plants you're growing. Most microgreens grow well at room temperature. You can get the exact information about temperature requirements from the seed supplier.

Harvest and Postharvest Factors

There are many preharvest factors that affect the quality of microgreens. The selection of species, among the commercial cultivators, is greatly determined by the popularity of individual varieties. Considering the enormous variety of microgreens when it comes to production, it's noted that the brassica family is the most user friendly and the most popular genotype for cultivating. It is popular due to its intense flavor, texture, appearance, and chemical composition.

Nutritional value is another important factor that contributes to the popularity of this variety. When measuring the total 25 genotypes, across 19 different species, in terms of the concentration of essential nutrients, the results showed great variability when it came to content of vitamins and nutrients under the great influence of different conditions. There was also a lot of variation when it came to micro elements and macro elements. These differences mainly apply to buckwheat, brassicas, and other varieties sensitive to environmental conditions.

Proper cultivation environment also seemed to affect the plant's antioxidant properties. Additional screenings were done on amaranth, which showed differences depending on harvesting status. The application of proper cultivation practices greatly affected nutritional value of the crops, with major differences found in broccoli crops, in terms of phenolic and flavonoid content.

Microgreens create an innovation in modern cooking specifically because of the popularity among consumers, with six species proving to be the most prominent when it comes to eating quality, texture, flavor, appearance, sweetness, sourness, and the abundance of tastes.

The brassica vegetables usually share flavors such as sour, bitter, and astringent, involving species like mustard grass and radish, which proved to be the least popular among consumers. The same can be said for the sweeter and colorful microgreens such as amaranth and beet. These foods have proven to be highly functional in providing high concentrations of phytonutrients and bioactive content, which is another important aspect of nutritional value when it comes to microgreens. The same was concluded for pepper cress and red cabbage, as well as cilantro and amaranth. However, these greens share intense tastes, which may or may not align well with the preferences of users.

Research showed that sufficient amounts of photosynthetic photons, the particle that is emitted through supplemental illumination, is necessary to provide the microgreen with the conditions for photosynthetic processes. An optimal level of lighting is necessary to provide both proper biological conditions and growth for economic purposes. Proper lighting will enable the plant to synthesize pigments, form leaves, and grow biomass. It's been proven that insufficient light interferes with healthy growth of the plant, resulting in hypocotyl elongation, and reduced leaf size and dried weight of the plant. On the other hand, proper lighting enhances the growth of different greens.

Species like bok choy and tatsoi grew healthiest under high LED lighting, which increases their sugar levels. Sugars are essential for the plant to grow and also improve the amount of pigmentation, particularly chloroplast pigments.

On the other hand, plants like lettuce grow healthiest under moderate LED light. A general consideration is that low levels of light reduce the amounts of chlorophyll in the plants, depriving them of one of the most beneficial compounds known to be able to rejuvenate and regenerate the human body. On the other hand, optimal lighting increases the development of this chemical, improving their antioxidant properties and yielding better biomass growth.

It's recommended to use higher lighting when growing brassica microgreens as well, as this improves their nutritional properties. The recommendation is to use an amount of light measuring over 400 μmol $m^{-2}\,s^{-1}$ (the number of photons in a certain waveband incident over unit of time on a unit of area).

When plants find themselves under stress due to insufficient lighting, they tend to release antioxidants. This is unfortunate, as we want them to preserve these cell-regenerating substances. However, improving lighting reduces this response.

One of the most important aspects of providing microgreens with appropriate lighting is a possible impact on their growth and nutritional value. If you plan on cultivating microgreens at home, giving them a proper amount of light will take some learning, as not all species respond to LED lighting the same way. It's been found that the happy medium, when it comes to illuminating microgreens, ranges between 320 and 440 μmol m^{-2} s^{-1}. This is the light intensity range that shows to yield the best results, provided that other environmental elements, such as soil, temperature, and the quality of air, are kept within the same optimal measures.

Maintaining a moderate amount of light is the best recommendation when it comes to microgreens, as too intense light is proven to alter their antioxidant responses, without enhancing growth or nutritional value. You'll best support the plants by supplying a steady source of even, moderate light that will keep the plant's naturally occurring chemical processes in balance.

When it comes to the dry weight of the plants, it's been shown that commercially sold microgreens range from 4.6 to 10.2%. Analyzed by species, pea tendrils lead in dry weight percentage, with red beet containing over 90% of water.

Nutrition/Supplementation

When it comes to nutrition and biofortification, it was proven that microgreens require a proper amount of nutrients so that they produce high yields and premium quality.

The growing medium plays a substantial role here, with supplementation and fertilization before sowing having a major impact on the nutrients that will later be synthesized in the plant.

Postharvest fertilization and presowing practices reportedly improve growth quality of these small plants. When it comes to fertilization, it is technically not necessary to produce good quality plants. However, it was proven to impact arugula and some other plants that respond well to additional nutrition. Fertilizers that are recommended include ammonium nitrate, which has shown to enhance the growth of these plants as well as improve their photosynthetic responses and their chloroplasts. However, some species can accumulate nitrates, which can then be considered an unfriendly factor that can reduce their taste and nutritional value.

The application of fertilization seems to enhance the growth of microgreens. Different practices can be used to adjust the content of minerals and reduce the amounts of antinutrients that the plant will absorb, which will then improve its taste and extend shelf life. The degree to which the plants are able to accumulate minerals depends on species and the genotype.

If you're interested in profiting from microgreens, you can contact restaurants or people who might be interested in purchasing from you. The most popular commercial microgreens include kale, broccoli, and arugula, which make for delicious salads. If you're interested in how to price your produce, you can always browse local stores and suppliers to see how much they charge for their products. An important factor to consider here is that you're producing fresh microgreens, that are far richer in flavor than those that have been refrigerated.

CHAPTER 5: HOW TO PREPARE AND CONSUME MICROGREENS

In the previous chapter, you learned how to properly cultivate and harvest microgreens. However, you are doing all of it for the purpose of eating well and enriching your diet. For this, it is important to know how to properly take care of your plants after you've harvested them and how to properly use them in your diet. While microgreens are nutrient dense, they are very sensitive to environmental conditions that can easily deplete them of their precious nutrients. For this reason, this chapter will give you more detailed instructions on how to not only store but also eat microgreens the right way.

First things first, we will briefly discuss storing microgreens after harvesting to preserve their freshness, flavor, and nutrients. Chances are that you won't eat the entire batch of your produce after they've matured. This is why you should only harvest and store the amounts you plan on using right away. It is usual for people to harvest the entire tray and then refrigerate the remainder of the plants.

However, this is not the best way to preserve nutrients, since these crops are highly perishable and will lose nutrients fast after they've been harvested. To preserve the maximum nutrients, it is important to either eat them fresh right away or store them properly. Before harvesting microgreens, it is important to have a precise, sharp tool. Preferably, you will use ceramic scissors or a ceramic knife. Ceramic is a nontoxic substance that is very light and gentle and won't chemically react with the nutrients in the greens.

The same can be said for metals. For example, if you use an old, rusty knife, it can contaminate your herb and reduce its nutritional value. Additionally, iron can transfer ions into the plant, which can accelerate the process of oxidation. After this, the plants might brown and lose their flavor and nourishing properties. It is also important to sterilize your growing trays after harvest to remove any biofilm or other contaminants that can appear during the growing phase. Use soap and water and scrub the trays with a brush, cloth, or pressurized water. Then you can rinse the trays with water and spray with a 3% peroxide solution or 5-10% vinegar solution or wash in a bleach solution. Then rinse thoroughly and dry prior to your next use.

Another important thing to consider is to moisturize and allow air to flow through the plants. This means that you shouldn't store microgreens in sealed bags. This will completely deplete them of air, and they will spoil and degrade quicker in these conditions. Instead, provide them with sufficient moisture and air flow. While you prepare your supplies for storing, you should lay out the produce onto a piece of paper towel or keep them in a container closet. One you store the microgreens, they should be sheltered from exposure to light, which can further deplete them of nutrients. If you won't be eating your crops fresh, you should keep them in shade and protected from direct light. When properly refrigerated, microgreens will keep their freshness for about a week. However, it is important to maintain the temperature of the refrigerator to 40 Fahrenheit, or roughly four degrees Celsius. You should never put microgreens in a freezer. In fact, some studies found that microgreens that are refrigerated at around 40 degrees Fahrenheit can last up to 21 days, while a warmer temperature reduces this time to up to 14 days.

However, this greatly depends on the variety, meaning that some will last longer than others. Keep in mind that the daily use of a refrigerator and opening it will briefly change the temperature. To check if your plants are doing well, keep an eye on how stored plants look. If they start to fade, become brown, or start to smell strangely, throw them out. This might be a sign that they've either started to rot or have grown moldy.

However, many users consider that microgreens can be well-preserved using plastic containers as well. While there's a variety of methods you can use to store microgreens, like plastic bags, plastic containers tend to prolong their shelf life. Clamshell types seem to produce the best results. Usually, microgreens will stay fresh up to one week in clamshells. But, it is possible for this time to expand to two or more weeks depending on temperature, moisture, and each individual variety. While bags are also useful for preservation, they come with a risk of developing mold, since it's a lot easier for moisture to condensate around the plants and create the environment for microbes to grow. On the other hand, clamshells will shelter your microgreens from being squashed and provide them with enough space and air. If you close the clamshells properly and keep the containers sealed, you will greatly extend the lifespan and freshness of your plants. On the other hand, glass containers have proven ineffective in preserving the gentle baby plants.

For this, it is important for the containers to be sterilized. However, they will still increase condensation, which can affect the quality of your microplants. The possibility of condensation also means a fertile ground for mold and bacteria. In addition, glass containers tend to deplete the plants of taste and smell while preserving freshness. It is also important to be mindful of using single-use plastic and Tupperware as well. While these containers can preserve freshness up to two weeks, it is possible for their quality to start to decline.

Another important thing to consider is to find the right place in your refrigerator when storing. Not all areas of the fridge have the same temperature. For example, if you put them on the top near the freezer, the low temperature can even freeze the plants. It is important to keep them away from the cooling vent, which is the place where the temperature will most often fluctuate. Preferably, store them on the lower shelves of your refrigerator. You should also pay attention to the humidity of your refrigerator. Pay attention to whether there is condensation and moisture surrounding your plants, because this can degrade their quality.

On the other hand, the surroundings shouldn't be overly dry either. Since there's not much you can do to modify your refrigerator for storing microgreens properly, you can always cover them with a paper towel, which will pass air but maintain adequate moisture. Last but not least, you should be mindful of different varieties. The quality of seeds and conditions they were grown in and the way they were harvested all affect how long your microgreens will last, how fresh they will stay, and how rich they are in nutrients.

If stored properly, your microgreens will last between two or three weeks. However, since this highly depends on each individual crop, the best way to determine how long you can refrigerate each individual species is to study the crop itself.

HOW TO INCORPORATE MICROGREENS INTO YOUR DAILY DIET

When it comes to implementing microgreens properly into your diet, you should consider that finding the right ways to consume them affects the nutritional benefits that you will receive. The simple fact that these plants are nutrient dense doesn't guarantee good results unless you consume them properly.

While all studies confirm that microgreens are essentially nutrient bombs and calling them super foods is quite justified, benefiting from their high antioxidant content will require making them a part of your daily diet diligently and consistently. Doing so will boost your immunity and reduce risks from heart disease, diabetes, obesity, and high blood pressure. However, if you don't stay regular when it comes to consuming microgreens, it is possible that you will miss seeing any particular results. Daily use is extremely important considering how easy and cheap it is to grow these plants at home. Here are a couple of ways to introduce microgreens into your daily diet.

Salads

The first recommendation is to eat microgreens fresh in salads. Microgreens are healthiest when they are eaten raw. The less you process them, the more nutrients that are preserved. Their delicate flavors will also remain potent if you eat them right after harvesting. Cooking microgreens will deplete them of nutrients, which means that coming up with creative raw recipes is the right way to go. For example, the sunflower shoot, a small lemony-green plant, is a perfect addition to every salad.

Wraps and Sandwiches

Next, you can make sandwiches and wraps using the freshly plucked herbs. You can use them to create intense, sweet, spicy, and overall fabulous flavors that will pack your meal with nutrients. For this, radish greens are usually the best condiments as they tend to go well with other fresh vegetables and meats.

While fresh microgreens will add some spiciness to your sandwiches and wraps, you should keep these recipes light and diet friendly, focusing on vegetables and greens instead of bread, meats, and toppings.

Cooked Meals

You can also cook with microgreens. There are many types of microgreens that retain a lot of nutrients even when cooked. However, keep in mind that the best recommendation is to pop them into the dish at the very end of cooking and not allow them to be exposed to high temperatures for longer than a minute. Since these plants are perfectly safe to eat raw, and cooking doesn't do anything to intensify the flavor, you can even think about adding raw microgreens to already finished dishes. They are good to combine with fried dishes, pastas, and as side dishes.

Juices and Smoothies

Another way to eat microgreens is to use them to create juices and smoothies. If you aren't a fan of eating raw plants, juices and smoothies are an easy way to incorporate them into your daily diet. For these purposes, wheatgrass has proven to be the most popular. If you add microgreens to a mixture of your favorite leafy greens, vegetables, and fruits in smoothies, they will add a touch of an individual flavor you enjoy. You can also create juices from microgreens on their own.

Keep in mind that you will need one part plants to three parts of water to create a refreshing drink that will contain enough nutrients.

COOKING GUIDE FOR BEST NUTRIENT PRESERVATION

One of the questions that's perpetually asked is whether or not microgreens are truly safe to eat raw. Generally, it is considered that raw microgreens are perfectly safe for daily use. However, removing the germs before eating is very important to eliminate the possibility of contracting fungus, parasites, bacteria, and other harmful microbes.

Cooking microgreens will definitely deplete them of precious enzymes and water-soluble vitamins. To make your microgreens as safe to eat raw as possible, it is important to maintain the hygiene of your growth containers and then rinse them properly before use. If you follow the guidelines for proper refrigeration, you will reduce the chances of bacteria and mold growing on your plants. Your plants will last up to a couple of weeks, preserving their taste and freshness (Mir et al., 2017).

Ideally, you'll eat microgreens raw. In this state, they contain the greatest amounts of nutrients, and they also have the most intense taste. However, you can also cook microgreens, as long as you don't boil them. If you don't want to add fresh microgreens into your meal, you can leave them to briefly steam. Preferably, this will be a couple of minutes before you take the pot off the stove. This way, your greens will retain taste and freshness but also keep the valuable nutrients.

When adding microgreens to your meals, you can use stems and leaves, as long as you carefully rinse them of any remaining debris and germs. Whether or not you'll use the roots depends on the species. You can also blend your greens prior to adding them into dishes or crush them to release extra smell and flavor. Don't forget that you can mix as many varieties as you want!

With this in mind, we will now present you with a couple of ideas for cooking with microgreens. In the next section, you'll find instructions for incorporating microgreens into your daily meals.

TIPS AND IDEAS FOR DELICIOUS MEALS

You can enrich any meal with microgreens, adding flavors of your choosing and extra sass to the most common meals. In this section, we'll give you simple and easy ideas to incorporate microgreens into your daily diet. Following are the simplest ways to turn any meal into a body-regenerating treat:

Microgreen Pizza. By definition, pizza is a simple dish, and we're not against it when it comes to good nutrition. However, stacking a regular pizza with cheese, sausage, and pepperoni doesn't result in the most stomach-friendly meal. Instead, replacing the fatty ingredients with microgreen arugula, basil, onion, or spinach will result in a tasty treat and healthy meal. However, it's important not to bake microgreens along with the pizza, or else you'll lose the majority of nutrients. Instead, add the amount you'd like a couple of minutes before taking the pizza out of the oven, which will give them a tasty crunchiness without killing the nutrients. Of course, you can always season a finished pizza with fresh microgreens, if that's what you prefer!

Burgers with microgreens. Burgers, sadly, have a notorious reputation for being unhealthy. However, if you prepare them with microgreens like arugula, kohlrabi, and cabbage, they'll have a rich flavor which will easily compensate for the lack of calories derived from carbs like buns or cheese.

Nourishing pesto. Aside from basil and onions, you can add pea shoots and sunflower to create a truly authentic, yet healthy and nutritious pesto. You can use this sauce either as an addition to pasta or as a salad dressing. You can also use this pesto to further season sandwiches and wraps.

Microgreen salsa. Salsa is yet another dish that's made for creativity and variety. Whichever microgreen you choose, from lemongrass, lemon, cinnamon basil, sunflower, or even spicier ones like peppercress, you can simply add them to the dish and create your own authentic recipe. This way, you'll come up with a perfect recipe that will go great with quesadillas, chips, tortilla, tacos, and many more.

Microgreen guacamole. Adding microgreen sunflower to your regular guacamole will make a super healthy dip for your chips and tacos. By all means, feel free to add any other plant you choose! You can also add this guacamole to salads, sandwiches, wraps, and any other meal of your choosing.

Microgreen pancakes. If you enjoy your daily dose of pancakes, you'll find pea shoot microgreens to be a great addition to your daily treat. Simply blend the plant, adding chives and other savory greens into the batter. This will result in a delicious pancake! In addition, if you're cooking for children who tend to dislike veggies, as many do, this is a good way to disguise them into a delicious meal.

Microgreen pasta sauces. It's very simple to turn your average pasta sauce into a treat for your blood vessels and immune system, much like for the palate. Lemongrass, arugula, basil, garlic, zucchini, and others add delicious flavors to numerous sauces, from Bolognese, to pesto and carbonara. There's no exact measure when it comes to adding microgreens to pasta sauces. You can choose the amount based on your taste and preference and decide between blending, crushing, or adding them whole into the sauces. In addition, popping the plants into sauces, while they're still cooking, for no longer than a minute, will enhance the flavors without compromising the nutrients.

Microgreen omelet. A morning omelet with a touch of microgreen is a great way to boost your breakfast with precious proteins, vitamins, and iron. If you further add delicious greens, such as microgreen spinach, onions, and basil to a simple omelet, you'll benefit from an abundant boost of nutrients before your morning jog or a workout. This will set you up for a productive day, improving your energy levels and focus at work. Furthermore, the flavor of this meal will add a touch of the exotic and Mediterranean into an otherwise plain breakfast. You can add microgreens to your omelet by blending them and mixing into the eggs prior to frying, or you can crush them and sprinkle over the dish.

Microgreen soup. Soups are a great way to hydrate before a satisfying meal. Furthermore, they are a great way to fight off viruses when you are sick and to boost your immune system. To add microgreens to your soap, add them when the meal is already cooked to preserve the most nutrients. Leave the soup to cool down slowly while the precious plants steam inside of the pot, releasing flavors and nutrients. Sunflower, beans, onions, lemongrass, basil, radish, carrots, and any other microgreens you enjoy can be a great addition to your regular soup.

In this chapter, you learned more about adding microgreens to your daily diet. With this knowledge, you can now proceed to enjoy your delicious crops, with full certainty that you'll know how to use them properly and maintain their beneficial properties. This will make your efforts worthwhile, as you'll soon be able to see the health benefits with daily use.

First, you learned how to store microgreens in your kitchen to best preserve their freshness, taste, and nutritional value. You learned that the best way to refrigerate your microgreens is to keep them in plastic bags, while protecting them from excess moisture and extreme temperatures. You learned that it's ideal to keep microgreens as far from the cooling vent as possible, and to keep the temperature of your refrigerator at the optimum 40 Fahrenheit.

In this chapter, you also learned how to properly cook microgreens. While there are some crops that handle high temperatures well, most of them aren't suitable to cook and bake. Instead, it's enough to add them to a meal that's already finished cooking, allowing them to steam and release their flavors as the meal cools down. In addition, you learned that you can also blend the greens into your juices and sauces to intensify the flavor of ordinary meals.

After that, you learned about the abundance of ways to incorporate microgreens into your daily diet. First, you learned that, in order to benefit from microgreens, you should consume them at least once a day, preferably multiple times per day. You also learned that the highest concentration and flavor is in the fresh herb, meaning that you'll get the highest quality use if you pluck the small amounts you need and use them right away.

You also can use them to make salads, sandwiches, wraps, and juices, and also add them to pastas, sauces, soups, and all other meals. With an abundance of microgreens to choose from, it is only up to you to decide which you'll enjoy the most.

Whichever your choice is, there's no doubt that you can use the abundance of flavors to enhance the taste and nutritional value of your meals. After that, we gave you some creative ideas about how you can incorporate microgreens into your usual daily meals. We focused on the simplest meals that most people have daily, aiming to provide you with simple guidelines regarding adding microgreens to common meals like omelets, soups, pizza, pasta, and others. With this in mind, it will be effortless for you to use microgreens, as you won't have to jump through hoops to discover new, complex recipes. We aimed for simplicity, which we believe is the best strategy to create a diet that is healthy, satisfying, and easy to maintain.

Now that you have everything you need to grow and use microgreens, perhaps you are interested in turning them into a business. The following chapter will further explain how you can start a business with microgreens, giving you simple and useful instructions on how to start your brand and which supplies to obtain.

CHAPTER 6: MARKETING MICROGREENS

If you're wondering whether or not you can profit from growing microgreens, the simple and sweet answer is YES. You can turn growing microgreens into a business if you are thoughtful, organized, and well informed. Starting a business can seem intimidating, but with the right guidance, you will find it not only manageable but also empowering. This is a great time to start marketing microgreens, as their popularity is at its peak. They are considered to be a completely new category of foods, with plenty of science to back them up. With enormous nutritional value, they can become a source of a profitable business.

In this chapter, you will find out more about marketing microgreens. The last chapter of this book will show you how to start a business with microgreens, giving you all the information you need for a good start and a profitable outcome.

When thinking about their profitability and costs, many farmers are already creating their six-figure microgreen businesses, and so can you. Microgreen cultivation can be highly profitable, and it isn't at all difficult. Once you learn how to cultivate your first crops, you will easily move on to creating bulk amounts.

However, the tricky question remains about how to sell them, how to create your selling price, and what exactly to do in order to profit from them. The calculations behind any microgreen business are important to weigh your profits against costs and keep your business growing long term.

First, we will answer the question of if and which microgreens are marketable. As you already learned, microgreens are popular, albeit very gentle and sensitive to environmental conditions. Everything, from production to packaging, needs to be carefully planned to yield the best quality product.

Profitability is an important part of every business, including this one. For this reason, we will give you insight into the production economics of microgreens. We will give you some advice on what you can do to save while growing bulk amounts. There are multiple reasons why microgreens can become an easy source of consistent income, mainly due to swift growth and easy harvesting, which can secure a steady supply of marketable produce all year long. Unlike other crops, microgreens aren't bound to seasonal conditions, as they can be grown in controlled environments. In this chapter, we'll explain the exact benefits of starting a business with microgreens and give you smart tips to leverage these advantages.

Next, you will find the exact calculations of profit and start-up costs. Moreover, we will review the exact list of tools and supplies that you need for bulk cultivation. With this in mind, you will easily prepare everything you need to start growing large quantities of microgreens that you will later market. A great benefit from starting a microgreen business comes from the low cost of tools and supplies, and we'll give you exact tips to obtain everything you need quickly and easily.

Aside from that, we will give you more information on selling microgreens. Selling microgreens isn't difficult as the demand for them is high. However, there's still some specific things you need to know about profiling your customers and advertising your business. First, we will tell you how to evaluate your competition to find out more about your own business goals, after which you will start tracing potential clients to present your business to. Moreover, we will show you how to use customer and client feedback to improve your own practices. Last, but not least, we will give you a detailed presentation about common legal requirements revolving around cultivating microgreens. Here, you will find out what the standards and certifications are that you need to follow for producing and selling microgreens legally and safely. This will help you consider the costs and efforts that will go into navigating the legal and administrative side of your business.

As you reach the end of this book, it's time that you find out how to make your efforts profitable and turn your kitchen hobby into a nine-to-five job. In the following section, we will give you the exact explanation for how and why you can profit from microgreens.

CAN MICROGREENS BE PROFITABLE?

When thinking about the profitability of microgreens, keep in mind that you do your math properly. So far, you've learned about the benefits of microgreens and the ways to grow them. But, from a business point of view, money is an important factor.

The Production Economics

When it comes to the economics of production, it's important to know that the majority of growers use inexpensive tools, such as trays, as well as benches and tables. You don't have to invest heavily into your supplies because the main things that affect the quality of produce include environmental influences.

The majority of successful cultivators use LED fluorescent lights. These lights are indoor-growing friendly. Also, experienced cultivators water the plants using filtered water, which removes harmful chemicals and chloride. Additionally, a part of good practice is to add seaweed extract to the water, which will provide additional nutrients for the seeds. You will need to provide dark environments for germination and then move the germinated crops to trays, moving them into locations that contain better lighting.

Most growers apply potting soil blends. They either use soil as a medium, or fabric mats like burlap, if they use hydroponic.

Gordon L. Atwell

Most successful growers say that retail buyers such as upscale grocery stores and restaurants chefs are their best customers.

How Much Can You Profit?

If you're a farmer, keep in mind that microgreens are among the most profitable crops for you to grow. They don't need a lot of space and usually average $50 in selling price per pound. This price can even increase depending on the demand and competition. Microgreens are also great for smaller growers and small farms. You can grow them in storage boxes or shipping containers and place them in common areas like basements and garages to earn potentially six figures.

Start-Up Costs and Supplies

Microgreens are a good business opportunity because the initial investment is very low, as you can use supplies you already have at home and obtain seeds very cheaply. In addition, the produce is ready for harvesting very quickly, meaning that you can see the first coin from your labor in only a couple of weeks.

When it comes to start-up costs, account for spending an average $2 per tray, including seed and soil. For starters, you can offer your services to only a single restaurant until you're skillful enough for larger scale produce. You can then expand to offering your produce in farmers' markets and increase production according to your own abilities. Another advantage of marketing microgreens is a fast turnaround time. As already mentioned, microgreens take only up to a couple of weeks to harvest, which allows you to maximize operational efficiency and experiment with different techniques and varieties. This allows you to quickly upscale your production or reduce it if your sales start to drop.

Another advantage of commercial microgreen growing is that they are a year-round supply. They can be a source of consistent income, particularly if you are already familiar with agriculture and farming. If you are a farmer, microgreens can be a great way to keep your business running during the winter and supply additional income. Microgreens are also high-value crops due to their enormous nutritional value. The plants are abundant with nutrients and vitamins, which makes them appealing to upscale restaurants as they make high end ingredients that serve as an incentive to selling expensive meals. This means that they are a very profitable product.

When it comes to the space you need to obtain, keep in mind that this business is very space economical. On average, growers produce around 50 pounds of microgreens per 60-square-foot space every two weeks with an average price between $20 and $50 per pound. This provides a profit of around $2,000 monthly. According to this math, you can profit around $100 to $160 per square meter, or $30 to $50 per square foot. Account for investing in your equipment, as well as optimizing your processes when calculating your price. On average, each individual tray that measures 10x20 inches in size will produce up to six ounces, which equals between 140 to 170 grams on average

You can take up microgreen production by investing anywhere from 15 minutes to a couple of hours every day. You will also need to account for the time that it takes to harvest and sell the products.

However, a six-figure business will require full-time work. You will also have to start thinking about employing people to help you with production. Microgreens are a great business opportunity because they are highly adjustable, and you can determine the amount that you want to produce depending on the income you want to achieve and the time you can set aside for growing them.

Here's a list of essential supplies that you will need to start your business:

- You will need a light fixture that uses two bulbs or four feet of fluorescent light. You will also need a couple of fluorescent bulbs.
- At a minimum, you will need 16 trays that average 10x20 inches in size. You will grow eight plates of microgreens on a four-foot setup per week, and you can increase this amount depending on the time and resources you have.
- Paper towels are another supply you will need. However, they are so cost friendly that you can obtain large quantities for only a couple of dollars.
- You will also need a spray bottle, which is essentially something that you don't have to invest in as you probably already have it in your home.
- You will need seeds, preferably starting with radish, as they are easy and fastest to grow. Invest some extra money into organic seeds because they are perceived to be of the highest value and will result in the highest-quality produce.
- You will also need a scale to measure produce well before packaging. You can use a regular kitchen scale to do this.
- Sharp scissors and knives for harvesting are also necessary.
- Regular potting soil will be enough for beginners.
- You will also need a timer that you will use to turn your lights on and off as needed.
- You will need a small fan to ventilate your crops, which will prevent contamination and molding.
- You can also get a regular, cheap watering can.

You can think about whether or not you want to get the new supplies or use the ones you already have.

HOW TO SELL MICROGREENS

The first thing I want to tell you is to account for every penny when turning your microgreens hobby into a business. You first need to realize that your selling price will be at least a 100% markup from your initial investment. Your price will have to cover taxes, shipping, production costs, and everything else that goes into growing and selling the product from point A, which is supplying seeds, to point B, which is getting the product to your customer and charging them for it. Everything needs to be accounted for in the price.

Adding to that, a portion must be included to compensate for your time and effort. After all, this is your profit for doing this business. Another thing to consider is that microgreens don't last long when refrigerated. Unless consumed fresh, they will lose plenty of nutrients and replenishing substances that will deplete them of their value. One way to overcome this obstacle is to sell your produce at local markets. This way, you will offer freshly grown plants that will contain the highest value. Many small farmers have grown their business to steady full-time jobs.

However, before you start, you have to be completely educated and aware of everything that goes into the successful production of microgreens. Your product needs to be of the highest quality to be marketable. You have competition, and that competition has many advantages over you when it comes to business knowledge and creating quality microgreen produce. Now, again to the business side of things.

Evaluate Competition

First things first, you will have to identify your competitors and customers. The former are the ones you want to exceed in quality of offering, and the latter are the ones you want to target when selling. To evaluate your competition, it is wise to first order a couple of batches from them and evaluate their businesses. Look into their prices, quantities, and quality of product. Other than that, look into their processes of growing, cultivating, harvesting, storing, and everything else to discover the things you want to emulate and the things that should be done better.

Reach Out to Potential Clients

Once you start your business, you can then reach out to local restaurants and offer samples as your first sale. It is your choice whether you want to offer small samples for free or introduce yourself as an existing business and suggest a business deal. You will have to target the restaurant chef, who is the main person to decide whether or not a particular supplier or a product is worth the investment. You shouldn't waste your time reaching out to managers and other staff. You can contact as many restaurants as you can manage, but preferably, you will target those that are most popular and most successful. Always keep in mind when planning your produce to preserve extra supplies for free distribution as samples.

Additionally, be willing to openly speak about your prices and storing conditions because this will present you as a reliable and honest business.

Gordon L. Atwell

Advertise Your Business

Present your products well by creating pamphlets or sheets that include quality pictures and descriptions of your products. Another important business tip is to underpromise when it comes to the quality of your product and then deliver more than expected. Long term, this can help you develop stable relationships with your clients. Also, keep in mind that, if you are offering to restaurants, their chefs are quite busy and won't have a lot of time for you. Instead, you will only have a couple of minutes of their time to taste your product and to share the most vital information, such as how much you can supply daily, and at what price, the shipping details, whether your produce is organic and fresh, and how soon you can deliver the desired quantities. Be prepared to give this two-to-three-minute presentation. Take some time to practice it.

Be Flexible

In addition, if you are competing with other suppliers for the same client, try to find out if they have any complaints and what they appreciate the most about their current supplier. If your potential client has complaints about their current supplier, look for those as a source of obstacles you want to surpass with your own offering, and use the information about features that they appreciate to emulate in your own production and surpass the competition. Take regular pictures of your farm and produce to make yourself as accessible and personable as possible. You want to advertise these photos in your online store, attracting companies, grocery stores, distributors and farmers' markets. For people to buy from you they need to be well aware of your presence.

Get to Know Your Customers

For your business to be successful, you really need to know your customers well. First things first, you need to be informed about their expectations and opinions on microgreens. You need to focus on what they perceive to be beneficial, and what they perceive to be challenging about their use, and then use this information to adjust your own produce. Once your business starts to grow, and you start to gain more customers, you want to frequently get updates from them to find out if they have any opinions to share or suggestions for improvement.

Observe customer responses religiously, and think about applying any criticism to improve your business. One of the biggest mistakes that business owners make is being defensive about criticism. Receiving criticism with a defensive attitude will show your customers that you don't care about them but instead want to preserve your own face, which is not a good look. While you should aim to preserve your reputation and standing, you should always apply customers' feedback into your own processes. Make sure to note any special requests from your clients and customers regarding quality and varieties you are offering. Are there any varieties that they desire that currently aren't a part of your production? Are there certain species you sell that aren't particularly popular? You want to consider these aspects so that you can offer it as the right product that your client needs.

Last, but not least, consider all other factors that affect profitability. Do your due diligence and research and discover what are the most profitable varieties to grow and sell. In addition, always be thoughtful of looking for better and more profit-friendly ways to grow and produce.

LEGAL AND OTHER CONSIDERATIONS

Before starting your business, it is important to be aware of essential legal considerations. If you want to be a successful business owner, there are plenty of standards and legalities you will have to abide by to run your business according to the law. First things first, it is important that, from a legal point of view, there are certain health risks associated with plant production (Riggio et al., 2019) Food safety will remain one of your biggest concerns when producing microgreens. It is important to be aware of all the processes and applications that are necessary to provide safe ingredients. When starting the microgreens business, you first need to learn more about food safety regulations. You will find plenty of documents online that provide information about different laws and duties you'll have to follow with production.

Depending on the government levels, whether the regulations are federal, provincial, or municipal, you will follow different requirements. To safely produce microgreen products for your consumers, when it comes to municipal standards, you will have to look into the individual laws and permits required in your own municipality. Usually, this includes development permits, local business licenses, and regulations.

You will also have to follow facility guidelines and requirements. Regulations often cover facility inspections and food handling permits, as well as safety training and courses for safe food production aimed at farmers. On the other hand, federal regulations often refer to safety and packaging requirements.

Whichever program you choose, you will have to abide by the OFFS program, as it is an essential part of providing your customers with healthy, safe, and sanitary products. Most customers and distributors require OFFS certification, which signifies that you follow legal requirements for safe and conscientious produce. You will also have to learn about food safety programs and requirements regarding plants, farming, preharvest handling, distribution, services, and provision of storage.

When it comes to microgreen risk assessment, it is intended to analyze potential safety risks and communicate them to growers so that they can follow the rules of best practice. These requirements cover potential hazards in terms of biological pathogens, pests and allergens, chemical hazards like cleaners, fertilizers, and pesticides, and physical hazards like water, glass, metal, nails, and debris.

When it comes to biological hazards, you will pay attention to risks associated with listeria, which is affected by ventilation and airflow. It also is impacted by the temperature of the facility. It is also relevant to whether the seeds you obtain possibly contain microorganisms. For this, it is important to source your seeds from a reputable supplier. When it comes to pests, like rodents, insects, etc., it is relevant which measures you will apply to prevent them from contaminating your produce. This includes measures such as cleaning, proper storage, and other protocols to prevent and treat possible past infections.

When it comes to chemical hazards, you will need to pay attention to whether you're storing any chemicals in the same area where you grow your microgreens. While this is not desirable, you should aim to clear your facility of any chemicals and instruct your staff to follow the best hygiene practices.

When it comes to physical hazards, you should pay attention to whether your growing racks can support the weight of the plants. You will also have to pay attention to the quality of lighting and whether it has been made with shatterproof materials. You will also have a mitigation protocol, in case your light bulbs shatter in the growing area. Also, this includes the protocols you will establish for disposal of microgreens that may have been contaminated, and to clear your production facility of any construction materials. Aside from that, further legal and taxation requirements depend mainly on the individual town, state, or region, which is something you can learn about by talking to local authorities.

In this chapter, you learned valuable information regarding marketing microgreens and creating your own brand and business. First you learned that you need to approach the venture with common business smarts by paying attention to profitability. While passion and vision are both important for growing a successful microgreen business, it is also necessary to pay attention to your profits, as they are what keep your business and income going.

First, you found out that microgreens are highly profitable because they only require the use of tools that you most likely already have. It's likely that you will only have to invest in a small number of trays and optimal lighting for your plants. Aside from that, you can significantly reduce your costs by planning the space in which you'll cultivate the plants for their best growth

You also learned that you will have to account for everything that goes into production and delivery of microgreens so that your business is sustainable. While microgreens have low start-up costs, these costs will increase as your business grows. To keep your business up and running, you found out that you will have to find good ways to present yourself. You learned that you will have to reach out to restaurant owners, chefs, and showcase your products in farmers' markets to advertise your business. You also learned the ways to make yourself noticeable, like printing out images and pamphlets, giving out free samples, and many more. Perhaps, the most important factor that will determine the success of your business is your relationship with customers. You will grow as a brand if you learn how to follow your customers' opinions and feedback regarding the quality and taste of your product.

You also learned that researching the competition and your potential customers will give you the information about how you should adjust your processes and the choice of varieties to best cater to the market. Last but not least, you learned about the important health and safety standards that apply across most states. When it comes to growing microgreens, you learned that you'll have to pay attention to different hazards, from physical and chemical, to hygiene factors that might contaminate your produce. Now, as you're finishing this book, I want to leave you with some simple advice to start small and slowly build up your own production. Before you get to know and practice cultivation of microgreens, you shouldn't order bulk quantities of seeds. Instead, do your research first, and discover what the most popular varieties are and start growing small amounts until you get used to them, and master small-scale cultivation. After that, you can move on to bulk cultivation and order a greater amount of seeds. This will ensure that you grow the plants with the highest level of success and quality, as quality comes first. It's essential that you remain devoted to giving your plants proper environmental conditions to thrive.

As you finish this book, we hope to have given you exactly the right information you need to start growing, using, and marketing microgreens right now!

CONCLUSION

Congratulations! You finished your manual on how to grow and market microgreens successfully. This book aimed to present you with the benefits of cultivating and using microgreens. Hopefully, we've given you all the information you need to understand the value of these gentle, yet powerful, plants, and how to include them in your everyday diet. The main purpose of this book was to show you not only the benefits of microgreens but also the simplicity and beauty of growing them on your own. Hopefully, while reading this book, you learned that microgreens are extremely easy to grow, if you follow the right steps and guidelines.

As you reach the end of this book, you now know everything you need about these small, yet valuable plants, to not only grow them for boosting your own health but to start your own business. This book is aimed to give you easy and comprehensive instructions on growing and marketing microgreens.

We started off by first explaining what microgreens are. In this book, you learned that microgreens are young versions of regular vegetables and herbs that are germinated and harvested at the young stage of their growth. You also learned that they have grown in popularity during the past couple of decades, mainly due to health benefits and their delicious taste. In fact, they're considered to be a luxurious condiment by high-end restaurants, and have been featured on television, in cookbooks, and even used to treat illnesses!

In the second chapter of this book, you found out the truth

behind that popularity. You learned that science shows that microgreens not only contain enormous amounts of nutrients compared to adult plants, but also have the potential to support healing from many illnesses, like kidney disease, weakness of the immune system, cardiovascular disease, obesity, diabetes, and others. You learned that these small plants may be tender in appearance, but that they are, in fact, up to a hundred times more potent than some of the healthiest vegetables!

In fact, as you found out, they contain enormous amounts of antioxidants, which are known to improve body functioning and regeneration of your cells. This important finding showed you that you can use microgreens to boost your body's natural ability to heal and rejuvenate. As you learned, antioxidants can help your body get rid of free radicals, the compounds that impair your health on a cellular level. Using microgreens, you can boost the health of your cells to help them get rid of faults and start growing fresh, healthy tissues.

You learned that microgreens pile up nutrients as they get ready to mature and grow into an adult plant. If you're careful enough to pluck them at the right time, you'll get a vitamin-packed batch of freshly harvested plants that you can eat raw, put in meals, or mix into smoothies.

You also learned that the nutritional value of microgreens greatly depends on their environment. You learned that lighting, temperature, handling, and fertilization have a lot to do with the quality of the end product. In this book, we presented you with research findings that showed that insufficient light, water, too high or low temperatures, and improper soil can completely deplete the valuable nutrients inside microgreens. For these reasons, we briefly described the optimal conditions needed for the healthy growth of microgreens. You learned that they thrive best at room temperature and in moderate light. You also learned that they need to be consistently misted with filtered water, but not too much, or else they'll start growing mold and bacteria.

You also learned that the choice of seeds can affect the quality of an adult plant. In the second chapter of this book, we explained all possible health benefits from using microgreens. Once we convinced you of the enormous possible benefits of microgreens, we went on to help you choose the best seeds and crops. We showed you how to decide on the crops you want to cultivate, by laying out the list of those that are most popular and most suitable for beginners. You learned that growing these plants costs next to nothing and that there are microgreens that are so simple to grow that they don't demand anything else other than soaking and placing on a paper towel! We also presented you with numerous types and individual species, describing their looks, taste, nutritional value, and methods for growing.

Knowing this will help you decide which ones you like best and which are the ones you'll choose to start cultivating. For beginners, we recommended growing a limited amount of varieties, preferably those you already enjoy as grown vegetables. This way, you'll be sure to like and enjoy your lush produce. In addition, we recommended growing only the amount you'll use up right away, as storing and preserving microgreens will take some exercise.

In this book, you also learned that purchasing the best seeds is extremely important to ensuring the quality of your plants. You learned that seed quality is important not only because of the genetic foundation for healthy plants but also for your microgreens to be free of toxic chemicals and be organic. For this, you learned that it's important to purchase only from reputable sellers. In addition, you learned how to distinguish non-GMO from organic and untreated seeds. We recommended purchasing only organic, untreated, and non-GMO seeds, since they have the greatest potential for high germination rates.

As you learned, germination rates determine how many of your seeds will sprout and proceed to grow. For highest germination, we recommended only top-quality suppliers, which you'll discover by researching brands and reading the information from their websites.

Once you fully understood microgreens and their benefits, we went on to explain and instruct you on how to properly grow them. In the fourth chapter of this book, you learned exactly how to grow microgreens. You learned that, in order to get all of the tools and supplies needed for this hobby, you will need plenty of containers, water, water filters, growth media, fertilizers, and sources of light to keep your seed growing and your plants well nourished. However, the process of planting remains simple, consisting only out of presoaking the seeds, filling a container with a growth medium, and transferring the seeds. However, different species, as you learned, differ when it comes to presoaking necessity, days needed to sprout, and harvest times. By looking into the information given in this manual, you'll be able to pick the plants that will be ready for harvesting roughly at the same time, making it easier for you to enjoy them all at once!

Next, we explained the exact process of growing microgreens. You learned how to plant the microgreens step by step, as well as to how to harvest them and care for them after harvesting to preserve their quality. After that, we showed you the best strategies for consuming microgreens. You learned about the abundance of simple ways to grow and include microgreens in your daily diet, such as to use them to make juices and smoothies, different meals, sandwiches, salads, and wraps, and also pasta sauces and soups. We gave you a couple of simple and sustainable tips and ideas for everyday meals that you will be able to use effortlessly. With these instructions, you'll add a variety of interesting tastes into your kitchen, while supporting your body as it regenerates and rejuvenates.

After that, we gave you instructions on how to turn your hobby into a business. We presented you with the reasons why microgreens are profitable and what you can do to start your own business. First, you learned that one of the reasons why microgreens are so highly profitable lies in the fact that they grow quickly, easily, and through the entire year. You can choose any species you want and grow them regardless of the season. As you are the one controlling the conditions, you have the power to grow as many or as few microgreens as you want.

However, in order to create a business, you'll need to calculate the possible profits depending on the amounts of produce you can cultivate and the quality you can offer. As you learned, it is of grave essence to first focus on growing healthy, delicious herbs. After you've mastered the art of microgreen cultivation, you can then move on to offering your produce to different clients, like restaurants, or sell them fresh in farmers' markets. As you learned, microgreens can easily become a full-time job. That is, if you're willing to learn and treat your crops with adequate care.

As you reach the final words of this book, we want to thank you for your time. Hopefully, we've answered all your questions, and given you all instructions you need for the successful growing of microgreens.

REFERENCES

Brazaitytė, A., Viršilė, A., Samuolienė, G., Jankauskienė, J., Sakalauskienė, S., Sirtautas, R., ... & Duchovskis, P. (2016, May). Light quality: Growth and nutritional value of microgreens under indoor and greenhouse conditions. *VIII International Symposium on Light in Horticulture,* Article 1134_37, 277-284.

Choe, U., Yu, L. L., & Wang, T. T. (2018). The science behind microgreens as an exciting new food for the 21st century. *Journal of Agricultural and Food Chemistry,* 66(44), 11519-11530.

Crispy Edge. (n.d.). *Why are microgreens such a popular ingredient?* https://crispyedge.com/2018/04/17/why-are-microgreens-such-a-popular-ingredient/

Di Gioia, F., Mininni, C., & Santamaria, P. (2015). How to grow microgreens. *Microgreens. Eco-logica editore, Bari,* 51-79.

Fresh Origins. (n.d.). *Microgreens facts.* http://www.freshorigins.com/microgreens-facts/

Kyriacou, M. C., Rouphael, Y., Di Gioia, F., Kyratzis, A., Serio, F., Renna, M., ... & Santamaria, P. (2016). Micro-scale vegetable production and the rise of microgreens. *Trends in Food Science & Technology,* 57, 103-115.

Mir, S. A., Shah, M. A., & Mir, M. M. (2017). Microgreens: Production, shelf life, and bioactive components. *Critical reviews in food science and nutrition,* 57(12), 2730-2736.

Mumm's Sprouting Seeds. (n.d.). *Growing a microgreen business.*

Sprouting. http://sprouting.com/growing_a_microgreen_business.html#a16558

Riggio, G. M., Wang, Q., Kniel, K. E., & Gibson, K. E. (2019). Microgreens—A review of food safety considerations along the farm to fork continuum. *International Journal of Food Microbiology, 290*, 76-85.

Samuolienė, G., Brazaitytė, A., Jankauskienė, J., Viršilė, A., Sirtautas, R., Novičkovas, A., ... & Duchovskis, P. (2013). LED irradiance level affects growth and nutritional quality of Brassica microgreens. *Open Life Sciences, 8*(12), 1241-1249.

Schiffler, A. (2019, March 6). The beginner's guide to start growing microgreens. Herbs at Home. https://herbsathome.co/the-beginners-guide-to-start-growing-microgreens/

Xiao, Z., Lester, G. E., Luo, Y., & Wang, Q. (2012). Assessment of vitamin and carotenoid concentrations of emerging food products: Edible microgreens. *Journal of Agricultural and Food Chemistry, 60*(31), 7644-7651.